SERMONS AND SERMON NOTES

BY THE SAME AUTHOR.

Self-Knowledge and Self-Discipline. Crown 8vo, 2s. 6d. net.

Laws of the Spiritual Life. Crown 8vo, 2s. 6d. net.

The Price of Unity. Crown 8vo, 2s. 6d. net.

Some Principles and Practices of the Spiritual Life. Crown 8vo, 2s. 6d. net.

Practical Studies on the Parables of Our Lord. Crown 8vo, 2s. 6d. net.

Fruits of the Life of Prayer. Short Considerations on the Seven Words of Our Lord from the Cross. 8vo, paper Covers, 3d. net.

LONGMANS, GREEN AND CO.
London, New York, Bombay, Calcutta, and Madras

Campbell Studios, New York.

Very sincerely Yr
B. W. Maturin

SERMONS AND SERMON NOTES

BY THE
REV. B. W. MATURIN

EDITED BY WILFRID WARD

WITH PORTRAIT

LONGMANS, GREEN, AND CO.
39 PATERNOSTER ROW, LONDON
FOURTH AVENUE & 30TH STREET, NEW YORK
BOMBAY, CALCUTTA, AND MADRAS
1916

All rights reserved

23/1011

PREFATORY NOTE

THE work of editing Father Maturin's 'Sermons and Sermon Notes,' undertaken by my husband, Mr. Wilfrid Ward, at the wish of the Rev. Charles Maturin, was nearly completed and the book was already in the press before his last illness cut him off from all literary activity. The sources of the materials used in this volume explain to a great extent the difficulties of the task. Of the eleven complete sermons five were preached by Father Maturin as an Anglican, of which four were reported at the time in the *Church Times* and elsewhere in the years 1890, 1891, 1893 and 1896, while the fifth—the sermon on Prayer—has no date. None of these reports have ever been reproduced or corrected until now.

Of the remaining sermons, preached after he had come into the Church, five were reported privately for his friends in 1904, and one, preached in 1909 at the clothing of a nun, was printed for private circulation and was corrected by himself. The difficulty of reporting Father Maturin was enormous. In fact, I have it on good authority that professional reporters in London considered him harder to reproduce than any other preacher of his day or than any speaker in the House of Commons. This was due not merely to the extreme rapidity of his utterance but to its uneven pace. It was inevitable that there should be mistakes and inaccuracies in the reports which required careful correction. Happily, Mr. Wilfrid Ward was so closely in touch with Father Maturin's thoughts and modes of expression that he was able to see and bring out the meaning of many obscure passages. On this work he spent time and care, and although the final touches from his hand were lacking to the correcting of the proofs, I think it will be found that his labours were brought to a successful conclusion.

The case of the Sermon Notes is different. Mr. Ward selected them from the mass of notes left in Father Maturin's handwriting. These notes were written in very small characters on the four sides of ordinary sheets of notepaper and have no dates. They were found in envelopes annotated with the text or subject of the sermon. There were usually three or four versions of what he intended to say on the same subject, and they gave evidence of the immense labour that went to his life work. Many of these notes unfortunately break off in the middle of eloquent passages and very few are brought to the conclusion. It was evidently Father Maturin's method to leave his peroration to the inspiration of delivery.

The proofs have been read since Mr. Ward's death by Monsignor Nolan, who thus continues his invariable kindness in revising proofs for my husband for many years past. They have also been read by Father Maturin's brother and literary executor, the Rev. Charles Maturin. He has very kindly corrected any verbal inaccuracies in the quotations from Scripture. Father Maturin, speaking *extempore*, for the most part used the English Bible, to which he had been so long accustomed.

PREFATORY NOTE

It is inevitable that comparisons should be drawn between the reported word and the memory of the spoken word by those to whom Father Maturin's preaching was one of the keenest joys and most invigorating aids to their spiritual life. Such a comparison must be to the disadvantage of all that can be rescued from the past and preserved in the cold printed word, and is only the inevitable tragedy that attends on all great orators. But those who feel the contrast with the living word the most strongly will also best understand the value of what is left to us, for in this volume they will find the impress of Father Maturin's great gifts of spiritual insight, of a most remarkable psychology and a penetrating candour which never failed.

I may say in conclusion that I have been tempted to regret that my husband devoted some of the short time left to him to editing these sermons and notes instead of using it all for original work, but I think that to himself the task was all spiritual gain. I can but hope that many others will find in this book the help and consolation that it brought to its Editor. If so, I trust that the names of both the preacher and his friend may not be forgotten in their prayers.

JOSEPHINE WARD.

Lotus, Dorking,
   July 1916.

INTRODUCTION

THE contrast between notoriety and real fame is a theme which gives food for much reflection. In the greatest names in history they coincide. In Shakespeare and Milton, in Pitt and Fox, in Galileo and Newton the quality of fame is coincident with its quantity—its extensive recognition. But among the mass of men and women whom we know it is otherwise—in our own day especially when advertisement is so common and so effective in creating newspaper notoriety. The names which every reader of the *Daily Mail* knows are for the most part not the greatest names. First-rate men do not condescend to the arts of self-advertisement. They exercise their gifts spontaneously and with little thought of general recognition. Thus the man of genius usually has his comparatively small circle made up of those whom his work affects directly. The writer has his readers, the artist his followers and admirers, the preacher his audience. That circle feels towards him as no one feels towards the far more notorious windbags and self-advertisers; but to the majority of his countrymen his very existence may be hardly known until or unless some accidental circumstance brings his genius unmistakably home to the general public.

Father Maturin was one of those men of real genius

who never advertised himself, but did his work quietly and thoroughly. His was not among the great historical names of his generation; but his gifts were placed very high indeed by those who followed his career as a preacher and came under his personal influence. The touch of true genius was unmistakable in him: yet I think his friends used to feel during his lifetime that though he was generally known to be one of our best preachers, the world at large had little conception of the quality of his mind which gave him so special a position among his own disciples and friends. And when at his Requiem the huge Westminster Cathedral was filled by some two thousand mourners it came to some of us as a surprise. It was a remarkable case where many individuals owed him a deep debt for his preaching, yet there had not been that open communication between them which leads to universally acknowledged popular fame. Each one who came said, ' I owe so much to Father Maturin that I must be among the mourners, though I fear that they will not be so numerous as such a man deserves.' Many hundreds in London alone said the same thing, where each man had thought that it would be said only by a few score.

I do not propose to say much of the external events of Father Maturin's life. They were not of great importance except as affording occasions for the real work of his life, constant personal influence. This work was really the beginning and end of his career. He was the son of a well-known Vicar of Grangegorman, who was almost the only high church clergyman in the Irish Church of seventy years ago. He worked in England and America as a Cowley Father; he did much mission work for eighteen years as a Catholic Priest. During all this time his influence was that of a preacher and giver of spiritual retreats and a guide to many individual souls. In his last years he seemed to have found opportunity for personal influence in a new field as chaplain to the Oxford Catholic undergraduates. But it was otherwise decreed, and one who was ever so keenly alive to the drama of human life died an heroic death in a great and terrible scene in that drama.

I propose to speak here of those gifts which enabled Father Maturin to win so many hearts and souls to a good and useful life, and often to a high spirituality.

Father Maturin was a man in whom missionary zeal, the fire of spiritual genius and penetrating psychological insight were combined to a rare degree. Both in the pulpit and from the chair of the preacher of spiritual retreats, first as a Cowley Father and then for eighteen years as a Catholic Priest, these gifts were exercised with a power which deeply affected many lives. I personally never heard any preacher of whom the word 'inspiration' could be more justly used. It was with him in the pulpit much what it is with many a great poet, whose conversation little prepares one for the immense sweep of imagination and passion or the power of vivid expression which are apparent when he takes his pen in hand. With the poet brooding thought in solitude as a rule kindles the fire and his pen is the instrument for kindling others. With Father Maturin the presence of human beings whom he addressed kindled the fire in himself and the spoken word was his instrument.

He was in private life a charming companion, full

of sympathy, a frank simplicity running through his conversation. He was fond of the society of young people, who loved him and delighted in his favourite ghost stories—for the mysterious was ever congenial to him. But the attractive characteristics of his companionship conveyed little suggestion of his deepest gifts. His Irish impulsiveness and want of balance, something one-sided in his judgments, his lovable boyishness, were familiar traits which made the mellow wisdom and the wonderful penetration of his pulpit utterances positively startling—so little did the agreeable *raconteur* touch the heights and depths reached by the preacher. It was as though a great spirit dwelt in the depths of his soul which only the presence of an audience of human beings looking to him for guidance could effectively evoke. And it was called out only gradually as a sermon went on and its theme developed. The text was spoken rapidly in a rather low tone and without emotion. The beginning was generally very simple. It made one feel that he was looking at the obvious practical facts of life and not any dream of his own. By degrees the thoughts and imaginings which his subject needed for its exposition and illustration shaped themselves. The fire was then kindled and there came forth the memorable utterances which left their mark for life on many of those who heard him.

To those who did not understand his sermons they sometimes appeared melodramatic, from the manner in which he delivered the most impassioned passages. But to those who followed his argument closely the most remarkable trait was a very fine psychological perception.

The most striking passages were those which showed his keen appreciation of the view of life which blunts the mind of the sceptic or the man of the world to the lessons of Christianity. He would first describe vividly all that could be said against the religious view of human life, and then, with a force immensely increased by such concessions, depict the Christian message as affording an explanation of life and a guide to conduct which cannot be found elsewhere.

Never will those who were present forget his sermon preached a year ago at St. Mary's, Cadogan Street, on the death of a friend deeply loved by himself and by many of those whom he addressed, the late Miss Mary Thesiger. How hard it often is to take quite firmly the Christian view of death when it comes near to our own door. We see the dissolution of all the powers and faculties. We are told to believe in their fuller life. We see the end. We are told to believe that it is only the beginning. How irresistibly at such times is the materialistic view apt to suggest itself. The physical aspect of death is so obvious—the fulfilment of the appointed cycle of growth, maturity, decay, and then final extinction. This is what we see in the rest of nature around us, vegetable and animal. Why should we think of a man as an exception ? The spiritual aspect of death, the conception of it as the entrance into a fuller and richer life is little suggested by what is visible to the loving watchers at the bed of death. We recite the prayers which presuppose this view of the case, but the haunting sense of utter extinction threatens to poison them with a feeling of unreality. The funeral preacher generally contents himself with dwelling on the past, with picturing him or her whom we have lost as they were on earth, with embalming the ever precious memories of friendship, touching only with decorous brevity on the question of where the mourned one now is, and what is happening behind that dark curtain of death. This last aspect of the case is at such a moment so hard to realise, so inevitably promotes a feeling of scepticism if it is pressed too insistently, that it is rarely dwelt on at great length in such a discourse.

But Father Maturin did on this occasion insist on it with a perfection of insight into the hearts of his hearers which enabled him to give full faith and comfort to many hearts, and brought consoling tears to many eyes. His success was due to his facing quite frankly in the first part of his discourse the sceptical thoughts which if allowed to remain sub-conscious might have poisoned the wells of faith and hope. He spoke first beautifully of the life of the friend that had gone, as a treasure left to the memory of those who loved her, as an eternal possession. He brought back to remembrance little incidents, ways and habits which made the picture true and living. Then he described with minute accuracy the impression left on dear friends at the bed of death, that all this gracious life with its happy memories was closed for ever—the career ended, the personality gone back to the nothingness from which it first came. This method was in reality the method of a surgeon who probes the wound to make real healing ultimately possible. Some of his words at the moment seemed almost unbearable. But they had probed the limits of lawful scepticism, and they had shown that when such limits were overpassed, scepticism had the nature not of reason but of feeling. It was a feeling caused by the ever present and pressing facts of this visible scene, absorbing and apparently exhausting all aspects of death that we can clearly imagine.

And then he passed to the view of death which Christian faith offers us. The half thoughts and unfulfilled aspirations and broken dreams which unanswerably suggest a self so far greater than this life can ever realise—these are wholly outside those categories supplied by animal and vegetable life which had at first suggested that death extinguishes man's individuality. If we must have a clear image in order to believe, of course we cannot get beyond the images with which earthly experience has supplied us. Then indeed are our beliefs the irrational slaves of our past history. On such a view man's birth from nothingness would itself be incredible before it had actually happened. But if we have faith to rise higher and let a view suggested by what is deep and unmistakable, though made up of obscure and largely unknown elements, gain entrance into our minds, then we can think of the dead very differently. The Communion of Saints becomes no longer an unreal dream. We can think of our dead friend, he said, as a mother thinks of her boy far away in India or China. She has never seen the country where he dwells; she cannot picture his surroundings; but she has testimony in which she trusts that he is happy and well cared for, and among kind friends of whom she knows much. The force and conviction with which Father Maturin brought home this Christian view of death to the hearts of his hearers were due entirely to the penetrating psychological insight with which he had first divined and faced those primary impressions wrought by the physical aspect of death which so often keep its spiritual aspect at a distance. That terrible haunting sense of death as mere extinction which comes spontaneously at the sight of it, lost its power by being boldly faced. The first part of his sermon effectively laid the spectre of scepticism, and cleared the ground for the entrance of the Holy Visions of Faith.

That was but one instance of this preacher's power which I have so often felt—not more remarkable than many another, but still fresh in the memory of those to whom it gave deep and lasting comfort. His genius had some of the uncertainty which usually attends on veritable inspiration. At times the 'spirit' refused to respond to his summons and he was left with the comparatively tame words at his command which suggest themselves to men and women when they do not realise the highest truths and yet have to speak of them. Sometimes a mere accident would put him off and an equally slight cause would kindle again the fire of his eloquence. He had the impressionableness which Irishmen so often have and which so often accompanies dramatic genius.

I may give one instance of this curious impressionableness. He was staying with us at Eastbourne some six years ago or more, and was to preach a sermon at the Sunday evening service. He was not very well and I think some trifle had worried him. He said that he totally lacked inspiration, that the sermon must be a wretched failure, and he wished he could avoid having to preach it. Our neighbour, Miss Agnes Zimmermann, the famous pianist, came to tea that

INTRODUCTION

day, and played to us afterwards for more than an hour. Father Maturin was an absorbed listener. The music so completely transformed him, working up his powers of imagination and realisation, that he preached that evening the finest sermon that I think I ever heard from him, the subject being the History of Job.

I have before me some notes made by a listener during one of his spiritual retreats. These notes will bring us nearer to the man in some ways than any general observations of my own on the character of his addresses, and I will here set down a few typical selections.

He was fond of the analogy between the order of nature and the order of grace, and he would insist that the systematic work of attempting to be good meant the employment in achieving a supernatural aim of just those moral qualities which are needed for success in any great work in human life. Self-denial, perseverance, singleness of mind are the conditions for success both in the order of nature and in the order of grace. Here is a passage in which this view of the case is set forth:

In the case of the *artist* ' strait is the way and narrow is the gate ' that leads to any success. . . . Self-denial, humility, patience, and love of the Teacher who is giving the lesson. . . . (Carlyle's courage and patient renewal of his labour after the burning of his volume on the French Revolution a lesson in the school of severe discipline.) . . . Another example; a genius for music has also a social genius; he must sacrifice one of them—give up his social distraction for art. Let him carry his self-denial a little further in a higher sphere and this artist could become a saint. . . . To learn a foreign language (to take another example) is to learn patience. . . . It is upon the principles of the moral law alone that we learn anything. We must be resolute and single-hearted, intent on seeing and learning the exact truth. Blessed are the pure in heart for they alone shall see truth. . . . In all nature— over each secret there stands its guardian angel. . . . None can enter here but the patient, the humble, the pure, etc. . . . Nature teaches moral discipline. . . . The world is the world of God, and the order of Nature is the order of God. . . .

But at once the difficulty arises that the devoted artist or the devoted writer has a most definite idea of the work he has to accomplish and his faculties are clearly adapted to its accomplishment. In religion it is otherwise : we work for aims the very nature of which is only fully realised in another world. We work with faculties which are more obviously adapted only to the world in which we live. With this difficulty he proceeds to deal :

For our work in this life we are equipped adequately. We are enabled by our faculties to do all that is necessary between birth and the grave on this earth. We set ourselves an earthly task and we have the power in ourselves to carry it out. But we are not only meant for this earth, but for the next world as well ; and for this we are not so well prepared. . . .

Tenacity of purpose, it has been said, is an intellectual rather than a moral matter. If *we see the end* we can go on. But we *don't* see the end clearly when that end lies in the other world. If we are beings of earth and heaven we are *not* fully equipped for this double work. God has not done His duty—it would seem at first sight. He has created us for creatures of Heaven and yet so dim is our

INTRODUCTION

vision of Heaven, and so attractive and strong the world all about us, it does not seem possible to carry on our work towards Heaven.

Is there any plan then for our further equipment, the equipment which we have not naturally? Two things we need for this struggle towards Heaven—light and strength. With rare exceptions, man has not these at his birth—he must get them supernaturally.

Objectively, therefore, God gives us Revelation.

Subjectively, He gives us faith.

The sun (Revelation) cannot be seen without the opening of the eyes (faith).

But is it enough to *know* the good? To read the Sermon on the Mount and acknowledge its beauty, is that enough to make us *act* the good?

Christ gives us *clearness of vision*, but he needs also to give us *spiritual power*.

To give us light is fairly easy; to give us *strength* is another thing. . . . God respects our *will*. The power that God gives us is a power that *we* have to lay hold of to secure it. The *will* is the thing. . . . God gives us power in a germinal state. . . . All our natural powers are greater than we know, but the depths of *spiritual power* in us are infinite. It is the power of Christ—not our own, and we *must go to the well* to draw the water. We are not conscious that the power is there until we try.

One means he frequently emphasised for making us realise to the full our latent spiritual power. Our efforts should, he often said, be in their form positive rather than negative. We should strive by prayer and meditation to realise the great spiritual aims and to fill the imagination with them, to make their attainment the interest, even the romance, of our life, rather than simply to avoid sin. To one who thinks chiefly of temptation and its resistance religion is apt to seem the negation of life. For the more we realise and dwell on the allurements of temptation the more our picture of life includes sin as a part of it. If, on the contrary, the imagination and purpose are concentrated on the image of positive good to be attained in life, religion becomes not the negation but the fullness of what is best in life. So, too, he would urge, the goodness which comes of ignorance is precarious and uninspiring and seems to identify virtue with shutting out horizons of knowledge which would enlarge the mind. Such goodness, moreover, may be easily put to flight by the inrush of some half-knowledge which might appear to contradict the Christian faith.

Let us, on the contrary, he would urge, boldly and frankly face all knowledge, confident that the whole field of God's truth—material and spiritual—is harmonious and consistent. This favourite theme of his is touched on in the following passage:

There are two theories of action in life:
1. Negative, abstain from evil doing.
2. Positive, do good and *crowd out* the evil.

Of course, to some extent the one thing necessarily implies the other. If we *do good*, we do not do evil. If we abstain from wrong, it implies that we do right. But the question is: which theory stands out boldly as the ground of our action? The old order under the Law preached, 'Thou shalt not'—the negative implying a positive; with the Sermon on the Mount it is the opposite, 'Blessed are the peacemakers,' etc., implying 'Cursed are the mischief makers.' Christ put the *positive* in strong evidence—the Old Law put it in the background.

Let us be *positively* good by action, not *negatively*

INTRODUCTION

good by abstention. So also, not ignorance but *knowledge* is the guardian angel of faith.

The forces we speak of as the 'discoveries' of science (e.g. electricity) are older than the Incarnation—were always in the world. God is the maker of them all and gives us all this scientific knowledge of His work. As He is the God of the Incarnation, why then fear Knowledge?

Jesus Christ was *positive*: 'I am not come to destroy but to fulfil.' 'Overcome evil with good.' (Of course at times there may be in the negative attitude—abstention—a use and a rightness, *but* we abstain in order that we may *more fully act* afterwards. The discipline of silence, e.g., is in order that speech may afterwards be more effective—either speech to God or to man. All *mortification* is *dying* that we may *live*. . . .

Merely negative goodness obtained by *not doing* wrong is a poor thing. At the Day of Judgment if we say to God: Lord, I have not told lies, I have not said hard things about my neighbour, I have not committed adultery, etc., God will answer: My child, tell me what you have *done* with all the faculties I gave you—with hands, eyes, speech, heart. . . . Catholics are not meant to keep their lives in a glass case and then transplant them straight to Heaven. We ought to use *all* our faculties *in the world for God*, in the very best way we can. Overcome evil with good. Theatre, Press, Society, etc.—*leave nothing to the Devil by abstaining* from these things, but *catch hold of them*, use them for God, make them Catholic. That is what God wants.

Father Maturin was very helpful to those who were tried by intellectual and moral difficulties against the Christian faith. And here again, as in the case of resistance to evil, he encouraged positive trust in God rather than the filling of the mind with difficulties themselves, some of which are, owing to our limited knowledge of God's great universe, insoluble here on earth. He preached that personal trust in God which the whole atmosphere of the Christian and Catholic Church does so much to make easier.

The two classes of difficulties meet us—those of *inner* life and those from *without*. Look at the latter. . . . They make life for all of us a *probation*, a testing: and the last great storm will be the worst of all; but if we pass through the others, we shall be able to pass through this. . . .

Of the outer difficulties and problems that meet us there are:

1. Intellectual difficulties. . . .
2. Moral problems. . . .

It is the office of religion to deal with these problems. Two ways of dealing with them.

1. By solving them completely (or appearing to) and thus giving peace—this can't really be done.
2. By creating an atmosphere of trust, calmness and peace we can wait in serenity for the answer.

This is what the Church does. She will *not* solve the difficulties—she can't often (her infallibility is *confined* to the sphere of revelation), but she will, if you give yourself over to her, create for your mind an atmosphere of perfect moral calmness and confidence. . . .

One great question that comes up often to the *most devout* minds is: why do we suffer so? (The misery of the world has taken away a man's faith sometimes.) . . . In zeal for God's reputation they ask that God should judge the world upon the highest moral principles, which He certainly does not seem to do. . . .

What are we to say to this question of suffering?

We sometimes come upon facts which mitigate the difficulty. For instance, a man with an awful cancer is often far more pitied and troubled over by those who look on his suffering than he himself is troubled. He is, very often, *happy within.* He sees and knows something of the good in the trouble that outsiders do not. We may think of God as of a father apparently to the outer world, harsh and selfish to his children ; but ask the children themselves if he is so, and they of the inner circle will feel the question an insult. . . .

There is an inner circle of people who *understand* God, because they have confidence in Him. . . . The *personal* element is everything in the intercourse of human beings. One person can influence another only as far as he can create an atmosphere of personal trust. Unless you have confidence in me I can't really teach you or help you, . . . nor can you do me justice in the views you will have of me. (*Cor ad cor loquitur.*) The personal element is the most mysterious and yet the most essential of elements to be considered in the intercourse of human beings. Only by being in sympathy with a person can we understand him. God is a person, and the same rule holds good. In sympathy with Him we shall understand His ways, and those ways which we cannot understand we shall trust. . . .

Dogmas are the garments of God ; dry, if viewed intellectually, but if viewed in the atmosphere of personal relationship, how different they will appear.

Come, therefore, into *contact* with God, into personal sympathy with Him. So will the problems become clearer.

These extracts are not specially chosen ones. They are not taken from Father Maturin's great pulpit utterances. They are extracts which chance has placed in my way—notes of a retreat which was given to a group of ladies at a convent in Sussex. But they tell us intimately something of his mind and method.

During his recent visit to New York I saw him several times. I dined in his company on March 14, at the house of our common friend, Dr. McMahon, the Rector of the Church of Our Lady of Lourdes, with whom he was staying. I never saw him in better health or spirits. He discussed his plans and was determined to sail by the *Lusitania*, which he thought from her speed the safest of all ships. Also he enjoyed its perfect equipment, which appealed to his imagination as a triumph of modern shipbuilding. I told him that I had received a warning that the Germans were determined on her destruction, and I was hesitating whether I should not myself sail by preference in an American liner. I had arranged to return to England on April 3. He laughed at my fears, and said that he himself was so determined to keep to the *Lusitania*, that although he could not accompany me, as he had engagements after April 3, he meant to delay his departure until her next sailing in May, although he would have preferred to return a fortnight earlier.

I met him again a few days later at dinner, at the house of Mrs. Augustus Paine, with whom I was staying. Mrs. Paine had been a devoted disciple of Father Maturin some twenty-five years earlier, when, as a Cowley Father, he used to preach at Philadelphia. She became a Catholic largely under his influence two years ago. He was on this occasion in even better spirits. He always delighted in congenial conversation, and that night he stayed long after the other guests had left.

I could not but see that the immense fruit borne by his sermons in New York had been a very real joy to him. He told me that he was far happier than on the occasion of his last visit to America two years ago. His buoyant spirits impressed me so much that I laughingly told him that he seemed to have

INTRODUCTION

grown ten years younger, and that I who was born nine years later than he felt myself quite an old man by comparison.

I saw him once more when I was staying with my friend, Mr. Thomas Kelly, at the Buckingham Hotel, New York. Mr. Kelly asked Father Maturin and Dr. McMahon to come on Maundy Thursday to a farewell dinner before my departure, which was to take place on Holy Saturday morning. Father Maturin was again on this occasion in remarkably good spirits and remained with us long after Dr. McMahon had taken his leave. When he was going I said, ' This is good-bye until we meet in England.' He replied, ' No, I mean to come and see you off on the *Lusitania* on Saturday.' On the following evening I received a message that he was so tired that he must give up this plan. He had, I think, been preaching at Dr. McMahon's church on Good Friday. Thus I never saw him again.

One of his American sermons I heard. It was, I gathered, the least successful he had given. Mrs. Paine described some of the earlier ones as among the finest she had ever listened to. The one I heard was not well constructed and for the first twenty minutes I was a little disappointed with it. But then the inspiration came, and though it could not redeem a certain absence of unity in the construction of the sermon, I carried away the remembrance of passages marked by that wonderful psychological insight which came to him often with the effect of great suddenness in the pulpit.

Father Maturin's end was that of a hero. And by a happy chance we know some of its details. After luncheon on that fated Friday, May 7, at about two o'clock he was seen on the deck saying his Office. The torpedo struck the ship soon after two. How long it took him to realise to the full what had happened we do not know, but we do know from a lady who survived that shortly before the ship went down, twenty minutes later, he was seen striving to keep people calm, giving Absolution to those who asked for it, fastening on lifebelts, and helping women and children into the boats. The lady who relates this was herself helped into a boat by Father Maturin, and just as the boat was putting off he threw a little child into her arms with the injunction 'Try to find its mother.' Then he stood waiting for the end, quite calm, but as white as a sheet. With his keen sense of the drama of life he probably realised vividly the approaching end. He put on no lifebelt. He did not take off his coat. He made no attempt to escape, but simply awaited death. We can picture him then as ever, intensely human and intensely spiritual—realising keenly that his own death was now a matter of minutes, yet eager to the last to do good and help others and throwing himself on God for strength and support.

His loss to us is, I think, greater than many realise. His power of entering into other minds is a very rare power, perhaps more rare among Catholics than among others because the extreme definiteness of Catholic traditions may stiffen smaller minds—may so completely fix their direction that the imagination loses its suppleness and cannot enter into any other view. Yet this imaginative understanding of other standpoints than your own is among the greatest gifts for winning souls to Christianity and to the Catholic Church.

INTRODUCTION

He was wholly out of sympathy with the excesses of Modernism. The publication of Father Tyrrell's Life was a deep grief to him, for he had greatly admired the spiritual lessons contained in Father Tyrrell's early books, and he had an old family friendship with the man himself. ' I shall nevermore take any interest in anything Tyrrell has said,' was his deliberate utterance after reading Tyrrell's Life. On the other hand, Father Maturin detested the narrow anti-Modernists and was keenly alive, just as Cardinal Newman was, to the necessity of facing new facts which must affect our view of the universe, and of saying old things in a new way for a new generation. His was a temper at once conservative and yet adaptable and plastic. His knowledge of theology was not detailed enough to make him fully realise difficulties in applying his principles, but his temper and principles themselves in this matter were very helpful to many who consulted him. His books do not adequately reveal the man's mind, but *The Price of Unity* will, I venture to say, in spite of literary defects, hold an important place in the Roman controversy of the future. Nevertheless what was greatest in him is not to be found in his written works. It was inseparably blended with his living personality, and can therefore never be replaced for us. The loss is thus quite irreparable. It can perhaps best be mitigated by the collection of notes from his sermons which, though they will not recall the magic of the spoken word, may keep a record of great thoughts begotten in moments of inspiration.

WILFRID WARD.

Reprinted from the *Dublin Review*.

CONTENTS

	PAGE
PREFATORY NOTE BY MRS. WILFRID WARD	v
INTRODUCTION BY WILFRID WARD	ix

SERMONS

THE MYSTERY OF SUFFERING	1
THE MIRACLE OF THE LOAVES AND FISHES	20
ON PRAYER	38
THE MYSTERY OF HIDDEN POWER	57
THE HUMILITY OF MARY (I)	69
THE HUMILITY OF MARY (II)	83
THE CALL OF GOD	96
SERMON PREACHED AT THE CLOTHING OF A NUN	114
CHRISTIANITY AND THE MODERN WORLD	131
SIN	143
THE LORD'S PRAYER	162

NOTES FOR SERMONS

NOTES OF A SERMON FOR THE RENOVATION OF VOWS	183
SORROW TURNED INTO JOY	187
THREE PARADOXES	192

CONTENTS

	PAGE
PERSONALITY	217
INTRODUCTION TO A RETREAT FOR PERSONS LIVING IN THE WORLD	221
INTRODUCTION TO A RETREAT FOR A RELIGIOUS ORDER	227
THE MANGER AND THE CROSS	233
THE TEMPTATIONS OF OUR LORD	242
THE LIGHT OF THE WORLD	261
ST. IGNATIUS	269
ST. THERESA	278
ST. MATTHEW	287
EVE	293
APPENDIX: FATHER MATURIN'S LAST SERMON	300

SERMONS[1]

THE MYSTERY OF SUFFERING

'Then Satan answered the Lord, and said, Doth Job fear God for nought? Put forth Thine Hand now, and touch all that he hath, and he will curse Thee to Thy Face.'—JOB i. 9 and 11.

OF every great question that stirs the minds of men, they naturally and instinctively ask and demand a simple, direct and reasonable solution. The instinct of the mind is not content with an answer which is not direct and simple and stated in a rational form. Yet we know, as a matter of fact, that in all the great questions touching on human life man does not get such an answer as that. The result is that among those who study the deep mysteries of life we find two classes: those, namely, who profess to have an answer for everything, and think that the thing for which they have not an answer is not worth answering; and those deeper and more thoughtful men who accept the mysteries as they find them, and stand before them with question upon question rising up, for which they have not the answer they fain would have, but who have something better and more reasonable, viz. that attitude of mind which is ready to wait till the solution comes. So, if we turn to those who stand as the high

[1] Sermon preached at St. Alban's, Holborn, March 26, 1893.

priests of science, we find that those who enter most deeply into the secrets of life have learned this :—a proper attitude of expectation before the mysteries which come before them; and this also, that while answers come in many unexpected ways—rising up from the depths below and descending from the heights above—yet that the answer as to the final cause of all, the meaning of the mystery of life, the solution of all the difficulties of science is not yet attained. We find the great high priests of science ministering before Nature, in the attitude not only of inquiry but of something more, of expectation and of faith. From deep study they have learned an attitude of respect and patient expectation and of faith.

It is the same with all the great mysteries with which we are brought into contact in religion. There are questions to which we would fain have answers: Tell me, what can you answer to this great question, for if you cannot answer I will have nothing to do with you. Some religions have given one answer, some another, more or less satisfactory; but every religion, in proportion to its truth, says : I cannot give you an answer to all questions; but there is something better—that same attitude before the mysteries of the unseen world, the mysteries which faith professes to solve and answer, as that of the student of Science before Nature—the patient expectation and faith of the saints.

There is that greatest of questions, which seems as if it must have an answer, the question why God allows the just to suffer ? It has been asked again and again through all the ages of the past, and solution after solution has been attempted. Some have said that

THE MYSTERY OF SUFFERING

there is no suffering at all—that is the solution which the Stoics have given. Others have said, wait in blind submission to the Will of God—that brings in a dreary fatalism. Others, throwing away the key of knowledge, tell us that the solution will only be found beyond the grave—a vague and incomplete answer, ignoring the fact that above all things the religion of Christ is a religion of the present. No such answers are satisfactory. The present is bound up so intimately with the future, that if sin on earth does not bring its hell on earth, I will not believe that beyond the grave it will do so ; if righteousness here does not bring peace now, I will not believe that it will bring peace hereafter.

In the first five Books of Moses we find no mention of the rewards of a future life : all is brought to bear on the present. Here is the school of character, the life worth living ; truth is truth, and righteousness is righteousness, whether there be a heaven and a hell or not. Earth and eternity are so closely linked together, the relationship between the two is so close, that all must begin on earth ; the kingdom of heaven begins with us.

We have again and again to turn away from speculation and from reason, and ask ourselves— what is the attitude of religion in relation to the mystery of suffering ? The more pious, the more religious, the more full of faith, the more thoughtful, men of the world have been, the more terribly anxious also have they been as to the relationship of God to the moral world. On the lips of Abraham there is the complaint, ' Wilt Thou destroy the righteous with the wicked ? ' as if he were almost afraid that God would do so ; as if the surface of life did not seem to show that God would not do such an unjust thing. David said, ' I see the ungodly in such prosperity.' Under the light of revelation we find that it is not the most superficial men but the most thoughtful, not the most irreligious but the most religious, who find that God does not seem to govern the world rightly, that He seems to punish the righteous and let the wicked live out all their days in peace. And they ask again and again of religion what light it can cast on the strange mystery of God's moral government of the world. When we test God's government of the world by our sense of justice, they do not seem to correspond ; God does not seem to be just in His government of all things. One man says : I never knew what suffering was till I began to be a Christian ; all went well with me, the strong man armed kept the house, but when the stronger, that is Jesus Christ, entered in, then came the struggle. Again and again we find it is a man's experience, that when he lived without God the world smiled on him, and that when he lived for God all seemed against him.

Is this world the world of God ? Does God care for His creatures ? Is it all the same to God that the righteous suffer and the wicked live in prosperity ? We must have a solution ; the question is so intense, we feel it burning in our conscience, stirring up our thoughts, appealing to our hearts—we must have some answer that is satisfactory. We look up to God and say : O God, Thou must not play with me ; if I am to worship and believe in Thee, above all things I must know that Thou art just, that Thou dost justly.

THE MYSTERY OF SUFFERING

If we turn from our own speculations to Holy Scripture, we certainly find that it does not shirk the question. When the Son of God came they said, 'Here is the Heir, come let us kill Him.' All the powers of evil gathered round the spotless Son of God; He met suffering on all sides, the thorns were woven in His Crown, His Hands were pierced, His Feet were transfixed with nails, His Side was opened and there flowed forth a stream of Blood, His Back was laid bare to the scourge. From the crown of His Head to the sole of His Foot He was covered with wounds and suffering. We cannot say that God shirked the question. Upon all the pages of Scripture it is the one thing which stands out as the characteristic of the All-holy Sufferer. We must bring the two words together, the *All-holy Sufferer*; and we must go further, for He was the Son of God, co-equal with the Father, consubstantial, co-eternal. When the spotless Son of God came down to earth it seemed as if suffering took hold of Him, rent His nature to pieces, and left His Body on the Cross, bereft of life and covered with the marks of suffering. We must say that at all events the Gospel does not shirk the question. And we find, from the sufferings of the Lord Jesus Christ, that suffering cannot be inconsistent with the love of God, however we may explain it, because God could not but love His Holy Son. If I am striving to live like His Son I must not be surprised if I am dealt with as He was. ' If they have called the master of the house Beelzebub, how much more shall they call them of his household?' If they treated Jesus so, how much more His followers; and the more like I am to the Son of God, the more I must expect to be dealt with as He was in this world. So whatever is the solution, it is not inconsistent with the love of God.

But we will not look to-day on the sufferings of Jesus and the great revelation which the Gospel shows. We will look backwards, and get some key to the mystery of suffering from a time before the Gospel was written. It is remarkable that there is one book in the Old Testament which is the history of the life of a man who was certainly not within the Covenant—he stands on the broader basis of natural religion. He was not a Jew. Some suppose the book was written before the Law was given to Moses; certainly the word 'Jehovah' is not found in it. There is no allusion to the Law or to the Covenant. Job was outside of it. The light which the Book of Job casts on the mystery of suffering is altogether unique and complete in itself. It stands on a prior basis to the revelation of the Lord Jesus Christ; it is written in such strange mystic language, with such sublimity of figure, that many have lost the key to its lessons.

We are as it were in a great theatre, and looking on at a great moral drama which is laid bare by the finger of God the Holy Ghost; and we, as from the very first we are let into the secret of it all, sit and watch the struggle which goes on in the heart of a great man when taken from the sphere of speculation to that of reality. He had his theory; will that Sciolism bear him up when he has to suffer himself? We see the test of the man's faith being brought to the point by the mystery of his own personal sufferings. We see all that was not true and reasonable and right in his faith going to pieces. We see his faith enlarged,

THE MYSTERY OF SUFFERING

broadened and extended, his religion taking a new aspect under the mystery of pain, and pain revealing to him the mystery of God in the world in a way that he never knew before. I will not give much for my faith till I have put it to the test of what it will enable me to bear. You go into the ward of a hospital and say to one of those who are lying there : my friend, you are bearing something of the Cross of Jesus. And the man answers : do you know what you are talking about ; I lie here in darkness and despair, and feel the ground-work of my faith failing under the strain of pain. I look up and say, is there no God ? Do you know what you are saying when you speak these platitudes of the love of the Saviour ? You do not know what it is to have your faith strained to cracking point, when God seems to have forsaken and left you in the solitude of the Cross. And then you tell me to rejoice to suffer with Jesus.

Job had his theory ; it was partly, but only partly, true, it did not cover all the phenomena of the truth. It had never been tested ; it was satisfactory to his reason and his conscience, but it had never been put to the test of his own personal life. Then comes the scourge, the flail is lifted and blow after blow falls, and the man is felled to the earth calling out to God, ' Why hast Thou forsaken me ? ' We watch step after step of the struggle, till at last the man comes out with perfect peace, with renewal of faith, with a larger, deeper holiness, with all that was inconsistent in his faith broken and tossed to the winds by the agony of his own personal pain.

We are first shown Job as a man who was upright and just in all his ways, surrounded with everything that could make life worth living. We know how hard it is for a rich man to enter the kingdom of heaven, but Job seems to have solved that difficulty. So we read, ' Hast thou considered My servant Job, that there is none like him in the earth, a perfect and upright man, one that feareth God and escheweth evil ? ' We see a man with every blessing of this world and the next heaped upon him. He did not know anything about pain or great distress or suffering, yet under prosperity his character had developed. The curtain falls, and it rises upon another scene. Two Persons are conversing together—God and the devil. We cannot deny the personality of the devil if we believe in the Personality of God—the personality of the devil is wrapped up with the Personality of God. We find in the Old Testament that while the Personality of God is insisted upon, so is that of the devil. The two converse together, and what is the subject of their discourse ? Their eyes are fixed on this little world here below, with all its mystery of sorrows and of troubles and of strifes. The eyes of God and of Satan are fixed on one man. God challenges His own enemy and the enemy of man. ' Hast thou considered My servant Job ? ' Satan's answer is remarkable : this Job—I don't believe in him ; I don't believe that Job is good, that he loves Thee, O God. But goodness, with Job, pays ; with him virtue is another name for utilitarianism, it has its own reward. Any man would be good while Thou dost bless his goodness like that. In the case of Job goodness brings a plenteous reward and a multitude of temporal blessings. Notice, the first person who brings up the charge of utilitarianism is the enemy of man-

THE MYSTERY OF SUFFERING

kind. He challenges God Himself. It is as much as to say: O God, I hate Thee, I have turned in rebellion against Thee, I cannot love Thee, neither can anyone else. Send suffering to Thy man who is so good, take from him those things that Thou hast given him, and he will curse Thee. You see the challenge against the character of God—if God must bribe love by giving temporal rewards to those who love Him, God is not lovable in Himself. So Satan deals a blow against the character of God. What answer is made? What answer would you wish to be made if the case were your own? If any person were to say to you that you love your husband because he has done all for you, all for your gratification, and that if he did not do such things you would cease to love him, what answer would you give? You would say: try me; and that is the answer that God makes when Satan says to Him, ' Doth Job fear God for nought ? ' Thou art bribing and winning his heart by prosperity, by money, by happiness. God answers: try him. Notice, God does not give Satan free play over His creature, He puts a limit. ' Behold, all that he hath is in thy power; only upon himself put not forth thine hand.' You may take his property, but you are not to touch himself. Test Job through his surroundings; you say he loves Me because of the family, the wealth, the large influence I have given him. Draw your cloud across his sun, take his friends, try him through his surroundings, but touch not himself.

As in all great dramas the audience are in all the secrets of the plot, so we watch as Job comes on the stage again. He has not heard the challenge. If he knew that he was being tested it would be no test at all.

The essence of a test is that the person who is being tried does not know it. You say: try me, O God. Then God comes and tries the soul, and the soul who is being tried does not know. But we are in the secret, and as the curtain rises we see Job surrounded by all the luxuries of life, happy in his family, respected by his fellow-men, and we watch to see if he will stand the test. Messenger after messenger of woe appears on the stage. The Sabeans have fallen on his oxen and asses and taken them away, slaying the servants. A fire from heaven has burnt up the sheep and servants. The Chaldeans in three bands have fallen on the camels and carried them away. A great wind from the wilderness has smitten the house where his children were, and they are dead. Blow after blow, but the limit is observed throughout. Job's circumstances, his surroundings, are all in the hands of Satan, but he so hides his hand that Job can never trace it. ' The Lord gave and the Lord hath taken away,' he says. It was not the Lord who took away at all, it was the devil, but so subtly was it done that Job traced to the hand of God what was done by God's great enemy. Now watch the effect on Job. In Eastern language we are told that Job ' rent his mantle and shaved his head, and fell down upon the ground and worshipped,' and said, ' The Lord gave and the Lord hath taken away ; blessed be the Name of the Lord.' In this test at all events Satan had failed. It was a proof to the devil and to God that Job's religion was sincere, that he was not one who loved God for temporal blessings, but for something deeper still.

The veil is lifted once more in the other world, and we again hear God and Satan conversing together.

THE MYSTERY OF SUFFERING

God says, 'Hast thou considered My servant Job?' —the very same words:—now do you not believe in righteousness for its own sake, that Job loves Me for My own worth? Satan's answer is remarkable: 'Skin for skin, yea all that a man hath will he give for his life.' Put forth and take his health; while a man has his health he can do anything. Job is a man of energy, of resource, he can make a new property. But put forth Thy hand and throw him on to a bed of sickness, with the prospect of never again regaining his health, and he will curse Thee to Thy face. It was an extreme measure, first to test him through his circumstances, then in himself. Job had stood one test. God was beginning to feel sure of His man, if we may say so with reverence. Here is a man, of whom I can test his heart and his reins. But again God puts a limit. 'Behold he is in thine hand; but save his life.' God seems to say, you may test him through his bodily health, but not through the taking away of his life. You may take him to the verge of the grave, but bring him up again.

The curtain rises on another act. Job comes on the scene robbed of his children and of his earthly possessions, a poor man, but full of resources and of power, and with strong religious faith. Then comes the next great blow: Job is smitten with an odious disease, a disease which in that country and age was always looked upon as a special token of the wrath of God. If we translate it into the language of Job's time, it was a disease only given to the man who was a very grievous sinner indeed. Job finds that not only were all his earthly possessions gone, but that God was pouring the vials of His wrath on his body.

For seven days he sits on the dung-hill, with ashes on his head and on his garments, in silence. His three friends come to meet him, and in the graphic imagery of the book we are told that 'when they lifted up their eyes and knew him not, they lifted up their voice and wept, and they rent their garments and sprinkled dust on their head, and sat down with him upon the ground seven days and seven nights; and none spake a word unto him, for they saw that his grief was very great.' For seven days he searches to the depth of his soul, for a great question has come to him to be answered; then solemnly Job opens his lips, not with querulous passion but with an outburst of passionate grief, as he curses the day that he was born. What was stirring Job to the depth of his heart, so that he bursts forth into all this tumult of passionate accusation against God and speaks the language almost of unbelief? Does God not care what a man does, will He treat all men as one? It is the hardest thing of all to say, God has forsaken me. What calls forth all this terrible outburst from the lips of Job? It is this. We find that his faith is shaken to its foundation; for in the primitive conception of religion the whole question of rewards and sufferings was brought to a single point, which was this: God always rewards the good with temporal blessings, and punishes the bad with temporal curses. Certainly if Job had known the Law he might have quoted the Fifth Commandment.[1] He might have shown how, when the people obeyed God, He blessed them, and when they violated the commands of God He punished them. He might have shown from the

---

[1] Vulgate Fourth Commandment.

THE MYSTERY OF SUFFERING

study of nature that God does reward the good with temporal blessings, and punish the bad with temporal curses. That was Job's religion. He had seen suffering before, men who had been scourged by the hand of God, and his answer was this: that a man who is suffering must be a bad man; but he felt himself to be good. Where he saw temporal blessings he attributed goodness to the heart of the man, and where he saw temporal curses he concluded that the sufferer must be a sinner, and that in proportion to the grievousness of the suffering. That was the test; but would this test bear out the whole of the facts? When Job suddenly found himself under the curse of God, all slipping from his hands, the storm breaking over him till he had forfeited his health and prosperity and his family and all, then the question was this: Is God good, or is God bad? My whole idea of my religion shows me that He is bad. For what was the fact? His conscience said to him, You are a good man; and his religion said to him, You cannot be a good man, or you would not be suffering. So his religion and his conscience were in direct antagonism. He knew that he did not deserve suffering; if he was to keep true to his conscience he must say, I know that I do not deserve it; God has no right to send it me. If God rewards the good and punishes the bad, He has no right to send me suffering, for I am not a bad man. Under such circumstances, if a man finds his religion in direct antagonism to his conscience, there is one of two things which he can do. If the man is weak he will throw aside his religion; we know there are many such men, who at the first difficulty that comes into their religious faith throw off their religion as a worn-out garment. The man who does that is not worthy of the name of a man. When difficulties come into your life it is not your place as a reasonable man to turn your back and run away; the more manly you are, the more you will fight it out till you get a solution. But there are men who fall into the error of Calvinism and say, if a man is among the elect he will be saved, if he is not among the elect he will be damned. Other men say, if this is my God I cannot worship Him; I cannot worship a God that is unjust. Rather should a man say to himself, There must be some element of truth in it; I will fight the thing out until I get the solution which will reconcile my faith and my conscience.

Thus Job might have thrown aside his religion. But Job was a religious man, and to say that he was a religious man is to say that he could not possibly throw away his religion, for it was the foundation of his life. Or he might have said: well, I suppose I am a bad man, I have been deceiving myself. There are some men who go on saying that till we are quite sick and weary. The first thing that comes is self-accusation. Their heart does not accuse them, but they get out of the difficulty in this way. If you do not know yourself to be a sinner, do not say that you are one; if you do not feel that you deserve punishment, do not say that you do. Do not get out of the difficulties of life by giving the lie to your conscience, saying that you deserve a thing which your conscience says you do not deserve. Job's religion said he must be a bad man, or God would not punish him; his conscience said he was not a bad man, so he breaks forth into

THE MYSTERY OF SUFFERING

what almost reaches the supremest blasphemy. He could see no token of God doing anything for him, no token of the government of God, all things were mixed and at variance; he bursts forth into open recrimination of the justice and truth of God, and then into deep pathetic words of prayer. He cannot let go his hold of his faith until he gets something strong to stand upon; he will not purchase his faith at the expense of a lie.

Behind the scenes Satan is saying: here is a discovery—a man who does not care for his health or his possessions; the one thing the man cares for is that God should be just: the strongest, deepest thing in him is his relationship to God. We see Satan behind the veil looking with wide-eyed wonder at a man who can love God more the more He takes from him; the one question of happiness and life is, whether God be just and true—I cannot live unless I can believe in and worship my God.

After many a page of struggle there comes a new person on the scene—Elihu. Some have thought him to be the Angel of the Lord, the appearance of Jesus Christ the Lord as the Mediator. He comes in to stand between the religion and the conscience, the Mediator who will give some hint of truth. What he says amounts to this: is the whole answer of the question as to suffering, that it must have to do with punishment and reward? May not suffering have another element, may it be not punitive but disciplinary? We know that when we punish our children we discipline them; but in that age it was almost a revelation, that suffering was not punishment for sin but a discipline of life, and as Job listens he begins to settle down.

In a later chapter God Himself stands before Job to challenge him. God did not explain suffering at all, but in one word what He said to Job was this— look out through the world of nature, and tell Me, can you understand My government of the world of nature in many matters? Tell Me, have you an answer to everything in the natural world? Have you a logical answer to every mystery there? Can you understand the animal creation? The instinct of the beast is wiser, more unerring than men. Can you understand My government of the natural world? If not, how can you expect to understand My moral government? And then, without one word of solution, for it would have spoiled the test, Job falls at the feet of God. 'My soul is even as a weaned child.' 'Shall not the Judge of all the earth do right?' 'Yea, let God be true and all men liars' —'that Thou mightest be justified in Thy saying, and clear when Thou art judged.' He stands before the greatest mystery, but without any solution save this—that which science gives—the solution of patient expectation and faith. But more than that, his whole nature gets tamed and disciplined, his mind trained, his will disciplined, his heart purified, and so the man under the mystery of suffering finds his whole nature in accord with his conscience. He says, I am not bad, but I was mistaken in my idea that suffering is for punishment only; everything is for the making and shaping of character, the formative principle of faith. So every element that is untrue is discarded, and all that is true deepened and enlarged.

THE MYSTERY OF SUFFERING

Such an answer as that God rewards the good and punishes the bad is all very well till a man has to suffer himself, and then he knows that it will not do. Job came out of the furnace of suffering with all that was true and noblest in his faith preserved, but with much added on, and above all with a mind set at rest, without a complete answer but this—certainly God is just. Above everything else suffering means moral development, and suffering is the witness that man on earth can give to the character of God in heaven, and before the vast world behind the veil.

You tell me you have brought the suffering on yourself, and that to know that Christ suffered that you might suffer with Him does not help you to bear it. You have not faith to accept it. But if I tell a man this, that through the unseen universe they are watching to see whether he can love God for Himself and be true to Him, then I appeal to the man's heroism, then he can stand. Poor man! you brought the suffering on yourself. Yes, he says; and I care nothing for a solution that is to be found in the next world. But if you tell him that one behind the veil has made a challenge that men will not love God but for what they can get, he braces himself up and says: I will show that enemy that my God is worthy of love.

We must pass through the testing of suffering, of which there are three kinds. Physical suffering, which is the lowest, keen and intense though it be. You have been in robust health, but then comes suffering; you are told you will perhaps never have your health again, then at once the strain of your faith begins. If you look behind the veil and hear the words, 'Doth he serve God for nought?' then you brace yourself up and say, 'The Lord gave and the Lord hath taken away; blessed bet he Name of the Lord.' 'Though He slay me, yet will I trust in Him.' Or there are deeper sufferings than sufferings of the body; the mother is suffering agonies of body, but she forgets them in the mental anguish over her child's pain. Mental pain, the loss of one dearer to oneself than life, to be separated from one who is our heart's better self, the sorrow that strips life of all its sunshine, it is the testing of God; but mark this: if you knew it was the testing of character it would be no test at all; it is the darkness, the incapacity to see, which is the trial. If we knew that God was doing it to test us it would lose its reality. We must go on in darkness, and hold us still to our God. There is a keener suffering still—those fearful moral sufferings, those scathing sufferings of temptation. We must suffer in our moral nature being tempted. The man says, I don't know what has happened to me, all my passions are wakened into new life, I know not where to turn from the torments of temptation. It is the testing of what we can stand for God. He looks up into the face of God and says: do with me what Thou wilt, for I know that Thou lovest me. 'Try me, O God, and seek the ground of my heart.'

So we can see that a special light is thrown on the mystery of suffering from the Book of Job: it is the testing of character, not merely here on earth in relation to men and women, in relation to our religion, but it is the testing of our character in relationship to God; and the essential element is that we cannot understand it, that we cannot see any reason why it comes. Unconsciously we trace it to a wrong hand—

we say it is God, and it is the devil; the devil is testing you, and God is watching to see. Satan is waiting to hear the first curse break from your lips. Man stands in his triple nature, and in his testing the character of God is set right before the world, which forgets or tries to ignore Him. Man stands in a middle place, in a vicarious position between the seen and the unseen, living by faith, holding on by faith to the mysteries of life, purified and sanctified by the Mystery of Suffering.

THE MIRACLE OF THE LOAVES AND FISHES [1]

'There is a lad here who hath five barley loaves, and two small fishes: but what are they among so many?'—ST. JOHN vi. 9.

THE multitudes had been following our Blessed Lord out in the wilderness—and had had nothing to eat. They were absorbed for the moment in their spiritual wants, and for the moment it seemed as though their material wants too were satisfied, as they gazed with straining eyes upon Him who had spoken to them words such as they had never heard before, that none had ever spoken before, words that had sunk deep into their souls. They were absorbed beyond the reach of ordinary human wants, they were absorbed for the moment in their spiritual wants; they had felt the thrill of the voice of Him Who was perfect Man and perfect God, of Him Who by His Manhood had touched the very lowest depths of humanity, and by His Godhead had reached the sublimest heights. In the wonderful link of that all-embracing sympathy they heard Him speak; and as He spoke they felt within themselves such a movement, such spiritual longings, such a capacity for spiritual things, that it seemed to them as though everything else sunk into the background whilst they heard the voice of the

[1] Sermon preached at St. Margaret's Settlement, Rotherhithe, December 5, 1904.

Son of God made man. And so they followed Him into the wilderness; they had a glorious Retreat, and the Conductor was the Son of God. They listened to words that stirred within them everything spiritual they had ever felt—the memories of long-gone days, the memories of early childhood, that since they had become men and women had fallen away. All came back upon them with an enthusiasm, a desire and a force they had never felt since the days of their childhood, and, as the Voice rang out, it touched the very depths of their souls. What can people do better? What can you do better? If you have to choose, what can you choose better than the life of prayer? What are the needs, what are the desires of this world compared with those of the other world? Do you feel, if you live only for a life of prayer and devotion, what matter if everything else goes to rack and ruin? There were men and women there who had forgotten everything; women who had come straight out of their homes, men who had come straight from their work, with their tools over their shoulders —who had forgotten everything, who remembered nothing but that they were spiritual beings; they seemed no longer material beings, but could only remember that they were spiritual beings come to feed their souls upon God. And then came the great reaction, the reaction that such things are bound to bring. Many a person, after coming out from Retreat, has found that he never felt the claims of the world so strongly before. The spiritual side had been to the front in the quiet of the Retreat, but, on coming into contact with the world again, he is conscious of other sides lurking behind, waiting to be drawn forth. And so these multitudes, 5000 men besides women and children—some 15,000 or 18,000 people, that is to say—had forgotten their bodily wants; they had forgotten, under the great and paralysing excitement, their hunger, and as soon as the strain was removed bodily nature reasserted itself, and they began to remember that they were men and women. Then came the great reaction, and it was our Blessed Lord who called attention to their needs there, in the wilderness, far away from shops and places where they could buy the food that was wanted. These people, in their religious enthusiasm, had become extraordinarily unpractical. There was the mother with the child at her breast, with no food wherewith to feed herself; the man who had come straight from his work, who had forgotten to bring any food with him into the wilderness. But, after all, was it not a wonderful act of faith? They were with Jesus the Son of God; they would remember that of old He had rained down manna from Heaven for them to eat, and that men did eat angels' food; and if the question of food had occurred to them at all, they would quickly have felt within themselves: we can leave that to the great Teacher. But Christ did not come to teach us that. We must not think that if we look after the spiritual side He will take care of the material side. We must not say: if I go to Church I need not mind my daily needs so much; if I look after God, God will look after me; if I pray, and if I come out into the wilderness without bread, or without even a drop of water to slake my thirst in order to follow Jesus of Nazareth, what will it matter? He will open the heavens and rain down bread from Heaven to eat. There is no doubt that if our Blessed Lord had done that, He would have taught us the worst lesson we ever learnt; He would have taught us that religion can save a person the trouble of thinking for himself, that religion can save a person the trouble of looking after his temporal affairs—his worldly business—that he need not look after them at all. If a working man goes to Mass every day, and remains too long and comes late to his business and says: what matter? God will take care of the business for me—if Christ had taught that, that would have been a fatal lesson. And why? This is why. Would it not be a splendid thing, you might think, if, in order to follow spiritual longings, you went to Church, and came home and found the table spread? What would be the result? That the more religious we are, the more unpractical we should become; we should feel that so long as we were saying our prayers we were doing our duty, not that we were neglecting our duty. In other words, we should forget the one great thing in religion, that God has tied up our souls in our bodies, and that that body of ours is intended to teach us a great lesson. We know, if we know ourselves at all, that we learn more lessons through our bodies than through any other part of ourselves. My body wants sleep and cannot get as much as it wants: my body wants food and has to learn to fast: I am always training my body. What is my body doing for me? My body is training my soul all the time, and my soul is learning many a great and splendid lesson of self-discipline, of self-denial and of self-sacrifice, many lessons of the Cross that I could not have learned if

I had not got a body. If our Lord had said to us: say your prayers, and I will look after your body; if you do not want to work, only say your prayers and bread will come down from Heaven—I cannot imagine a more disastrous lesson. As we Catholics look back and read the Gospel history of that 5000 in the wilderness, who had forgotten to bring any food with them, we must feel that if our Lord had said: never mind, I have the keys of Heaven, and there is bread enough; nobody ever asked me in vain: follow me into the wilderness and you will find food enough there—that would have been a very bad lesson.

But He did not say it. What He said was: there you are. You have come out into the wilderness, and now that you are here you will have to think for yourselves. What are you going to do? They had forgotten their hunger, and it was our Lord called attention to it. They were so spiritually carried away that they had forgotten they were hungry, and the Son of Man was the first to refer to it. Even the disciples had forgotten they were hungry; the representatives of the Catholic Church had forgotten it; the Son of God made man first called their attention to it. And our Lord said: now you have to feed your body, to look after it. All the religion in the world won't give you food. You have got to work for it. If you go out into the wilderness, you won't get food by merely praying for it. Prayer without work won't get food. By working without prayer perhaps you won't get it either; and if you only pray without work you may not get it; but pray with all your heart and work with both your

MIRACLE OF LOAVES AND FISHES

hands, and what is the result? The mere struggle for food will do a great deal of good. Some of you here, my dear children, could teach many of us, perhaps, great lessons of extraordinary patience and wonderful faith, because you have gone to bed at night heavy of heart, saying: God knows what I am going to do to get food for the children to-morrow morning. You know that if you sit with your hands before you, you will get nothing; but you also know that there is a God, and that, if you pray, somehow or other God will help you. It was your body taught you that lesson. If you had no body you would not have learnt that lesson. What lessons these bodies of ours, which so often bring us so much trouble, teach. We think it would be so grand if we had no bodies, if we had no need to sleep or to eat daily. What a splendid life it would be: but what splendid lessons we should never learn! The angels know nothing of the troubles of life; they are kindling with the love of God, but they have not had to fight the battle of life. One small trial, and then they saw the Vision of God. I remember seeing a wonderful picture of an angel feeling, with tender fingers, the sharp pricks of the Crown of Thorns; and the angel's face wore an expression of surprise. They do not understand pain as our Lord understood it. Ah, we could teach the angels some lessons! Just think, the angels of God beholding the face of their Father in Heaven, sent out as ministering spirits, guardian angels—some are perhaps standing behind you at this very moment—those angels of God look down with wondering eyes on the bitterness of our life, and on the hardness of our toil. Some, perhaps, feel our hands and say: how hard they feel; what a curious thing that body is! But God says: yes, but through that body man is trained, often through hunger, often through thirst, often through pain, often through weariness. Sometimes that body is so tired that he can scarcely drag one leg after another. But the splendid spirit looks up, and the angels look down, and feel they could almost worship the strange beings that God loves so much.

And so, my brethren, I think we must see that what our Blessed Lord did in the wilderness when He called attention to the fact that people had bodies, was meant to teach us that people must not be careless, because they are religious, as to whether they do their business properly. We must not think that it does not matter whether we keep our accounts or not, whether we answer our letters or not. I think we learn that lesson. I remember a good lady once saying to me, 'It is a most extraordinary thing: my husband is such a good man, he goes to Mass every day, he goes constantly to Holy Communion, he spends a great deal of time in the parish, and does a good deal of parish work, and yet his business is going to the dogs.' 'Well,' I said, 'I suppose so. If he spends all that time in Church, and looking after other people's affairs, he must neglect his own business.' All the religion in the world will not keep his accounts for him; a business man must do his business, for if not you may be perfectly certain that the business will fail. All the religion in the world won't make up for that. It is a fact that you have to learn book-keeping if you are going to keep books. All the religion in the world will not keep your books for you; it cer-

MIRACLE OF LOAVES AND FISHES 27

tainly will help you to do it, and help in such a way as to prevent your sinking under any trouble, but it will not save you from the trouble. We are always dividing our lives into water-tight compartments, and religion is the most water-tight of any. Religion, as an end in itself, is very much the same thing as living for eating or sleeping as an end in itself. There is more harm in it perhaps. A man may live to eat and become a glutton, or he may live to sleep and become a sluggard; but if he makes religion an end in itself he spoils it, and the greatest force the world has ever known becomes a thing like a wild animal from which the teeth and claws have been extracted, and which has become a mere plaything. Religion is to push you upwards, to help you upwards, to force you upwards and to help you in looking to God. The troubles of life will force you to look to God, and religion sanctifies every department of life. The man of business, by looking after his office, may be gratifying God just as truly as a priest saying Mass, or as St. Paul when he went preaching through the world, because he is sanctifying the actions of his daily life. That was the lesson really taught in the wilderness. But let us look further—that was not the whole lesson.

Our Lord turned to the Apostles, who were looking on, to those twelve men who followed him, and asked them what they were going to do. Our Lord Himself was in the midst; not one of them had any money to spare; Jesus of Nazareth the carpenter's son, Matthew from the receipt of custom, James and John, fishermen, and so forth. They were all working men, their faces burnt with the sun, their hands hardened with toil. So they looked over the multitude—perhaps 18,000 people, all hungry—the women with the children crying at their breasts, the men beginning to feel rather ashamed that they had been so stupid as to have forgotten to bring food, and when our Blessed Lord began to speak to them about food, feeling the cravings of the body, and feeling too that it was a very foolish thing they had done to forget the needs of the body because they were saying their prayers. And then our Lord turns to the Apostles, and asks them, What are you going to do? And one says: Master, send them home. Whence shall we buy bread here in the wilderness? Send them home. My dear brethren, we are always hearing of that despairing problem of the impossibility of dealing with the feeding of a great mass of people. Your parish priest came here six months ago, and looked round upon this great parish with its need for the care of souls and bodies too, and said: here am I and my assistant priest, what can we do? How can we ever reach them? I give a few shillings here and there, but it is like dropping a pebble into the ocean with the idea of filling it up. And they feel almost as though they must turn to the Lord, and say: Master, send them away: we may deal with a few, how can we possibly deal with the multitude? We are striving after the impossible. Let us do the best we can with a few. And then our Lord says: no, you must not do that either. Here is a problem; you must solve it. I am not going to solve it for you by sending you bread from Heaven, nor must you solve it by sending the folk away. Perhaps the people may be thriftless, they may have come without bringing food for themselves; but there they are, and there is the Catholic church.

MIRACLE OF LOAVES AND FISHES

He turned to St. Peter, He turned to the twelve Apostles and said: what are you going to do? And St. Peter and the twelve Apostles say: send them away, and let us forget them. And some of you, my daughters, who have perhaps come down here for the first time to-day, and looking on these streets see them full of tokens of poverty and of hard work, feel pained, and you go home and try to forget it. You go home and you say to yourself: it is perfectly ridiculous: I am only one person: I can only give a few shillings. I will go home, and talk about it as much as I can, and get the needs of the people known; but as for my trying to do anything for all those thousands of people —10,000 perhaps, as there is in a neighbouring parish here—what can I do among such people, what can I do among so many? Send them away. Let me forget them. My dear brethren, there are numbers and numbers of people who have never even thought of these problems. There are numbers of people who have lived in this world with plenty, with more than they need, and it has never occurred to them to think that for every sixpence they have, for every sixpence that they waste, they will have to give an account. It seems to me an extraordinary thing in a world where other people are sweating and labouring and agonising, that such are doing nothing but amusing themselves, nothing but spending money on themselves. There are very few people who cannot deny themselves a little, who cannot do something, if only for an hour a week. I know not, when they come to stand before the Judge and see the marks in the hands of that Judge and behold Him as He is—I know not what they will say. I know that life is a serious thing, and that the responsibility of possession is a great responsibility ; and I know that no man possesses anything that he will not have to give an account of ; no man possesses sixpence more than is necessary for his actual needs that he will not have to render an account of. We have that bond with God Almighty : unity of the great human race, of the great mass of humanity ; all our infinite divisions are just to draw souls together and make that bond a reality, that by one giving and another taking the whole shall be bound more closely together. We think it is perfectly useless to cope with such miseries, therefore we make efforts again and again to forget the multitudes, and we feel hopeless and try to escape from our responsibilities. We are told that we are going to have an unparalleled hard winter. People are using their brains to find out what can be done. What are we to do ? Here are people who are suffering and in great poverty, unable to get work. They are perfectly willing to get work, if they can find it. One does not see what is to be done, how they are to be helped to help themselves and keep their families together, and one feels it is an almost despairing job.

What did our Lord do ? What did He do ? He said to the Apostles : you must not turn your backs upon this grave question. I have opened your eyes to see ; now go and do something. And Philip comes and says, Master what are we to do with all this multitude ; we would fain do something. They have nothing of their own. And our Lord says : listen ; go to everybody in that multitude, and ask them what they can do for themselves. Make them do their very best for themselves. Gather together

MIRACLE OF LOAVES AND FISHES

every scrap of food you can. Ask every one of all that mass of people. If there is a woman with a loaf of bread, let her give it for the good of others; if there is a person with a bottle of wine, let him give it for the good of others. I can do nothing at all until they help themselves. They must contribute all they can. Bring together all they can give, and then I will see what I can do. And the Apostles went about amongst the multitude, and said to this one and to that: what have you got? And they answered, nothing—nothing at all. And what have you? Nothing. Nor you? No, I have nothing. Nothing. Always the same reply. At last the twelve Apostles came back, and Andrew comes up to our Lord smiling, with the five loaves and two fishes in his hand, and he says: this is all that the multitude can give—five loaves and two small fishes. They have nothing more at all. They have done their very best. I have gone to every man, woman and child, and they had nothing. But I found a little boy and I said to the lad: well, my lad, and what have you got in this basket? And he told me, I have five loaves and two small fishes. Well, I said, will you give those loaves and fishes to Jesus of Nazareth and see what will happen? And the boy gave them to me and here is the lot. And then there came a great movement among the multitude, and the Lord said: make them sit down. And they all sat down, and He took the five loaves and the two fishes, and when He had given thanks He gave some to each of the Apostles, some to Peter, some to Philip. He kept on breaking, and they kept on coming back; and each time they returned

He said: here is more, more still. And still they kept coming backwards and forwards; there were more hungry mouths still. No, He said, it is not all gone yet. Is it not extraordinary how much there is in a little thing when once it is touched by the hand of the Son of God? At last the Apostles came and said, Master, they are all filled, and every one of them says they have never had such a splendid meal before. And where did it all come from? It all came from the five loaves and two small fishes. And the little boy stood beside with beaming face and said: my little lot fed all that people. And the people looked at Jesus Christ, and they could not make head or tail of it, that between the Teacher and the little lad they were all filled. But they were more than fed, and the disciples looked about and brought back twelve baskets full of remnants which remained, upon which the Apostles probably lived for many days after. Now what is the lesson?

The lesson is this: God won't do anything for those who won't do something for themselves. It is only when human aid fails that Divine aid comes in. If you want £10,000, and can only bring a couple of pence, somehow or other it is accomplished; Divine Love does it. Divine Love does wonderful things. Go to the United States; go to Ireland. Where did the money come from to build those great churches? It came from the few pence saved by hard-working men, pence earned in the sweat of their brow; they gave the money that was the result of their hard labour, and God blessed it. Ah, if we could only realise that in every sphere of life. A person says: well, but I can only earn a sixpence here and there, and

MIRACLE OF LOAVES AND FISHES

what is the use of that when the children are starving and my husband is going steadily to the bad?—often through the public-house. I answer: when God sees a person doing his very best, then at the last moment man's despair is God's opportunity. But God won't do anything until you help yourself.

It would be a disastrous thing if God came in and saved people the trouble of looking for their daily bread, because they had faith, because they were Catholics, because they had prayed. Prayer will make the impossible possible, but if you give nothing you get nothing. You take a handful of seed, and you throw it upon the earth; in a few years you have acres and acres of growing corn that will feed many people. If you put in no seed you get no corn. Here is a farmer: he harrows and ploughs the land, preparing it for the sowing of seed, and people say: what are you going to do? He says: that is all I can do. Then he puts in a handful of seed. And if you put that seed into the hands of God, what comes up? In a few years it covers acres and acres of ground, if somehow, somewhere, you commit it to the hand of God. If I, as a farmer, do not do the work, do not sweat and labour and toil, the seed will do nothing whatever. If I do not work hard, the seed of itself will do nothing. And therefore so it is with those who have to work and with those who strive to help the workers. Be sure of this. You say to yourself sometimes: here is a great colony, a crowded parish; I could only give one hour a week to work amongst these people, what is the good of that? What is that among so many? You say, perhaps: I am only a poor frail girl with no very great capacities, though I have a heart capable of loving God; but what is that among the great mass of work that needs to be done? That is exactly what the Apostles said. Yet you and I have seen what a very little thing can do when given into the hands of Him who is the Maker of all things. I suppose many people have often felt almost afraid when looking at quickly growing works—things begun with a great splash, with a great sound of trumpets—that they will not go on as they have begun: it is the little seed first planted in the earth that brings forth first the blade, then the ear, then the full corn in the ear; that brings forth first thirty, then sixty, then a hundred-fold. It was that one woman, who was ready to consecrate her life to hard work, to work that seemed ridiculous and at first impossible; but who prayed and worked, and worked and prayed, and gradually began to draw people who could give their time, till the thing grew—men knew not how, but God knew: there again it was the five loaves and two fishes that brought that great blessing. It was the heart that loved Him and the heart ready to sacrifice itself that brought about this result. That work is now a thriving work, and is full of greater developments and possibilities still. One person said: there is a tremendous business here, there is a great work to be done here. See what it began from. It is a tremendous business down here: it is an enormous parish: it takes away your breath to look at it. And you think: but what can I do? One thing I am going to do, I am going to do the very best I can. And that one person, doing the very best she could, in a quiet, simple, unostentatious way—

MIRACLE OF LOAVES AND FISHES

gathering a few here for a Mothers' Meeting, a few there for a Club, a few to undertake certain kinds of work—has met with response, and people look on, and the angels say: Oh Lord, we saw Thee do this in the wilderness 2000 years ago, and it is the way still. People must give of their time, if it is only a few hours, and when they give into Thy hands, with loving faith and confidence and trust, we know what Thou canst do. Though the workers are few, the results are beyond measure; we are amazed. That, my brethren, seems to me the lesson of the miracle.

You remember the poor widow putting into the Treasury her two mites that made one farthing. I read once that the offerings in the Temple were so tremendous, that the great coffers were so full the people had absolutely to be prohibited from giving any more. Think of it. Think of the clergy refusing to take any more offerings! They had more money than they knew what to do with! Among all these great gifts a woman dropped in two mites that made a farthing. And our Lord said:—I tell you that this poor widow hath cast in more than they all; for they have given of their abundance, have given of their riches in proportion, but she has given all that she hath. Let me tell you one little story in conclusion. A priest was working up in Liverpool, where a poor old woman was to be seen at Mass every morning of her life. One day she was not there, and they sent to the priest and told him she was dying. He went to see her and found her very near death; and she said to him, 'Father, you will find in that drawer some money; I put in whenever I could spare a penny.

And sometimes things went very hard, and I was often tempted, when I had to go to bed without supper, to open that drawer and take a few pence out. But thank God I did not. I want you to buy something for the Church with the money I have saved by this means.' The priest opened the drawer, and do you know what he found? He found £18. And he said, 'But I cannot take all that.' The woman burst out crying, and said, 'Won't God take it from me? You won't refuse a thing that I have been working for all these years.' And the priest took the money, and bought a beautiful chalice to hold the precious Blood. She has gone, but the chalice is there still. If a person who had barely enough to keep body and soul together could do this, it shows how little things grow—how the five loaves and the two small fishes grew and multiplied in the hands of Jesus Christ. Let us take this lesson at any rate. Nobody's work is too little to be neglected. If you can give but a few hours a week, then take that work and do it, and do not let any other engagement take the place of what is offered to God. If you have only a few pence, give them generously. Make a resolution that you will sometimes walk when you might take a bus, and so save money, and send it to the Settlement. If you do little things like that, you may say: it is only a few pence, and what are they among so many? But put by faith into the hands of Jesus Christ, they will grow and grow. So let everyone do their best and let no one feel that life is of little value, because nobody can do more than their best; nobody can give more than they have to give. And you, my children, on the other hand, are not to stand and simply wait for the work to come. Your business is to do the very utmost you can, to offer the little things that you can, and then see whether, offered in the spirit of prayer and faith, God does not take that small offering, and, somehow or other, make the five loaves and two small fishes satisfy all your daily needs.

ON PRAYER [1]

'Oh Thou that hearest the Prayer, unto Thee shall all flesh come.'—PSALM lxv. 2.

THERE are not many contrasts more startling and bewildering than that which exists between the promises of Holy Scripture and their fulfilment. From the first promise vouchsafed to Abraham down to the last promise of our Lord Jesus Christ, it always seems the same—the rich and ready outflow of the promised gift, never or rarely fulfilled. We close our Bibles, having read of the blessings given us through Christ, of their greatness and power, the supernatural grace and life of the Church: how glorious she is to be, 'without spot or wrinkle,' how unwavering in her teaching, 'the pillar and ground of the truth,' how powerful in her discipline, 'If he hear not the Church let him be unto thee as an heathen man and a publican'; how close and intimate the relation into which the soul is brought with Christ, we are made 'members of His Body.' By Baptism 'we put on Christ,' in Holy Communion we are fed by His Life: 'Except we eat His flesh and drink His Blood we have no life in us.' Great and wonderful gifts and powers! And then we turn from reading of them to see their practical working. We see a Church weak and torn asunder, we see Christians, who

[1] This sermon was one of those preached by Father Maturin as an Anglican, but the report is not dated.

are members of Christ's Body, not even knowing their great privileges, altogether ignorant of their supernatural powers. We look into ourselves and we feel the strength of passion and the weak or stifled voice of conscience remonstrating, and the feeble movements of grace so weak that we ask : is it grace, or is it only the excitement of nature ; and then we wonder, is this all ? Is this the only realisation of all those great and many promises and gifts of God ?

But perhaps in nothing is the contrast more striking than that which exists between the promises of prayer and their fulfilment. Again and again our Lord urges upon His followers, ' Ask and it shall be given you.' ' Whatsoever ye shall ask the Father in My name He will give it.' ' Ask and ye shall receive that your joy may be full.' No less than five times during the last discourse in the upper chamber does our Lord reiterate the charge to the Apostles to pray : ' Without Me you can do nothing.' ' If ye abide in Me and My words abide in you, ye shall ask what ye will and it shall be done unto you ' ; and yet when we turn from these promises to see their fulfilment in the world around us, how sad, how bewildering the contrast. Even the Bible itself records signal instances of prayer of some of the holiest men being apparently rejected. Moses besought God that he might enter the promised land, that he might live to see the fulfilment of all his hopes and of the unwearied labours of his life, but it was denied him. St. Paul besought the Lord to remove the thorn in his flesh, ' The messenger of Satan to buffet him,' a trial which he had borne fourteen years, but he was refused : and which of us has not had far more experience of prayers to which we got no answer, at least none that we could see, than of prayers which were answered as we desired. The very language we use of any answer to prayer that we cannot doubt shows how little we expect it. We speak so often of a *wonderful* answer to prayer, whereas if God were as true to His promise as we might expect, we would rather speak of any failure of prayer as far more wonderful.

Now there is no doctrine more practical and that so affects the Christian life as prayer, and it will not do for us to have a doubt on the subject. In the great progress that has been made of late in physical science, and in the open speech in which our age glories, when thoughts that were sometimes whispered through the soul in moments of doubt have been formulated and uttered loudly, when questions are presented to us that seem impossible to answer, and that overthrow all our ideas of the simple way in which we thought God played with and altered the laws and forces of nature in answer to anyone's prayer, there is often left in the mind a feeling of uneasiness.

The intellect is half converted to doubt, while faith still lingers on in the heart. There is a feeling that it will not do for us to ask too many questions, and that a wide knowledge of nature must necessarily lead to unbelief in prayer, and that if we would preserve our faith in all its simplicity, then it will not do for us to know too much of the workings of nature. If God were to break one of the laws of nature, we are told the consequences would be almost infinite. The world would be thrown into chaos. We could not tell what results would happen. I suppose that is true, says

ON PRAYER

many a one, but still, we are bound to believe that God can and will do it; and yet there remains naturally the lingering feeling of doubt and uncertainty. Are we to expect God to set aside His own laws. Are we to believe that there can be no reliance upon the laws and forces of nature, because all over the world one may be needing one thing and another another, which can only be granted apparently by setting the laws of nature at nought.

Therefore it is necessary for us often to adjust our faith to our growing knowledge. Our faith indeed must never change, never can change; but it may happen that we for want of knowledge explained amiss many matters of faith. We must never be afraid of truth, from whatever source it comes. If the scientist is an absolute unbeliever, yet if what he tells me of nature is true I must believe it. Faith is not worth purchasing at the expense of an untruth. If God reveals anything to me, I know it is true and I know it will harmonise with all other truth. What God says through revelation He cannot contradict in nature; therefore the vast progress that has suddenly been made in the physical sciences may oblige me to alter my theories as to the way in which God can answer prayer without in the least affecting my belief in prayer itself. I am bound to have a reasonable faith. I am certain that faith does not need ignorance to hold its shield before it for protection, rather I believe that it is ignorance that is the great enemy of faith.

Now the arguments that are brought against the possibility of answers to prayer may briefly be summed up under two heads, theological and scientific.

I. It is said: do you suppose that God is like a

weak man moved and governed by emotion ? Can you imagine that He will change His plans or purposes because He is appealed to by one of His creatures ? Does not such a supposition entirely overthrow our idea of His majesty and wisdom ? Has He not made the world and ordered all things as He knew to be best, and if He were to alter anything in answer to man's entreaty, would it not imply a defect and a weakness ? Surely, so we are told, we must believe that He who is upon the throne of the universe is beyond any such weakness as we might pardon in a creature. Is it not the height of irreverence, not to say presumption, to imagine that the God, who upholds all things by the word of His power, can be stirred or moved or changed from all His purpose by any need or prayer of ours ? Look rather at God in His majesty, the Maker and Ruler of all, to whom you must submit, but whom you can never hope to move ; a God as great and mighty as the God I worship, prayer and petition cannot move, for in wisdom He hath made all things.

Now to this argument two answers may be given :

1. We never supposed that prayer could change God; the effect of prayer is purely subjective. By prayer I do not expect to change God, but I do expect to change myself. Whether we ever get anything through prayer or not, the effect upon ourselves is so beneficial that it is worth cultivating a spirit of prayer.

Or again, if we do receive answers to prayer, it is not because God has been moved or touched by our entreaty, but because prayer is the condition which He has laid down for obtaining certain gifts ; but the prayer is really no appeal to His will or His heart, it is simply the fulfilment of a condition. Then all the passionate appeals to God for mercy, for help, all the trustful casting of oneself in weakness upon Him who is so strong is utterly meaningless, nay, nothing but an effort at self-deception; it has no power to touch Him nor to move Him. So far as God Himself regards me in my great earnestness and faith, I might just as well appeal to a block of stone. St. Paul was wrong. He is *not* ' touched by the feeling of our infirmities.' He only waits till His creature has fulfilled the conditions He has arbitrarily and without any reason laid down, and when those conditions are fulfilled He will, with cold indifference, grant what we have asked.

If this were true, I can only think that the evil effects of prayer would far outweigh any advantage that might be gained by answers to our prayer; for there could be only one result—the more earnestly we prayed the more completely we should deceive ourselves and try to fancy God altogether different from what we know Him to be. In my prayer I entreat Him as though He could be touched, while my theory of prayer has taught me that He is altogether emotionless. Which of us, in time of great sorrow, or great need, when we are ourselves most real and most intensely in earnest, could bring ourselves to pray, if in such prayer there was no room for the outpouring of our hearts, no room for the expression of our trust; if we were taught, before we went upon our knees, to remember that the God to whom we were about to pray cannot be moved by our tears or appeals, but that if we fulfil our side of the arbitrary condition He has laid down He will fulfil His.

No, my brethren, you will not pray if such is your

belief; no man who ever really prayed will believe in such a theory of prayer as that. I would rather never pray than force myself to believe, that when I succeeded in praying most earnestly I only succeeded in a most perfect piece of self-deception. It is only to a God who can be moved to whom men would care to pray, ' O Thou that hearest the prayer, to Thee shall all flesh come.'

We must believe then, if we believe in prayer at all, that it is not the merely mechanical fulfilment of a condition that is purely arbitrary, but that it is a direct appeal to God's Will, that the end of prayer is to move God, that God *is* touched with the feeling of our infirmities. True, indeed, prayer has its subjective effects, and they are great; but at the close of my prayers I don't ask myself merely or chiefly, has that prayer done me good? but has it reached, has it touched God? I expect God to be moved, even as man is moved, by the helpless appeal of weakness to strength.

And therefore the question has to be answered: is not this an unworthy conception of God's character? Does it not imply weakness? Is it not beneath our idea of the Ruler of the Universe to suppose that He can change His purpose because man has asked Him? In other words, is not emotion rather a defect than a perfection, and should we not believe a perfect Being to be above such weakness?

2. In answer I would ask:—what is our idea of a perfect man? Should we imagine a man, the more perfect he became, to become more entirely emotionless, and a man who was absolutely perfect to be beyond all power of being moved, to be ruled by reason

and conscience alone, helping indeed the needy and suffering, but not because he pitied them or was touched ? Do we think that if the judge's voice trembles when he passes sentence of death it is a defect, or that it was a defect in the prodigal's father to be moved with pity for his returning son ? Certainly our highest ideal of man is of One Who was touched with every sight of human sorrow and suffering, Who healed, not as a duty to the sufferer, but as the Evangelist tells us, ' being moved with compassion'; Who wept by the grave of Lazarus ; Who was won round by the appeals of the Syro-Phœnician woman for her suffering child ; Who seemed to be the only One to think of the bodily needs of the multitude who had followed Him into the wilderness to hear His teaching. What would the life of Jesus be if all those acts of pity and tenderness were omitted ? Do we think His life less perfect because He mingled His tears with ours and felt for all our woes ; does it not rather add to His perfection ? And He Who is our ideal of manhood is God Himself. He Who stopped by the wayside to heal the blind man from very pity was God ; He Who was touched by the tears of the widow of Nain and, so to speak, out of compassion for her changed His purpose and restored her son to life, was God. Certainly then, Holy Scripture does not hesitate to describe for us a God Who is ' full of compassion, long-suffering and of great mercy,' Who ' like a father pitieth His own children'; if we believe the revelation which Scripture gives of the character of God, it is of a Being most readily moved by the appeal of suffering and needy man.

We then, as Christians, believe, not only that it is not a defect, but that it is one of the Divine perfections that ' He is full of compassion and mercy, long suffering and of great kindness,' and this compassion is elicited in a peculiar way by prayer. Certainly it is so among men. The claim which the sufferer has upon us is increased by the fact that he has besought our assistance. What should we say of the parent who had no desire to grant his child's request simply because it is his request? I think that we should call him a hard man. I think that we should feel towards such a character some portion of the moral repugnance which would be evoked by a character wholly devoid of emotion, and this repugnance is of the nature of moral disapprobation. Doubtless we should condemn the parent who always yielded to the wish of a child, but we should also condemn the parent who felt no desire to yield and who refused his child's earnest petition without some degree of pain. In a word, *desire* to comply with a child's request is a motive which we expect to find in a parent's heart, and we would regard as morally defective a nature from which it is wholly absent.

Now if we examine the elements of which prayer to anyone consists, or rather, the feelings of which prayer is the natural result, we shall find no difficulty in understanding the desire to comply with an earnest petition which exists in every kindly nature.

Their component feelings are two—desire and trust. Prayer is the result of earnest desire for the thing asked for, combined with trust, more or less firm, in the person from whom it is asked, that he will be disposed to grant the request. It is this latter element

—often very weak but never wholly absent—which I conceive distinguishes the case of one who prays from the case of one who desires without praying. It is the presence of this element of trust which disposes a man to prefer a supplicant to one, quite as deserving, who does not supplicate. In man, we know as a fact that there is nothing which more powerfully affects a generous mind than trust reposed in it by another; and I may add, it is an emotion of which our moral sense entirely approves, and if among the shades of human guilt we would distinguish one of surpassing darkness, it is the guilt of trust betrayed.

Now, in reasoning from the case of petitions addressed to man to that of petitions addressed to God, the principles already laid down allow us to conclude that the presence of the element of trust will justify a preference on the part of God for the person in whom that element is found; so that he might fairly receive a blessing which was withheld from one equally deserving in other respects, from whose mind the element of trust was absent. How entirely this principle pervades the New Testament I need hardly remind you. In truth, it is the groundwork of Christianity.

It is not then contrary to our idea of the perfection of God's character that He can be moved to grant us our requests; it is even according to all our analogy from human perfection that He is moved especially by the fact that man trusts Him enough to appeal to Him, and therefore, because we so believe we say, 'O Thou that hearest the prayer, to Thee shall all flesh come.'

II. The second class of argument against the

efficacy of prayer is of entirely a different nature. The first, as we have seen, is drawn from its supposed inconsistency with the character of God. The second is deduced, not from any idea which we may have of God, but from what we know of nature. They who so speak make no assumption as to the attributes of God, or even His existence. They maintain that the answers to prayer are impossible as inconsistent with some established principle, and they endeavour to show that the claim of those who believe in the efficacy of prayer is not borne out by facts. You ask, they say, for what is impossible, and you cannot prove that you obtain more by prayer than we do without prayer.

Now the most popular form of the argument against the efficacy of prayer on the scientific side is this,— such a theory is contrary to the principle of law. In past years men thought that the various phenomena of nature were a number of disconnected facts; now we know, and the more our knowledge increases the more we learn, how all creation is under the dominion of law: ' Thou hast set them their bounds which they shall not pass.'

Forces which are in their essence and their source utterly mysterious, are always being found to operate under rules which have strict reference to measures of number, to relations of space and time. Not even a drop of water can be found, except under rules which determine its weight, its volume and its shape with exact reference to the density of the fluid, to the structure of the surface on which it may be formed and to the pressure of the surrounding atmosphere. Not one of the countless varieties of form which prevail in clouds, and which give to the face of heaven such

ON PRAYER

infinite expression, not one of them but is ruled by law, woven, or braided, or torn, or scattered, or gathered up again and folded, by forces which are free only within the bounds of law. It is wonderful to find that even in such a matter as, for example, human speech, the unconscious changes which arise from time to time amongst the rudest utterances of the rudest tribes and races of mankind, are all found to follow rules of progress as regular as those which preside over any of the material growths of nature.

And those phenomena of nature which at first seem wholly separate and disconnected we find to be closely bound together and interdependent, one upon another. Nothing in nature stands alone. Gravitation is a force which prevails through all space, but it does not prevail alone; it is a force whose function is to balance other forces. Each force, if left to itself, would be destructive of the universe; were it not for the force of gravitation the centrifugal forces which impel the planets would fling them off into space; if it were not for these centrifugal forces the force of gravitation would dash them against the sun. The orbits, therefore, of the planets, with all that depends upon them, are determined by the nice and perfect balance which is maintained between these two forces. Again, the revolution of the seasons, seed-time and harvest, depend on the law of gravitation in this sense, that if that law were disturbed or inconstant they would be disturbed or inconstant too. But the seasons equally depend on a multitude of other laws—laws of heat, of light, laws relating to fluids, to solids, and to gases, and to magnetic attractions and repulsions—each one of which laws is invariable in itself, but each one of which would produce utter confusion if it were allowed to operate alone, or if it were not balanced against others in the right proportion. It is very difficult to form any adequate idea of the vast number of laws which are concerned in producing the most ordinary operations of nature. Looking only at the combination with which astronomy is concerned, the adjustments are almost infinite. Each minutest circumstance in the position or size or shape of the earth, the direction of its axis, the velocity of its motion and of its rotation, has its own definite effect, and the slightest change in any one of these relations would wholly alter the world we live in. And then it is to be remembered that the seasons as they are now fitted to us, and as we are fitted to them, do not depend only on the facts or laws which astronomy reveals, they depend quite as much on other sets of facts and other sets of laws revealed by other sciences, such, for example, as chemistry, electricity, and geology. The motion of the earth might be exactly what it is, every fact in respect to the planetary position might remain unchanged, yet the seasons would return in vain if our own atmosphere were altered in any one of the elements of its composition, or if any one of the laws regulating the action were other than it is. Under a thinner air, even the torrid zone might be wrapped in eternal snow; and so it is through the whole of nature. There are laws everywhere, laws in themselves invariable, but so worked as to produce effects of inexhaustible variety by being pitched against each other and made to hold each other in restraint.

What presumption, then, not to say what folly, is it to suppose that by our prayers we can change or cause the violation of these intricate and interdependent laws? It might have been comparatively easy to believe that our prayers might effect the desired change in the climate or temperature when we believed that the wind blew where it listed and as it listed, and that the cloud gathered and poured forth its waters as it drifted in its lawless course through space, and that this and that might happen without effecting violent changes in other things that seemed disconnected and alone. But when we know the close and intimate relationship of all the laws and forces of nature, how absurd it is to imagine that by our prayers we can tamper with these strong unbending laws and forces without bringing all around us into chaos and confusion. The passing cloud is governed by law, and to break that law would cause such infinite confusion that we cannot tell where the result would end. All science, as well as all security for the present and future, depends upon our firm belief that the laws of nature remain unbroken and unchanged.

Therefore, we are told, to look for answers to prayers which imply any physical results is unreasonable, and to grant them would be to sacrifice the security of multitudes to the desire of a few.

The question, therefore, that we have to answer is, do we in asking God for such things ask Him or expect Him to violate a law of nature ; do we, in petitioning for a change in the weather ask for a miracle which, if granted, would involve changes so vast and so unmeasured in the working of the physical laws that it becomes impossible to conceive what the results would be and where they would end ? I think not. No one asks God to upset the whole constitution of things because some change may be beneficial for them or their land. We do not believe that God would. Nor do we ask Him to break any of His laws whatever we may ask of Him. It is true we seldom ask God for anything that is not, in a certain sense, a miracle, that is to say, an effect produced by a method different from any that man is able to use; but a miracle is not a violation of law.

Let us take one or two instances. There is a protracted drought that threatens a famine; we Christians betake ourselves to prayer and ask God to send us rain. Nonsense, we are told, the rainfall can't be affected by our prayers, it is under certain and fixed laws. We can calculate the amount of rain that fell in this country last week, and we can trace it accurately to certain atmospheric changes at the equator and the poles: these changes have been going on through past ages, and to change to-day's rain you would have to go back almost to the beginning of the world.

Now is this true ? Is it true to say that last week's rainfall is dependent only upon the great movements at the equator and the poles, which have been going on for ages. Certainly it was true in the past ages; but the presence of man upon the earth, we are told by these same men of science, has materially affected the rainfall; let him cut down the forests and clear the swamps and the climate undergoes great changes: that is to say, that between the steady and unbroken movements of these forces of nature the will of man has stepped in and by stronger forces has suspended or checked their operation. The showers would come and go according to the forces by which they are

ON PRAYER

ordered, unless another force, man's will acting upon the forests, intercepted and wrought a change. I tell my friend that I will ask God to give or to withhold rain in its season. That's folly, says my friend. Very well, I answer, I will not ask God to interpose His will and give me what I want, I will effect it by my own will and acts which carry my wishes into effect. Is this a miracle as it is generally understood? Is this a violation of law and a bringing in of infinite changes, and a disorder that can never be set right? Certainly not. The laws and forces of nature move with their grand and steady rhythm the moment that the force stronger than they has been removed.

Again, in praying for restoration of health to the sick, we are calling for no violation of any law of nature; the skill of the physician seeks to stay the course of disease by remedies which he knows and has tested, but how very limited is the knowledge of the most learned. In praying, we ask God to stop the course of the disease by the interference and application of a stronger power—His own will.

Or to take one other instance. I am walking upon the edge of a precipice and lose my footing; shall I pray that I may not fall into the abyss below and be killed? What folly, I am told. You don't suppose that God will violate the law of gravitation for such a purpose. Very well, I answer, I won't ask God, I will ask you. Will you save me as I fall? You stretch out your hand, and catch me, and I am saved. Yet you didn't violate any law. You interposed a stronger *force*, the muscular force of your arm, which suspended the weaker force of gravitation; that is to say, your will stepped in amidst the forces of nature, and, acting in strict obedience to law, suspended for the moment one force by another. Why then should it be any violation of law that God should do the same and by the interposition of His will effect the same result ?

The wider our knowledge of the laws of nature, the more we are able to do what a few years ago would have seemed contrary to law. I tell a savage that I can send my thoughts in a moment across the Atlantic ; he says it is impossible. We should have said a few years ago that such a thing would be a miracle, and in opposition to the laws of nature, but as we have learnt to understand nature's laws better we found it possible.

Why then should not many things that seem to us contrary to law, be to Him Who knows and has made all law but the most perfect accommodation to law.

In prayer, then, for anything which demands external physical results we do not ask God, even if we ask for what seems absolutely miraculous, to violate any law, we appeal to God to exercise His will on nature, and what the effects of that will can be, who will dare to say ?

In conclusion I would make two remarks—

1. We have no right to limit prayer to entreaty for spiritual blessings. ' Ask what ye will '; the danger is, not that we should ask too much, but too little. Such a limitation is really a lack of faith ; it springs partly from the feeling that the ordinary events of our life are unworthy the notice or interference of God, forgetting that ' not a sparrow falleth to the

ground without your Father,' that as everything affects all character for good or evil everything is of interest to God, and that prayer is not degraded to earth by the expression of any of our wants, but earth is raised to heaven. And again, there is a feeling that it is more difficult or implies more for God to interfere in the ordinary temporal affairs of life than in the spiritual. Are then the forces of nature stronger than the moral forces? Is the force of gravitation in its sphere stronger than the force of habit? Is it easier to convert a sinner than to change the temperature from cold to hot? No, my brethren, if there be any greater or less, the moral miracles are greater than any that can be wrought in the material world.

Learn rather to come to God for all you want, to lay before Him all your needs and hopes, temporal as well as spiritual, 'casting all your care upon Him, for He careth for you.'

2. Prayer is not intended to dispense with the use of the ordinary means for assisting ourselves which God has given us. 'If a man will not work, neither let him eat.' We have no right therefore to expect God will hear our prayers if we do not do all in our power for ourselves. A man has no right to sit with his hands before him and pray for food and clothing; prayer in such a case would be a curse, not a blessing. And so when God has given us remedies for sickness, we have no right to set them aside and pray instead. We might just as well sit down to an empty table and pray for our food. Such a doctrine of prayer carried out logically into life could result in little short of the most disastrous effects. We may pray,

but we must work too. And so in sickness we must pray, but the prayer must be that God will bless all the remedies He has put in our hands. Our Blessed Lord Himself in many instances in the Gospel used remedies for the sick, anointing the eyes of the blind with clay and laying His hands upon the diseased part.

Let us then in prayer draw near to the throne of Grace, knowing that the God to whom we come is full of compassion and mercy. Knowing that all things are possible to Him, and that all His power is under the dominion of His love. Knowing too, that the more helpless we are, the more demands we lay upon His loving heart.

THE MYSTERY OF HIDDEN POWER [1]

[1] And this shall be a sign unto you; ye shall find the Babe wrapped in swaddling clothes, lying in a manger.'—St. Luke ii. 12.

THIS, my brethren, is the great anti-climax of the announcement made to the shepherds by the Host of Angels, as on Christmas Eve they gathered in the open heavens and declared to the shepherds that the Desire of all Nations was come, that the prophecy was now fulfilled, that the seed of the woman that was to bruise the serpent's head was born, that the object and end of all prophecy would finally manifest itself in the coming of the Messiah. It was the central fact of the history of the world, and the interpretation and manifestation of the force that underlay the development of the whole Jewish nation—that unspeakable power that came from the doctrine of the Messiah. Something was always expected, and that something took more and more the shape and form based upon the first prophecy in the Garden of Eden, and widened and unveiled itself as ages went by, until at last the Son of God made Man stood before men and they beheld Him face to face. The moment of the fulfilment of prophecy had come, and the incarnate Son of God stood upon the threshold of the door of human life, ready to enter in, ready to say

[1] Sermon preached at the Convent of the Assumption, December 23, 1904.

the word, ready to manifest God to man, to manifest man to himself. And the angels could no longer contain themselves, but appeared to the shepherds on that eventful evening, exclaiming in a grand burst of song: 'Glory to God in the highest, and on earth peace to men of good-will.' Then they summed up their great announcement to the shepherds, and to the whole world, by singing those startling words—the great anti-climax of their song—their Gloria in Excelsis: 'And this shall be a sign unto you; ye shall find the Babe wrapped in swaddling clothes, lying in a manger.'

The faith of those poor shepherds is marvellous; it does not seem to have been a great strain or a great astonishment to them. Few things that touch upon faith are an astonishment to the poor, they have the greatest faith of all. Their knowledge of the power of God is perhaps greater than we can really imagine, depending day by day upon His hand, and relying day by day upon His bounty. We are not told that the shepherds expressed great surprise, at the anti-climax, when it came, but that they went with great joy to Bethlehem, and there beheld Mary and Joseph and the Babe, wrapped in swaddling clothes, lying in the manger.

During the whole history of the past up to that time every act and scene in the life of Israel gathered round and found interpretation in the hope of the Messiah. We catch frequent glimpses of this here and there: take especially the instance of the woman seated by the well side, to whom Our Lord spoke. When He told her of the great things to come, she answered, 'I know that the Messiah is to come who

THE MYSTERY OF HIDDEN POWER

will tell us all things.' We know that all classes, even the poorest, the most degraded, were looking for the Messiah to make clear the words of the prophets of the restoration, and later the great prophecy of St. John the Baptist himself, ' There cometh One after me whose shoe's latchet I am not worthy to unloose.' The whole hope of the Jews was centred in the Messiah. If any emergency took place, if any great need occurred in their race, they looked to the Messiah to supply that need; in any time of trouble, such as their captivity, the Messiah was to set them free. And now, when they were under the heel of Rome, it was of the hope of the restoration of the kings of Israel that the Apostles were speaking: they could not disentangle the two ideas. When trouble came the Messiah would help them; when the Messiah came He was to set them free.

From the time of the first prophecy uttered in the Garden of Eden, prophecy divided itself into two parts. One set of prophets took up the great and joyous songs of triumph, they spoke of the serpent and his seed and the woman and her seed, and the crushing of the serpent's head. Other prophets took up the sterner side, and spoke of the bruising of the heel of the woman and her seed by the serpent. We see the two lines of prophecy separating wider and wider, till one speaks of the bruising of the serpent's head and the other of the seed as under the dominion of the serpent. And these two became more and more irreconcilable as time went on, till at last, at the time of the coming of Our Lord, there were two schools of interpretation, as it were, two Messiahs looked for. We know that the truth was that the two were to come together in one. He was to conquer through suffering, through the cross—the true emblem of power. Here was the blending of the prophecies again. The intellectual Jew looked to the Messiah for some great manifestation of moral and physical power in conquering his enemies. This was the great hope of Israel; and he looked to see this great and wonderful manifestation, but what did he see? Only a Babe wrapped in swaddling bands, lying in a manger.

In the presence of Our Lord there was always something disappointing. He did not in His coming rise to the standard that men's hopes and imaginations had set up. And it was the same later on in the history of Christ's life. We hear that the whole country was filled with the rumours of the greatness of the events He had done: how He had raised the dead to life, had touched the eyes of those who were blind and made them see, how He had touched the raging waters and there was a great calm. All the forces of nature seemed to bend themselves before the voice of this strange Prophet of Nazareth. Those who heard of these wonders longed to see Him. And when the people did see Him they found a man in all things like unto themselves, and there was something disappointing—there was something disappointing always in the presence of our Lord—the scorn of men and the outcast of the people. Yet under the form so humble and so scorned, there lay all the majesty and all the power of the Eternal. There was nothing to appeal to the imagination in the presence of Our Lord. He based His mission on an appeal to faith. You can imagine hearing of some great politician, some great artist, some great general whose fame

THE MYSTERY OF HIDDEN POWER

is bruited through the country, and when you see him you are most frightfully disappointed and you say: this man is not at all what I expected to see. That must have been only a ten thousandth part of the disappointment felt by these men when they came into the presence of Our Lord. They had heard that He could not only speak great words, but that all nature was submissive to Him, and that He might do what He liked with the forces of nature, that the devils were subject to Him. When they came and saw Him, they said: ' He hath no form nor comeliness, no beauty that we should desire Him: a scorn of men and an outcast of the people.' St. Paul, writing to the Galatians, says they were surprised, for though his letters were weighty and powerful his bodily presence was poor and weak, and his speech contemptible. So, with all reverence, we may say that in a certain way that was so with Our Blessed Lord. There was a staggering of the imagination. People said, this cannot be the Holy Prophet of Judah, the Desire of Nations, the Lion of the Tribe of Judah. And they were offended because His presence did not rise to the appeal of their imagination. What faith must it have demanded, when the shepherds heard the first message of the angels: And this shall be the sign: the Son of God is made Man: the Desire of all Nations is come—a Babe wrapped in swaddling bands, lying in a manger. Poorer than ordinary infants, absolutely beggarly, absolutely without anything to set off his appearance, with no obsequious servants, no home—only a little infant lying in a manger in a stable.

Now, my brethren, we must always look deeper

down than the mere surface of the words. When the angel said to the shepherds this was to be a sign—not only a sign to them, but a sign to all mankind; not only a sign of the Incarnation, but also a sign of the work of the Incarnation—we see that there was, as I said, a staggering of the imagination, a falling back of ideas previously formed. And if we were to ask: what is the Incarnation? the answer is always the same; the great antiphon of the Incarnation is the sign of strength under the form of utter feebleness and weakness. Under this surface, under this weakness of the infant, was the strength of the mighty God, wrapped in the swathing bands of a baby lying in a manger. My brethren, we shall always find, whenever we come across any mystery, that it fails to be something that appeals to our imagination. Therefore it is hard to believe. If the angels had said: you see a great light, that will always be a token of the Incarnation, then the whole history of Christendom would have been different. All men would readily have believed in the power of faith and prayer. God does not act thus. When Our Lord was in Gethsemane He said, 'Thinkest thou that I cannot now pray to My Father, and He shall presently give Me more than twelve legions of angels. But how then shall the scripture be fulfilled?' Our Lord said: no, this is not the way I am to do it. If our Blessed Lord had done it in that way, there would have been no manifestation of His special power. It would not have helped man in his probation. When surrounded by enemies we should have expected God to give us legions of angels to win the victory. If we thought we could draw down legions of angels from

THE MYSTERY OF HIDDEN POWER

heaven to dissipate the powers of the evil one, then the whole history of your soul and of mine, the whole history of Christendom, would have been different. We should not have brought down the power upon ourselves by our faith. God designed rather the unfolding of a mighty force, from the very smallest beginnings won by the exercise of our will, sanctified by Divine Grace. It would not have been that. We should have walked with a magic power around us, untouched by evil, and we should have looked to that power of God to set us free from the curse. Such would have been the case for us if the great antiphon of the Incarnation had been different. And such would have been the history of Our Lord's own life if He had cast Himself down from the pinnacle of the Temple. It would have been an appeal to the imagination. It would not have been the most spiritual appeal, but it would have been the most imaginative appeal. People would have all crowded into the Catholic Church. God's plan was other than this. St. Paul said, 'Not many wise, not many great, not many noble men are chosen. God hath chosen the weak things of the earth to confound the things which are mighty.' You are not necessarily nearer to God because the imagination is kindled by a wonderful picture; it is an act of faith to see nothing, to feel nothing, but to believe. And so what we look for in the Catholic Church is the carrying on of the prophecy of the Incarnation. It is first of all the sign, the Babe wrapped in swaddling bands, God under the token of infantile weakness. Is it not an extraordinary thing, men say, that intelligent people should believe that a few crumbs of bread are going to do them any good? Is it not an extraordinary thing that the sprinkling of a few drops of water, a few drops of oil touching the forehead, should make a difference in anybody's welfare? It is not in the least astonishing if you take the Incarnation as a sign and interpretation of it all. The sign of the Incarnation is power, in the lowliest and most unworthy forms. What would those shepherds, what would the mind of anyone have been led to expect as to the way in which God would become Incarnate? If they had been asked, they would have answered: He will rend the heavens when He comes down; so shall the coming of the Son of Man be. We know that they were quite wrong. It was to be a sign— the sign was to be one little infant, more lowly, more shabby than ever before, lying not even on His mother's lap, but on a little straw on the hard boards of the manger. That was to be the sign of the Incarnation. And when people say: are you not astonished, can you imagine that God is going to give Himself to us under the forms of bread and wine, under the form of a few drops of water in baptism? I answer: no, I do not feel surprised. What I should be surprised at would be if there were a great flash, and then the Presence of God upon the altar. What would lead me to doubt would be a great manifestation, a manifestation of anything that would appeal to the imagination. The prophet said, there were horns coming out of His hand—the emblem of strength. The power was there, but it was hidden. Who could have told that the little Infant, lying there stark and naked in the bitter winter's night, was going to turn the world upside down, going to bring into existence virtues

THE MYSTERY OF HIDDEN POWER

that men had never dreamed of before. Who could have thought that Rome, after all its mighty strength, the exercises and the intrigues of years, that all traditions, man's every act, man's low passions, were all to be vanquished by this Infant—a Babe wrapped in swaddling bands—from God Most High.

So, my brethren, you may say it is as it were the motto for the Catholic Church: you may expect the Babe in swaddling bands lying in the manger. You are to see nothing striking to the eye; it is all the mystery of hidden power. What you are to see is something that staggers you, because it is something that you would not expect to find as the sign or mark of power. The power is all hidden under the form of weakness. And so Our Blessed Lord, when He takes the Bread, says: look what I take, it is scarcely matter at all, it is matter in its very thinnest form, but I must use some material thing. The power, the spiritual power underlies the finest, thinnest almost imperceptible material. When I take this child, and want to make him an heir of the Kingdom of God, a partaker of the Kingdom of Heaven, what do I do ? I take a few drops of water, matter in its very poorest and weakest form, and so a fit token of the mightiness of God. And, therefore, when the Blessed Sacrament is lifted up and all Catholics bow down, and somebody who does not understand stands at the door, with perhaps a smile containing something of pity, perhaps almost something of contempt, we say to him:—but why should you be surprised ? You would not be surprised if you believed in the Incarnation. Why should you be surprised when the Mighty God came wrapped in the swaddling bands of a babe ? Would it not be more staggering to your faith should it appeal more to your senses ? What could be in more direct contravention to the way in which He did come, than if God were to give us His great gifts in a magnificent semblance of power, as in the Shekinah of Divine Glory, so that when the High Priest went into the Holy of Holies he veiled his face, lest he should behold the face of God and die ? We Catholics see, under the swaddling bands of an Infant, the Presence of the Most High. We look for God in the feeblest tokens of infantile weakness. The instinct of the Catholic faith leads Catholics to look, not for great, but for lowly things, for in the lowliest forms we see the mightiest manifestations of God. Therefore it seems to me that the idea of the sacrament, that manifesting of power under the form of weakness, is exactly what the angels pointed out when they sang, ' Ye shall find the Babe wrapped in swaddling bands, lying in a manger.' Always look for that : here is the Founder of the Kingdom of God, and the symbols of His birth will always be manifested in all His deeds. Always look for strength under the sign of weakness, under the sign of infancy, under the garments of a babe.

And once more, so it is to be in ourselves. We say : Oh, if God would only do something great in me. If I could put my heel upon that sin and crush it once and for ever. How often have we felt, as we have knelt in confession, the burden of some little fault, of some great fault, that we have found cropping up again and again. Why, we say, why can I not crush it out and have done with it once and for all. And the answer is, it is always the sign of God, the working by

THE MYSTERY OF HIDDEN POWER

little actions that gradually produce great results. Great results are not produced in a moment. Great sweeping reforms, magnificent and amazing conversions, such things are possible, but they are not God's ordinary way of working. The sower goes out and sows the seed, and the seed lies dormant in the earth, and nothing happens for a few days; then the seed comes up, first the blade, and then the ear, and then the full corn in the ear. And so it is with Our Lord in the Kingdom of God; so is the working of the Most High. Therefore we are to be rather afraid when we find any great and sudden change taking place in our nature. Our Lord was not looked upon all at once as Wonderful, Counsellor, the Mighty God, the Everlasting Father, the Prince of Peace; but grew up like the Babe at His mother's side, never dissociating Himself from us for one single moment, in order that He might experience in that human nature all that man may experience, and pour out through the soul the well-spring from on high. And so with ourselves. We must knead the gifts of grace gradually into our heavy, stupid, dull nature. We must take the golden threads of grace and weave them into our nature, until the whole garment is complete from top to bottom without seam. God has given us the powers of the world to come, the powers that were first manifested in the Infant of Bethlehem; we are to take these powers and, helped by them, to check our temper, to control our irritability, to lift ourselves out of our sluggardly ways, to be stimulated to do this thing and that. We have to knead that stimulant into the whole structure of our character, until the whole character is transformed. As the flower is part of the seed put into the earth, so it is in the Christian life. The character is partly human, but every virtue there comes from baptism and the sacraments of Divine Grace. These are the forces that cleanse and transform, and make men in very truth sons of God.

THE HUMILITY OF MARY—I

'And there appeared a great wonder in heaven; a woman clothed with the sun, and the moon under her feet, and upon her head a crown of twelve stars.'—REVELATION xii. 1.

YESTERDAY, my brethren, we were keeping the Feast of the Immaculate Conception, the fiftieth anniversary of the definition, as an article of divine faith, of the Immaculate Conception of the Blessed Virgin. And in order that we may understand what that doctrine really is, and what it involves, we must be quite clear as to the nature of the fall, we must consider what happened to the first Eve, what she had lost. Mary was given back what Eve lost, and more.

God might have created man in one of two states: He might have given man everything that belonged to human nature and nothing more, just as He gives to animals the things that belong to the animal nature and nothing more, just as He gives to the trees and the flowers the things that belong to their nature and nothing more. Every tree, every plant, every bird is perfectly satisfied with itself; it has no restlessness or discontent; each is perfectly happy in its own position. Now God might have made man like that. But in that state man would never have wanted to get any nearer God. There would have been no such thing as revelation, there would have been no such thing as rising into a higher sphere; if man had died, he would possibly have entered into a state of perfect happiness, where he would have known God, but he would never have seen Him, or wanted to see Him any nearer, any more than man wants to be an angel. He would have found himself a limited being, like any other animal; man would have been a higher form, but, like any other form of animal creation, he would have been limited and confined within one sphere. Think what it would have been if God had made man like that! He would never have known much about God; he would have had enough to satisfy all his wants, but he would never have cried: ' My soul is athirst for God, even for the living God; when shall I come to appear before the presence of God?'

Within the limitations of his own nature man would have lived perfectly happy, and would have passed into the natural beauty of the other world, where he would have grown in perfect happiness and perfect peace. If God had done that it would have been a wonderful act. But God did not do that, God did something more, something greater: for, from the very moment when God created man with a body and a soul, He united him to Himself. The light of God shone within his soul and illuminated it with supernatural knowledge. The love of God burned in his heart, and kindled it with supernatural love. God raised him into union with Himself and gave him the possibility of beholding Him face to face. And man, looking round upon the world, saw all nature kindling with the light of God's love; and, looking within himself, saw his soul all radiant with the presence of God, and knew that he himself could never rest until he had seen God face to face.

THE HUMILITY OF MARY—I

This was the gift of original justice, the lifting of the creature up off the plane of the earth to the region of the supernatural, into touch with Himself. That was the free gift of God to man. And now it was perfectly fitting that God, having given that gift to man, should give it under condition. That condition was that man should obey God, and not eat of the fruit of the tree of the knowledge of good and evil. Round that tree there hung the shadow of a mystery which strongly appealed to man. Whenever our first parents looked at that tree, there stirred within them the antagonism between desire and duty; and when temptation is once stirred up within the soul, there is only one of two ways out of it. You either do the act and sin, or you don't do it and you gain the victory. When a thing comes to be done or not to be done you cannot get out of it, you can't compromise. We may make compromises with ourselves, and try to look as if we were not doing this or that, and play tricks with ourselves, and persuade ourselves we are doing what is wrong by accident, like Aaron making excuses to Moses when he tried to forget his own desire. We may try to get out of scrapes and difficulties; but whenever the antagonism between the law and desire rises up within our souls, at once it becomes a case of either yielding or standing out against it. We must remember this. A temptation, a trial, what does it mean? what kind of thing is it? There is only one kind of trial that is of any importance, that is a moral trial, a trial of character. You may be very clever, and at the same time very untruthful and very insincere. The mind, the intellect, may be something entirely apart from the person himself—an adornment, just like some personal adornment that belongs to you. A person is a character, and you every one of you have a character, and that character must be tested before God can make use of you. If a person is going to take a high position—if a person is going to be appointed to hold a position of trust, even in the convent, you test that person. People say: so-and-so should not be put into this position of trust until we know something about her, until we know whether she will stand the trial and do her duty. What is the meaning of the trial? That you test a person through and through, from the crown of his head to the sole of his foot, that you know, if tempted, he will say: that is wrong; I am forbidden it; I will not do it. That was the testing to which Adam was put. That was the only kind of test God could give him. God had in His eternal plan lifted him up to the very throne of Heaven, and before admitting man to high and lofty positions God must try man.

It is all very well, if you are asked whether you would succumb to a temptation, to say: no, I would not do it; nothing would induce me to do this or that. We may be like Hazael in Holy Scripture who said, ' Is thy servant a dog that he should do this thing? ' but within a very few years he went and did the very thing he had said he would not. He did not know himself. Sometimes we think we won't do a thing, we do not know ourselves; but when the thing comes, when the temptation comes, we are surprised at our own weakness, and we yield, and finally we do it. If God had said to Adam: I give you to-day all things, but there is one thing you must not do, Adam would have exclaimed: Oh my God, it

THE HUMILITY OF MARY—I

is impossible that I should disobey Thee. 'Whom have I in heaven but Thee; and what have I in earth that I desire in comparison with Thee?' But, as a matter of fact, when the test came, he fell and ate the forbidden fruit; when he fell he violated the commandment of God and chose the creature rather than the Creator. And thus began the taint that has been handed down from father to son, from generation to generation. As soon as Adam did that what happened? This is what happened. Nature was left alone, and the supernatural was withdrawn. The free gift that God gave, the gift of Divine grace that God might have made man without, was withdrawn, and man's whole nature fell down to earth again, and he became a natural instead of a supernatural being. Suppose God had raised up one from among the animals, and had given it power to speak and to act, and that then that animal had fallen back, it could never be the same again as the other animals. It would have a wistful look towards man, it could never rest content, it would never have the sense of peace that belongs to all the other animals, it would never rest content with the conditions of their nature; it would always be striving for something else, would be restless, discontented. And so no sooner had Adam fallen and lost his crown of glory, the gift of original justice, and with it lost the crown of beauty which God had given him as an adornment of his position, than man became restless, discontented and dissatisfied, and there he was, crawling about upon the earth, this child of God. There he was, who had once tasted the gifts of Divine wisdom, feeding upon the husks that the swine did eat, and feeling that while his father's servants had enough and to spare, he perished with hunger. This is what the Fall was: it was the loss of the supernatural in man; man fell down to the natural. But man still feels longings for God, and that feeling for God often tries vainly to satisfy itself on the most beautiful things of the earth. The trouble with man is that he has tasted the supernatural gift of God and never quite forgotten it. Since man has seen the beauty of heaven, he never can be satisfied with the beauty of earth. The human race fell down deeper and deeper, and forgot the presence of God. Men made to themselves idols of wood and of stone, and bowed down to them saying: these are our gods. And when they began not to keep God in their hearts, God gave them over unto a reprobate sense, as St. Paul tells us, and they became more and more immersed in the desires and the struggles and vices and miseries of this life.

And then God came on earth to give back to man the gift he had lost.

If anyone were to ask you: what is original sin, what would you find in the soul of a new-born child if you could see it? the answer is: you would find nothing at all. All you would find is that the soul had lost something. It would be like a lamp from which the light has been removed. Man's soul is like the monstrance without the Blessed Sacrament. The monstrance without the Blessed Sacrament is nothing, the essential thing—the presence of God—has gone. The light was withdrawn from the lamp; the lamp was left. And as the light was gone, the inner nature became disturbed, the passions broke

THE HUMILITY OF MARY—I

loose. Before God's presence was withdrawn, everything man did he did together with God : everything was done with his whole being, body and soul worked together in every act he did. At first the whole person did the whole act ; now man wishes half-a-dozen different and opposite things at the same time. Before the Fall this was not so. That was original sin. If you were asked : what is original sin ? what would you answer ? The answer is this : the loss of the presence of God, a lost grace, a privation, a man being born without something that his father lost for him through sin. And that loss brings a kind of stain upon the soul—the guilt of Adam's fall. There is nothing in the soul that would not anyhow have been there. It is simply the loss of the presence of God in that soul. That was the Fall. That is original sin. Now, my brethren, God came to give back to man the gift he had lost. Then two things must happen : God Himself must take our human nature again, and purify it in Himself, and He must impart once more to man the gift he had lost. God Himself came down, and the entail of sin was cut. Our Blessed Lord in the Incarnation was conceived by the Holy Ghost of the sinless Virgin Mary. He had no human Father, and so the seed of evil, transmitted from father to son, was stopped when He was conceived by the Holy Ghost. God could not take any impure thing into union with Himself. God could not touch, could not unite with Himself, or take into union with Himself, the thing that would kill Him— sin—if I may say so with all reverence. And in order that He might take our nature into Himself He united Himself with man, and, through that union, poured out upon the whole human race the gift man had lost. Human nature had been purified.

And how did that purification happen? It was in the very moment of time in which the Blessed Virgin was conceived in her mother's womb; in that moment, aye, in that very moment of conception, the Holy Spirit was there, watching the building up of the fabric of the holy Temple of God. And because God was there the gift was given back. That was the Immaculate Conception. It was the perfect purity of a human being, from the very first moment of her conception, streaming over with the gift of Divine grace. That was the Immaculate Conception. On the one hand, Catholics and every Christian say, ' He was conceived by the Holy Ghost.' He had not any earthly father; the entail of sin was stopped on the side of the father. Therefore it seems to me that, on the other hand, it was only the natural thing—what we might have guessed if we had not known it by the teaching of the Church—that human nature, before God could unite Himself with it, must be cleansed. That cleansing took place in the Blessed Virgin, when the grace of God united, at the moment of her conception, with human nature, and built up the fabric from which He was to take the substance which was to build up the life through which human nature was to be restored. And note this: that with the original righteousness with which Adam was united with God, God gave various gifts— God gave him immortality, immunity from suffering, a knowledge of all things needed for the poise and perfect balance of all his powers. These gifts were taken away for ever, but man could be united with God without these; man had lost the crown of original justice, but that crown was given back in the Blessed Virgin, even though immortality was not given back and immunity from suffering was not given back; for the Blessed Virgin was the Mother of Sorrows, she suffered from her childhood on. But she had that greatest of all gifts, she had never tasted sin. Here was one human being that was as God had intended man to be. Only she did not live in the Garden of Eden, in places of peace, like the first Eve; but she came out into the world, where forces were raging which were all against the purposes of God. She came out into a world (though God never intended it to be a world of sin), into a world of wickedness, this pure maiden with her instinct of purity, with the perfection of her nature, endowed with those rich gifts and every moment increasing in grace. This maiden found a world in rebellion against God. Sometimes, in lesser degree, one good person finds himself among people who do not care to be good. A number of Catholics living in the world will find themselves in many cases among persons who are not Catholics, Christians find themselves living among those who are not trying to serve God at all. Here was this pure child of Adam, unspotted by sin, living among the storm-clouds that gather through the sin of Adam—the whole world rebelling against God.

What strikes us most of all in that peerless life of ideal womanhood, a woman such as God had originally intended Eve to be, is its extraordinary simplicity. We do not see anything very striking, anything very amazing that she ever did. She merely followed the ordinary course of Divine Providence. She always stayed where her Child was ; if her Child suffered—and the Child must suffer—the Mother suffered too. If the Child had to go down into Egypt, the Mother went down into Egypt too. If the Child came up to Nazareth, the Mother came up to Nazareth too. Her whole life was perfectly natural, perfectly simple. It is good for us to remember that the holiness of the most holy is not unnatural. Sin is unnatural. When God gives us the gift of grace it is not unnatural, it is to restore nature. You cannot do anything more unnatural than sin ; you can do nothing more natural than be good. And what strikes us most in the life of the most perfect of our race is her extraordinary simplicity, her extraordinary knowledge. She quietly went her way, and things yielded to her ; if not she broke her way through them. She never for one instant failed in obeying, in following the Will of God, in fulfilling the purpose of God. Oh, it is wonderful when we think of it, when we think of the way in which we put ourselves to all kinds of contortions to try and do right. How often we strain ourselves and put ourselves into a state of mental anguish, in our efforts to try and get ourselves right, when the rightness is so simple, for it merely consists in realising that God is Love, and in living for Him.

And so we just see these three things in the Blessed Mother of God ; let us remember always that she was perfectly sinless. Read the Magnificat : you do not find one word of penitence ; she never had anything to repent of ; you cannot imagine that she took any part in the deeds that caused the Crucifixion of Her

THE HUMILITY OF MARY—I

Son. And first of all, notice the extraordinary humility. If a person has the least touch of pride in them, they cannot be really lifted up. There are many people for whom God might do great things, but for this reason it would not be good for them. Many a person craves the gift of prayer; but God knows that if they had it they would be very proud, and so God does not give them that gift : He holds it back. Many a person would like to be in a position in which they feel they could do a great deal of good; but God knows that in that position they would begin to be very self-conscious and self-satisfied, and so God withholds the gift. Perfect humility can be raised to any height. The Blessed Virgin said : ' God putteth down the mighty from their seat, and exalteth the humble and meek.' Because she was so humble God exalted her. The strange thing about her humility is, that she could glory in the fact that all generations should call her blessed. In the Magnificat there is a great deal of praise of herself. The reason of that was, that she so perfectly felt that everything in herself was the gift of God, not her own possession. You may say : is that not a most lovely landscape ? Is not that mountain splendid, is it not magnificent to climb ? But you are not proud of it; the reason is that it is outside you, that it does not touch yourself. But as soon as it touches yourself, that you feel it is your own, then you are proud of it. When once you realise that everything you have is not your own, then you will cease to be proud of your own gifts. God gives us certain gifts. You say : I know that people like me, I know that I have the way of making myself popular with people. But that is God's gift to me, and why should I be any more proud of it than of the mountains or the flowers? God gave her that perfect humility, that realisation that her wonderful qualities were the gift of God. It is not true humility to say that you have not got certain gifts that you know you do possess. If you have perfectly true humility you realise that the gifts of God are not your own, but are God's gifts; and so you do not feel exalted. A being who realises that, who is rich in all kinds of magnificent, intellectual and physical gifts, as the Blessed Virgin was, who could realise that all those gifts were the gifts of God—such a person was capable of being great, such a person could be made use of; and so she was capable of being made the Mother of God, for there was no fear that she would take to herself the gift of God and look upon it as her own.

Mary's whole life was, from first to last, the simplest of all lives. When the angel came and told her what her vocation was, she at once realised it, she never swerved; she did not want to do anything else. She realised at once that it was the Will of God. That is so simple, and yet the hardest of all things: 'This is the Will of God—even your sanctification.' We know what the Will of God for us is —it is just to be perfectly simple. There is a beautiful road leading one way, and there is another beautiful road leading in another direction, but that one road is the road that God wills, and therefore I will follow it. It was so with Mary. What position might she not have filled in the world if she had used the great gifts which God had given her for herself; but she chose rather to use them all for God, to fulfil His purpose. These two things should always go together the Will of God and the will of man; and if you obey the Will of God you help others to obey it too. No person has ever been good without making others better; no person has ever been bad without making others worse. Let us thank God for all the good people in the world. Often we hear of people doing much active good in the world; but goodness itself is a great power quite apart from active beneficence. Many people do not realise that a person can do a great deal of good to his fellow-creatures by prayer, by simply praying for them. They do not understand the self-denial of the great Orders, those who lock themselves up and spend much time in prayer and penitence; they do not realise, they forget that there was one who lived a life of retirement from beginning to end, whom we scarcely know a single thing about, whose words were only recorded seven times, but who is the best known and the best loved woman in the whole world. For where has the name of Christ gone, that the name of Mary has not gone too? Wherever Christianity is found in the whole world, there is the name of Mary too; and who is there but knows what she has done for the human race? And let all honour and love her.

As we think of the Immaculate Conception, we think of the ideal of womanhood, we think of the highest height to which created woman has ever reached. Think of the Blessed Virgin, think of what her life was, so extraordinarily simple; you cannot think of her committing sin—it would be like their saying of Our Blessed Lord, her Son, 'He casteth out devils by Beelzebub the Prince of the devils.' It does not seem to many of our countrymen that Mary was extraordinary. They do not realise that her life was miraculous and supernatural, and they deny to her the graces she has attained, because all those graces run through simple streams. The life of the Blessed Virgin was such a life of simplicity; it ran on such regular lines, lines according to the Will of God, that it needs the light of faith to realise what her life really was, a life so wonderful that her own cousin could say, ' Whence is this to me, that the Mother of my Lord should come to me ? ' Mary realised at once herself. As she stood at the door of Elizabeth's house, before anybody realised, before anything had happened except what she herself knew, as she looked round she exclaimed, ' Behold from henceforth all generations shall call me blessed!' Was there ever such a marvellous fulfilment of marvellous words ? Wherever we hear the name of Christ, there we hear the name of the Blessed Mother of God, who was born without sin and who lived without sin, and who gave to Him that flesh by which He saved the world.

THE HUMILITY OF MARY—II

'Clothed with humility.'—1 PETER v. 5.

THE Feast of the Immaculate Conception, which we have just been keeping, passes almost immediately into the Feast of the Coming of Our Lord at Christmas. These two festivals together teach us this one great moral lesson—the lesson of the greatness of humility in the spiritual life, the lesson of the greatness of humility which is the dawn of all virtues. It was through humility that the Blessed Virgin was capable of being raised up. It was through the humility of such a person that the coming of Our Lord Jesus Christ became possible, through Whom the whole human race was lifted up. If there had been one taint, one touch of pride in the Blessed Mother of God, how would she have received her high vocation? Had she looked downwards, at once she would have seen on what a height she was standing; when the angel came and said that she should conceive and bear a Son she would have reeled as she stood; but, looking upwards in her perfect humility, she could gaze as high as she pleased, with no danger of giddiness. Lucifer stood upon a height with all the Angel Host around him, waiting for a breathless moment before the vision of God was permitted. He had gained more light and knowledge and wisdom than the other angels from his greater nearness to God;

but as he stood upon the utmost steep of creation, waiting to behold God face to face, for one moment he looked downwards and he lost his head, he plunged down into the abyss, plunged down from the heights of heaven to the abyss of hell. Our Blessed Lord— He Who humbled Himself that He might make us rich with the riches of God—said: 'Learn of Me, for I am meek and lowly in heart.' He might have said: I am very holy; I am very courageous; I am very truthful—but what He did say was: 'Learn of Me, for I am meek and lowly in heart: and ye shall find rest unto your souls.' Humility, as it were, fills the atmosphere at this time; it is the atmosphere of the Feast that is just coming, the humility of the perfect creature, the humility of God made man.

There are various spheres in life in which we do not need humility at all, where it would, in fact, be somewhat in the way. If you want to get on very much in the world, humility is rather out of place. If you think a good deal of yourself, people will think a good deal of you; in this world, people are taken at their own estimate. People who think well of themselves have the way of making others think well of them. When you are pushing your way through the scramble of life, humility has not much place there: if you are humble you will probably be pushed out of the way. When I say that humility is necessary, it does not follow that it needs humility, in any sense of the word, to get on in the affairs of this world—in the natural sphere, humility has not much place; but when we come to the supernatural sphere, the sphere into which the Second Adam lifted us when He came to give back the gift which

THE HUMILITY OF MARY—II

the first Adam had lost through eating the forbidden fruit, we find there is not a single step we can take that is not hampered by pride.

The first element of approach towards God is humility; somehow or other humility must enter into our souls. That is the first step. There are certain sins we all know we have. We know what it is to give way to temper, we know what it is to tell lies. But pride is a much more subtle thing than that. You may be very proud, and yet not know it. You may constantly be committing many sins that are the direct fruits of pride; you may be very proud, and perhaps think all the time that you are very humble. It is a comparatively easy thing to meet tangible faults and fight them. You know that you are inclined to say unkind things about people; you say: I am not going to do so any more, and you determine to conquer that fault. That fault is difficult to fight; but you *know* that fault. Many persons do not know that what is hindering them from making a step upwards in their spiritual life is the lack of humility, the presence of pride. Humility is like an atmosphere. And pride is like an atmosphere. In which of the two does your soul really live? You look up on a soft summer day, the whole air is tinted and sunny, and you see the whole blue sky above you; you look up again a few minutes later and you cannot see the sky, it is clouded over. And you wonder: where do the clouds come from? They were there all the time. The air grew chill, the atmosphere became condensed, and the sky clouded. And so you look into yourself, and you see your soul clear; you look again, and you see thunder-clouds raging. Where did they come from? They were in the atmosphere of the soul. You look, and you see your soul with eyes of self-satisfaction; you look again, and you see a definite fault. Where did it come from? It was there all the time. People go about feeling raw and sore and bitter, and they do not know what is the matter, and then out it comes in a burst of temper. A person goes on in an atmosphere of self-congratulation, he thinks people are so nice, and that things are going smoothly and pleasantly; and then in the midst comes out some horrible untruth, and that lie was the outcome of pride.

Therefore, we may be certain of this, that except in so far as pride is giving way fundamentally, and the atmosphere of pride in the soul changing into the atmosphere of humility, humility reigning where pride used to reign—there cannot be any real fundamental spiritual progress. Because the idea of the whole spiritual life is, that the soul should be conscious of its own incapacity to rise without the presence of God. I cannot rise unless God has lifted me. A man could as well fly without wings, as a soul rise in the supernatural life without the help of God, without the aid of Divine grace. Many a time God will allow a man to fall into terrible sin, in order that he may come to repentance. Many a time, when nothing else will help, when a person walks alone, entirely independent, feeling no special need of God, no special need of the Sacraments, and having no sense of incapacity within him if he misses the Sacraments, God will allow him to fall very badly. Many a person has plunged into a life of wickedness, because God allows him to fall very low in order that he may

THE HUMILITY OF MARY—II

rise again, through humility. Humility is like a lever in the hands of God, that God may lift you up; humility allows God to work in you. It is not saying: I can do this, or I can do that. It is admitting to yourself: I can of mine own self do nothing, but—'I can do all things through Christ who strengtheneth me.'

There are two or three striking characteristics in pride that make it such a difficult thing for us to meet. One is the sublety with which it works. Pride will enter into all our actions, sucking out, as it were, the real sap, and putting the poison of self-love into its place. If a man in such a state of self-deception were awakened by some horrible fault, he would know exactly where he stood.

The danger of pride is that it flatters and soothes self-love, and does not allow a man to know where he stands, and will put him on the defensive against the truth. He may say: you cannot accuse me of being selfish, or of not doing my best to help others. Nobody does accuse him of not helping other people; but the real reason why he helps other people is some personal motive. God says: get your motive from Heaven, not from earth. Get your motive from Heaven and your power from Heaven.

As long as I get my motive from God my act is raised; but so long as I get the motive from myself I may do the act a great deal quicker and easier, but the act falls to earth. It is, for instance, a very pleasant thing for me to feel that one person appreciated my kindness to him, and that when other people were saying unkind things about me, I could go away and visit that poor old man or woman, and have all sorts of pretty speeches poured into my ear. I feel that that person really understands and appreciates me ; while, all the time, that was just the one person who did not understand me at all. It does not follow from my doing that kind act that I have any love for God, any faith in God ; I did it from the motive of self-love. Acts done from the motive of self-love cling to self and fall to earth. Such acts are not inspired by the spirit of humility, they are inspired by the spirit of pride. So long as the sap circulating through the soul is not the sap of Divine grace, but the sap of self-love, there is secret poison in those actions. All the fruit of pride is found to be tasteless and poisonous. It cannot bring forth the fair blossoms of Christian virtues, for that which alone can bring out those virtues is the grace of God.

The Christian life is like a tree, growing and spreading its roots in the earth ; bringing forth first the blossom, then the leaf and then the fruit. It has a slow, gradual growth ; and it is not until the years go on that you see the fruits of the Spirit—love and joy and peace—richly endowing and beautifying the soul. You see another tree growing up much more rapidly, and apparently much more beautiful, putting forth leaves and blossoms ; but when the time for ripening comes, when the autumn comes, the fruit is all sour and you cannot eat it. The one is inspired with the love of self in some form or another ; the other is inspired by the love of God, and that is of far slower growth.

Another curious characteristic of pride is that you often find that the people who are the most proud are those who have least to be proud of, and that the people who are the most humble are the people who have a great deal to make them proud. You will find an extremely learned and clever person not nearly so proud as one who has a little smattering of knowledge. You will find a man with practically no knowledge at all, much more intellectually proud than one who is really learned and wise. A person goes about a good deal, and is very popular in the world, is very attractive, has many gifts, and is liked by everybody; but he may not be nearly as proud as one who does not enjoy half as much popularity, who has not half as many gifts, nor so much reason for pride. It is a curious thing that anyone can be proud of so little. Why is this? I think it is because we are too apt to limit and circumscribe our views, and to make a little world for ourselves. We do not look out into the big world, we only look into our own little narrow world. A great thing for us to remember is that we must always be comparing ourselves with people bigger than ourselves; we must not always be like the Pharisee who thanked God that he was not as that publican. We must be always looking upwards, not downwards, looking at the people who do far more than we do, and comparing the little we do with the great things those other people do; not looking in at ourselves and saying, I can do this or that well, and therewith be perfectly self-satisfied. As a contrast, think of her whom all generations shall call blessed, walking to all appearances within the limits of ordinary human life, but in truth going forward along a path, a track that no human being had ever walked on before, guided only by the Spirit of God, and never making a blunder or mistake. There was no comparison in her mind with anything except the very highest—the will of God Himself.

It is possible for us to be inspired by the pride of self-love when our lives are very small. Pride is eating the heart out of everything we do, even out of our very prayers, and the soul is not wakened up to consciousness. Often it needs that very sin of sins, that would seem to drive a person into despair, to drive him to the very feet of Our Lord.

If then there is such danger in pride, how are we to develop the very opposite of this pride, which is humility ? The first thing we may be sure of is this, that pride won't go out of our life just because we want humility to come in. We may say to ourselves : I hate this pride, and mean to conquer it ; but it is one thing to conquer a definite fault, and another to recognise and conquer a subtle thing like pride. A person says : I have stolen two or three times, and I am determined I won't do it again. You cannot say the same of a habit like pride ; it slips through your fingers, it is always coming up, it is—as I have said—like the atmosphere, it lurks in a place. You think you have conquered it and have driven it out of the sphere of your spiritual life ; but if you oust pride in one direction, you become proud of something else. Pride creeps noiselessly about and tries unconsciously to get a footing. The battle with a secret foe is very difficult. Consequently pride is a much harder sin to overcome than a tangible overt sin, and takes a longer time. I think that the only way in which pride can be conquered, is not to destroy it but to replace it. Every thread of pride that is unknotted must be replaced with a thread

THE HUMILITY OF MARY—II

knotted with humility: for every breath of pride breathed out, a breath of humility must be drawn in: for every atom of pride cast out, an atom of humility must come instead of it. Nature abhors a vacuum; so does the moral life; so does Divine grace abhor a vacuum. You can only conquer evil by doing good; you can only conquer pride by being humble. Everyone is either proud or humble. Every person who is no longer proud is humble, and everyone who has been proud and is so no longer, is humble, because humility takes the place of pride. Therefore we must be patient with ourselves, struggling always for the possession of that virtue which cannot co-exist with pride.

We must always remember, in striving after humility, that we may be perfectly certain that we can never become humble at the expense of untruthfulness or insincerity. Pride is always a lie, always untruthful, always exaggerating. Pride will always fix its mind, not upon the person, but upon some quality in the person. Pride will always say: I can do this or that; humility says: I *am* this or that. Pride is taking a bit of myself, and keeping my eyes fixed upon that and forgetting the rest. Pride says: I know that I am not very clever, or very attractive, or very popular; but I know that I can do something that somebody else cannot do. Pride keeps on thinking of that one thing. But that is only a talent, a gift, it may pass away and leave you without it. It is like a tree which has not much foliage and not very strong branches saying: I have this beautiful blossom. But the blossom is not the tree; the blossom dies and the tree goes on. Humility takes in the whole person: I *am* lowly! Pride says: I have this or that. Humility *is* the person; pride is partial, pride takes the partial view. And therefore pride is untrue, and is satisfied with one thing and exaggerates the importance of that one thing. Humility takes in the whole. And consequently humility is always true. It is not humble to say: I cannot do this, when you know you can. It is not humble to say: Oh, do not tell me that I have this or that gift, when you know you have it. That is pride. If God has given you a gift, you have to use it, and you cannot use it unless you know you have it. We hear over and over again in the Old Testament that God was always saying to the ancient people :— remember that I have dealt with you as I have dealt with nobody else, with a mighty hand and with a stretched-out arm. I did this for you, and this for you: I did not do it for anybody else. The reason He impressed this upon them was that He meant them to understand: I have done so much for you, now you must do a great deal more for Me. And so, when a person says: I do not like to think I have this or that characteristic, that I have such and such a gift, for fear it will make me proud, the answer is: you cannot be truly humble without realising that you have that gift, and you must use that gift for the glory of God. You cannot use the gift unless you recognise it, and if the recognition of it makes you proud, you are not recognising it as God's gift. And so humility is perfectly true. Mary said, 'Behold from henceforth all generations shall call me blessed'; Saint Paul said, 'I am not a whit behind the very chiefest of the Apostles'; and the Meekest and Humblest of Men said,

' I and My Father are One.' And so it is no use to shirk facts. I know that I have the gift of music, I know I can play well, I know I can sing well ; I know I have the gift of making people like me ; I know I have the gift of influencing people. But that does not make me proud. I know if I have these gifts I have got to use them ; and if God has given me these gifts to use I must cultivate them, and therefore humility always comes in and recognises everything in the person. And so you will find that a very humble person can say things that nobody else but a very conceited person could say. Sometimes a little humble person will talk about themselves in a way no one else could who was not frightfully conceited. It is just because they have ceased to be personal ; they now look upon these things entirely as God's gifts, and feel responsible for the exercise of those gifts, and use them for the glory of God. There is no room for pride.

Therefore it is good for us to remember this. Pride always looks at part of oneself, humility always looks at the whole. Pride always looks down, humility always looks up. How is it, when I know I can do a great many things that other people cannot do, and have the gift of making myself more pleasant and popular than many others, when I know that somebody else would give all they possess to have the gifts I have, how is it I can keep all that without a shadow or an atom of pride ? How can I do it? By comparing myself, not with somebody below, but with somebody higher, and that somebody higher Our Blessed Lord Himself. Until Our Lord came down to earth pride was not known to be a sin at all. In the old heathen times humility was looked upon as another name for weakness. Possibly we are ashamed of being humble. Look at the little hill set in the level land; it thinks itself so high, it is so proud. But put that little hill in a mountainous country and you will see how small it is: it is nothing but a little rise in the ground. I remember in the flatlands of Lincolnshire there was a tiny little hill; we used to talk of it as a hill, we always looked upon it as a hill, because the surrounding country was almost level land. So a little person stands all alone, a little bit more attractive, a little better looking, a little cleverer than others. It is like the little hill in the lowlands; but take that little person, and put her among great folks, instantly pride becomes irritated in her. Therefore instead of saying: I am not attractive, I am not so good looking, I am not so clever as I thought, but I must do the best I can; it is for me to fulfil my duty towards God wherever I am, she begins to feel sore and bitter when comparing herself with bigger people. Pride remains; but the person has found her level, has found that she is not the kind of person she thought she was at all. But humility says: I have always looked up to one so much greater than myself and striven to fulfil the Will of God in me, and comparing myself with the Son of God, comparing myself with our Lord Jesus Christ, there is no room left for pride.

And so, my brethren, it is by perfect truthfulness, by living in the Presence of God, that pride is to be overcome. By comparing ourselves to our Lord Jesus Christ, by living closer to our Lord Jesus Christ, and by seeing Him in the whole of His moral splendour

THE HUMILITY OF MARY—II

—in the greatness of His real character—we see our own puniness and pettiness, and feel that the things we can do are so trifling and small that there is nothing to be self-satisfied about in them, but much to be ashamed of. Consequently, as we look through our whole nature, as we take stock of everything we have, we recognise every gift God has given us, and we strive to develop that gift to the glory of God by living in the Presence of God. Pride is always living in the presence of self; humility is always living in the Presence of God. It changes the whole centre of one's life when we try to find God's Will. I used to think, if I did such and such a thing what would be the effect upon such and such people and towards myself? Now I think: is that right? What does God want me to do? Conscience becomes a clear, strong, resonant voice that ever fills my soul, and controls and rules me; while gradually the soul sinks into its place, and finds itself in all its greatness small indeed in the Presence of God.

THE CALL OF GOD [1]

'A certain man had two sons; and he came to the first, and said, Son, go work to-day in my vineyard. He answered and said, I will not: but afterward he repented, and went. And he came to the second, and said likewise. And he answered and said, I go, sir: and went not. Whether of them twain did the will of his father?'—St. Matthew xxi. 28, 29, 30, 31.

We are not likely to be allowed soon to forget all the great advantages and discoveries of modern science and the knowledge we are gaining of the physical world. One after another the great difficulties in the physical world have been met by science and have yielded to man, owing to the indomitable energy and will with which he has faced them. As we understand more and more of the problems of the material world, as our progress in the domain of physical science grows wider and wider, we often wish that our knowledge was growing in other spheres proportionately, for real progress, to be thorough, must be all-round progress.

A man may be perfectly well grown in one direction, and deficient in another. We have it on the testimony of Charles Darwin that the result of too great a devotion to one branch of knowledge is that, while one side of

[1] The date of the preaching of this sermon was November 20 1904. The substance of the last part of it is to be found also in one of Fr. Maturin's sermons on the Parables, but so much in this version is new and important that his readers will be glad to have it included in this collection.

THE CALL OF GOD

the nature becomes too highly developed, the other side may become atrophied. It is quite possible that a man may so throw himself into the study of physical science, that other aims—other powers—far greater, far higher, far wider, may all pass from his mind, and the nobler side of his nature may die of atrophy.

True progress must be an all-round progress, not merely a growth in one direction. Progress is not true progress if a man, while growing and developing in one sphere, is dying in another.

So we say as we look around : would that man knew as much of human nature as he does of material nature. Has man really progressed ? Has he really advanced very much in the knowledge of his higher nature ? We have advanced very much in the knowledge of material things, but we have not advanced much in the knowledge of spiritual, of psychical things. I doubt if we know very much more about ourselves than our forefathers did. I doubt if we have much more knowledge of human nature. We stand with the most fascinating of all studies before our eyes, and yet we are standing on the threshold still, unable to enter, and unable to understand. What revelations lie in the human heart that do not lie in the physical world around us ! What strange possibilities ! What wonderful paradoxes ! Man so great, and yet so small ; aiming so high, and yet falling so low ; so persistent in his efforts after something which he cannot attain ; ever struggling and striving after the impossible. How splendid he is in his indomitable perseverance, how crushed he is by constant and perpetual failure, and yet he will not take failure as an answer. He will not be beaten back, he will not be crushed. As we look on, as we watch these struggles, do we not recognise the same movements within ourselves? It is by looking into ourselves that we get to understand other men better, we gauge other men, we feel the pulses of others' lives as they throb and beat in our hearts; we get to understand other men better through ourselves, though our progress is slow, faulty and imperfect, and we stand on the threshold still.

The knowledge of human nature is always an interesting study to man, and the study always presents startling paradoxes; yet, perchance, the study and knowledge of myself, on which the study of man in the aggregate must always depend, is more interesting still.

I can understand that you have the power of drawing a veil between your character and mine. You do not want me to know you as you are, and you can close yourself in, so that you seem a person entirely different from what you really are. The whole failure, the whole trouble we have known even in the closest and most intimate of human relations, that between mother and child, arises from the fact that neither can quite understand the other; for it is almost impossible to penetrate one mind by another, to study one personality from another.

But when I turn away from others, I say, how strange a thing it is that I who have been living with myself all my life, ever since I was born, should fail to know myself. Oftentimes I think, the longer I live and the more I watch, the more absolutely ignorant I become of myself. So much is this the

THE CALL OF GOD

case, that often we believe ourselves to be perfectly different beings from what we really are, different in body and mind even from what our friends know us to be. We do not recognise our own personal appearance, any more than we recognise our mental or our spiritual state. It is strange that a person does not understand his own personal characteristics; but that, in our mind and in our nature and in our physical state, we should think ourselves to be something that everybody knows we are not—when we come to recognise this it is very startling. We have constantly to be correcting ourselves by other people's judgment of us, and by this and perpetual introspection come to find we are not the kind of men and women we thought we were at all.

We understand more easily that new states, new conditions, new circumstances of life may bring about new revelations to ourselves of what we really are. I can quite understand that if a strong man loses his health he might undergo a strange change, and discover a new side to his nature, a new strength, a new forbearance. We know perfectly well—which of us is not conscious?—that outside things have a great power, an immense influence on the inside nature of a man. We have some great shock, some great sorrow, and we find a new side to our character, a side we never saw before. Some new fault or some new virtue, that has been lurking within, waiting for an opportunity to show itself, comes to the front, brought out by some special circumstances.

A man passes from health to sickness, who has never known what it was to be a day ill in his life, and he says: I never knew what a grumbler I was till now. A man passes from popularity to unpopularity, and you hear him say: I never knew what a fund of bitterness I was possessed of before. It only needed circumstances to draw out what was latent all the while. A man passes from living amongst sympathetic friends to dwell among strangers, and he says: I never dreamt what a selfish person I was till now. In all these cases, the man is an entirely different person from what he imagined himself to be.

Is it not true, that the more we know ourselves the more we are convinced that there are conflicting forces working under the surface of our nature? How often a person can be intensely worldly and then intensely religious! Sometimes we find ourselves going quickly from an alternative of intense self-indulgence to extreme asceticism. Who does not know the reaction from sensuality to saintliness? These strange upheavals of our nature, these strong currents will come to the front. When all looks calm and peaceful, we know these currents are still beneath, powerful, intense, of a strength we cannot measure, into whose power, if we fall, we shall be carried away, for we lack the force to resist. At times one of these currents comes to the surface, at times another; and, this being so, it is all-important that we should try to get to know ourselves, to be prepared for these changes.

Many things at different times in our lives may help us to this knowledge; but before all and above all, there is a factor in life so great that there is none other to compare with it in helping a man to know himself. It is the call of God, and it is described in the words I have taken for my text from the Gospel of St. Matthew.

I am not going to stop this morning to prove the possibility of God's call, or even to explain what I mean by God's call. Everyone knows that God does interfere in his life, at some time or another, in some way or another, sometimes by suffering, sometimes by allowing terrible temptation, sometimes by permitting a man to fall into awful sin, sometimes by sorrow; but, in one way or another, God does interfere in our lives. There are probably not many here who have not felt this interference, who have not heard the Voice of God speak in their lives. If there be any here who, in the days of their youth, have not yet heard God's Voice, who have not yet felt God's Hand, be sure of this, that at some hour or another, some time or another, in some way or another, God will come into your life, God will interfere in your life and will speak to you, and you will know the truth as He speaks, and from that day forward your life can never be exactly the same as it was before. The vision may have departed; the solid earth goes round in its course; but the man who has come into contact with God, who has heard that voice—like Saul of Tarsus on the way to Damascus—may follow it, or may reject it and turn away, but he can never be exactly the same man again.

Now, when that call of God comes, there are various ways of meeting it. There are some people who are always straight, always direct, and if the call of God comes to them—or, in other words, if some new ideal of life comes before them—they will at once and most readily make up their minds, they will at once reject it or at once strive to follow it. There are men and women who will say: I only want to know what I ought to do, and they do it. There are others who will say clearly: I know what I ought to do, but it is too hard, too difficult. Life is too pleasant for me, and the things of life, as they are, are too dear to me; and to tell me that I must turn my back upon them is to tell me a thing that I know is true, but which I have not the smallest intention of doing. I can perfectly understand that. If you say: I am going on doing wrong, I am determined to go on doing it, because I like it. I know well that I shall have to bear the consequences, that I shall have the penalty to pay by and by. Well, my friend, I understand; but I think you do not understand what the payment will be sooner or later. Another man says: I am struggling with all my might; I know what I ought to do, and I am struggling to do it. We cannot doubt that he is struggling towards doing what is right. But in the parable we have two typical characters, quite different, and yet both show us the character of the man who is not straightforward with himself. Many people put themselves to torture, many people labour here, who will have neither the full pleasure of this world nor of the next. They cannot make up their minds to do what they are told. They cannot enjoy this life because their power of faith is too strong, and they cannot let themselves go and do what God tells them. They are consequently always on the edge, always standing between light and darkness. They have no full enjoyment of one life or of the other.

THE CALL OF GOD

Here are two types; and I think if we study them we shall find, though they lived two thousand years ago, and though they did not speak our tongue, that each represents in Biblical language the kind of thing that goes on in your heart and in mine every day. The master called his sons to realise his ownership, to realise that he had something he wanted them to do for him, the working in the vineyard of the Lord. I do not know, I do not care, what it was they were to do. This is the point: they were called to do something for him. In other words, God came and interfered with their lives and said: Let your life have something of obedience towards Me; now go and do something for Me. When a person is living only for himself, and then feels the claim of God on him, when he hears the Voice of God calling to him, 'Go, work in My vineyard,' I want you to go and do something for Me,—that will wholly change his life.

Now, as the master of these two men—the father of these two sons—comes and calls them, and interferes in their lives, and says: I want you to do something for me—go and work in my vineyard, the answer of the first is, ' I will not,' and afterwards he repented and went. The answer of the second, perfectly polite and apparently obedient, is, ' I go, sir,' and he went not. The question of Our Lord was, not what did that man intend, what did that man mean, but which of those men went, which of those two men did what he was told? That was the question for judgment. Our Lord turns round on the multitude and says: you see this man had magnificent intentions. He agreed to go with the utmost politeness and obedience. He had a great capacity for realising spiritual things; he took the greatest pleasure in the Voice of God speaking to him; but, my friends, what did he do? I asked him to go and work in my vineyard, and he did not go. See the other man, who answered rudely and roughly, who had not the smallest intention of obeying. To the voice of the master, he answered: I will not go; I do not want to go. The man had not the smallest intention of obeying, but somehow or another he did it. When the call came, which was it who obeyed? It was the rough, rude, impertinent, rebellious son that brought himself upon his knees.

It would have been easy to understand anyone who said, ' I go, sir,' and went; or, ' I will not go,' and went not. Here in each case is a man who makes up his mind and brings his will into action at once. But in the parable each man knows perfectly well what he wants to do, but he does not do it. We are shown two men exactly opposite as to character, whose first answer is exactly opposite to what they do. The first says, ' I go, sir,' and went not; the second one says, ' I will not go,' but he goes. What does it mean? I think it means this, that everyone of us has a depth to his character. Now, what I mean by the surface of my character is my inclination. What comes to the surface is inclination. Inclinations work one way, will works another. People are not responsible for their inclinations; there is nothing good or bad in inclinations. You tell me that it is your inclination to be lazy in the mornings. Ah, but, my friend, the question is, do you resist your laziness? Do you get up early in the morning?

Oh yes, you say, I get up early. If you resist your laziness, if you get over it, that tells character, the inclination is not your character. Again, a man says: I am not at all inclined to pray. For my part, if it were not for the fear or the love of God, or a sense of responsibility, I do not know that I should go to Church at all. It's not according to my taste. My natural taste and inclination is to the things of the earth. Ah but, my friend, the point is, do you go to Church? Oh yes, I go. The inclination goes one way, the will another. If you were to put it in other words, what is the difference? There is a vast difference, all the difference in the world— the difference between wishing and willing. You cannot help what you wish, you can help what you will. God won't judge you for what you wish, but He will judge you for what you will. Do you say you wish these fast-days weren't coming next week? I don't like fasting at all: I very much prefer feasting to fasting. I always feel I shall be very glad when the fast-days are over; I look forward to their being over. Well, my friend, you cannot help that; but the point is, do you keep the fast? Oh yes, I keep the fast, but I sometimes scarcely think it is worth while keeping it for a man who is wishing all the time he were feasting. But do you keep it? Yes, I do. That is the point. Perhaps a man says: I don't like going to Holy Communion; but if you ask me why I don't like to go, I am almost ashamed to tell you the reason. I don't like getting up early in the morning; I don't like the prayers of preparation; I don't like going to confession. And so you never go to Holy Communion? Oh yes,

I go; I always go; I never miss it. Well then, my friend, you are not responsible for your inclinations; but you are responsible for your actions. It makes all the difference in the world whether you are ruled by your inclinations, or whether you get the upper hand of them and are ruled by your principles. You are not responsible for your inclinations; you cannot help the fact that if you were left to yourself, and that if you were a pagan, you would be the very lowest kind of pagan, the most lawless kind of pagan. You cannot help the fact that God has broken into your life, and you cannot be a pagan even if you wished it. You may be a pagan in your mind; but if the law of God rules your life, I don't much care what your feelings are, you are a Christian. Here is a person who says: if you ask me what kind of a man I am, I will tell you in a few words. I like good living, I like good clothes; I like the comforts of a comfortable home; I like never to be disturbed, never to be interfered with; I like to have my own way. But if you ever saw a man who cannot live as he would like, I am that man. I am always being interfered with; my home is not particularly comfortable; I am often obliged to put the comforts of life away from me. All my inclinations tend downwards, while my will is struggling upwards.

Well, my answer is, my friends, which of these two men did what he was able to do, did the will of his father? Not which wished to do it, not which liked to do it, but which did what he was told? Now look. Here is a man of strong passions —for, mark you, sometimes the very best men have the very strongest passions—they might have been

THE CALL OF GOD

the worst. For think, it was touch and go, so to speak, whether we ever had a Saint Augustine; we have it on his own authority. He was born sensuous; he had it in him to be a Doctor of the Church, and he had it in him to be a sensualist. Read the account of his conversion. He tells us in his writings of his inclinations, what they were: how he clung to the things he hated, and how the toys he loved and played with called him away from God, and he finally broke with them. The very best men may have the very strongest passions, and it is certainly true that some of the very worst men have often had the very best inclinations. These people are so impossible, because they are always intending so much and never doing anything.

Here again comes a man whose inclinations are to take life easily. He does not like difficulties, he likes to have things his own way, and the call of God seems to pass unheard. Then some time, perhaps, he loses his child, or his wife, or he has some other great sorrow; or perhaps he has some powerful temptation, and he realises for the first time how easily he might fall and never recover himself. I am not going to argue as to whether this change is the Voice of God or not; I am talking of men who knew what they ought to do, who knew what kind of life they ought to take up—to them such knowledge was the voice of God. The man was called. To him the work in the vineyard was God's work. He must turn away from the selfish life to the life of service, and the first thing he was called to do was to go and work in the vineyard. When he was first called, the first thing he said was, 'I will not.' That was the answer of inclination: I won't go and work; don't ask me. Go and ask that brother of mine. He is religious. He likes to be in Church all day long. He can pray by the hour. Go and ask him; I am not going. I don't like these things. I will not go and work in the vineyard. Why don't you leave me alone? 'I will not go.' That was the answer of inclination. That was the answer he could not help. He was simply saying: that is my nature; that is the way I am made. That is the way, if it were not for the grace of God, I would always go on. Leave me alone to my selfishness, to my self-indulgence. Let me sink into my corner. Leave me for the flesh I am. I cannot be otherwise. That was the answer made to the master when he called. Then the son went away, and began to think it over, and somehow or another conscience began to work. Conscience begins to call to him; and the will rises up in obedience to the conscience, and stems the tide of inclination, and he goes and does it in the end. That is the point. You say to that man: I hear that you have changed your life altogether. I hear that you are working in your father's vineyard. Oh yes, he says, I don't suppose my father cares a straw for what I have done; I don't suppose he cares a scrap. I did not want to go. I did not mean to go. I was positively rude when I was asked; but, somehow or other, conscience was too strong for me, and I went against all the currents of my nature, and my will stemmed the tide of inclination, and I went and did it. I don't suppose it is of much use my doing it. And then the father looks down, and says:—what do you think of this boy? He did not want to work

THE CALL OF GOD

in the vineyard; he did not want to do it; but he went and did his father's will.

Now look at the story of the other type. The father goes to the other son, whose inclinations were all of the very best. He gives a little flutter of excitement when he hears his father's voice. He likes going to Church. He likes the stained-glass windows, the sweet perfume of the incense. He prefers the pleasant stillness in contrast to the roar and rush of life outside. All his inclinations are for spiritual things; he could talk for hours about good deeds. He could tell you by the hour together about the splendid lives of some of the great saints, and the doings of some of the monastic orders: he likes this kind of thing. Then comes the test of facts. What are you going to do? The master says: I do not care one straw whether you like these things or not, whether you like doing them or not. If you like them they help you, that is, if inclination bears upon the will and forces it to action; but if the will is not moved and holds back from action, then I would rather have your rough, rude, surly brother, who openly says he does not like these things, but feels the power of conscience and goes and does them. So the master comes to the son who has spiritual inclinations. My dear friends, I do not suppose if you had spoken to that young man, you would have found he had the smallest idea how shallow these spiritual things were. They never acted as a force, they never formed a current. If you had talked to him about sacred things, you would have thought how intensely spiritual he was. You would have said: it is amazing to me where that young man gets his spirituality. It is surprising how much he knows, and how he can put his own feelings almost into the language of the saints. Yes, that is all very beautiful, but what we want in this work-a-day world is men who will do, not the men with inclinations only.

I come in special need to a man, and I say: I am in terrible trouble. I should be so grateful if you could help me. I am in great poverty; a few pounds would help me now, and steer me over into quiet places. Will you lend it to me for a few weeks? Will you help me now? And he says: my dear fellow, I am truly sorry, I feel so intensely for you. Anything I can do in the way of kindness and sympathy I shall be only too glad to do. But what are you going to do in the way of giving me money? Oh, I am sorry. I am afraid I can't afford that. And then you go to his brother and ask him, and he says: Oh, don't ask me for anything. I have nothing to give. Go and ask my brother; he's got plenty. Oh, here—here are a few pounds, if that is any good— here you are. The other man was very kind indeed. I felt every moment his purse was going to be opened; but it remained closed. It was all inclination. You could not depend upon him for doing one hand's turn. It was all inclination, all feeling. And so when the father asked him to work in the vineyard, he replied, ' I go, sir.' Oh, I shall be delighted to go. There is nothing I should like more than to work in my father's vineyard. Only give me plenty of work to do, and you will see how I rejoice in doing it. Then the night comes, and the father asks: well, what have you done? And he says: well, upon

THE CALL OF GOD

my word, I am ashamed ; I intended to go all day long. But somehow or other, I have not gone. He meant to go, he had the wish to go, but he did not go. And then comes the judgment. Christ asks of the people standing round: which of those two did the will of his father ? And the answer of the whole world is the answer of those who stood listening to Our Lord :—that rude son is the one you can depend upon in the long run after all ; he will do the deed, though he does not like it. His conscience spoke truly. His will was strong. The other was all inclination.

This, my friends, is the last Sunday of the old year ; for next Sunday will be the first Sunday in Advent— the beginning of the new Christian Year. It is good for us to look back and to ask ourselves what we have done since last Advent. What did we intend to do? What have we done ? Many people intend to do so much, and never do anything more than intend. Somebody has well said: when the devil cannot tempt a man to give up God, or make him do wrong, he tempts him to make a resolution. The man makes a resolution, and he thinks that is enough, and he never thinks about it again. Never conclude from the best intentions you have that you are a bit better than the man who has not any intentions at all. Never rest upon the fact that you have good inclinations. It is not the inclinations, it is the will you have to judge, and what it acts upon. Do not at the end of the day be content with saying : I felt devout at my prayers. That is not enough. The person who gets into a stupor of emotion, an ecstasy of prayer, and comes out of Church and goes on exactly as he did before, does not do enough. Emotions may be only deception, unless they end in an act of the will. I am not merely a reasoning, not merely an emotional being, but both. I am above all things a man with a will ; but until that will is set into action, all is entirely without result. The meaning of all emotion, all desire, is to act upon the will, and set it acting. Let us look back on the past year, and say to ourselves: what did I intend to do ? What did I do ? I intended to go to Holy Communion more regularly. Have I done it ? It does not matter if you intended to do it ; if you have not done it, you are no better than if you had not intended to do it at all, possibly somewhat worse.

On the other hand, there are men and women in this world who see only the evil, only the worst of themselves. They are always afraid of themselves. They are always underestimating themselves, and saying : I am not a man of strong religious emotions, I am a man of action. Meantime the will has to fight hard, has to strive hard against all the downward currents of a man's nature which are setting strongly in another direction, so that in the very act of doing good it seems to them as if it was worthless, because they feel nothing. Such a man as that will be astonished before the Judgment Seat of Christ to find that Our Lord looks at and judges by, not what that man felt, but by what he did. That man, in spite of all his feelings against doing right, makes that right action of more value because of his difficulties, because of his hard struggle against many infinitely great odds. Let us take ourselves as we are. If we are men of strong religious feeling, let us thank God for that strong feeling ; but

THE CALL OF GOD

feeling itself is no good—is worth nothing—unless it ends in action. If we are men of no religious feeling at all—men of the earth, earthy—who, if left to ourselves, would go rapidly downhill, let us thank God when we feel the power of God's grace, when we feel the claims of conscience. At times the strength of our nature, in revolt and rebellion against conscience, seems to debase every act we do. It does not. It raises it. The final question on all life is not merely what was the inner state, what was the inner struggle, but, what did it proceed to, what did it end in? He who knew his Lord's will, and did it, though all his nature and inclinations were against it, was blest. He who knew his Lord's will, and did it not, though all his nature was clamorous with approval, shall know the curse of that servant 'who knew his Lord's will, but prepared not himself, neither did according to His will, and shall be beaten with many stripes.'

SERMON PREACHED AT THE CLOTHING OF A NUN[1]

'I found Him whom my soul loveth, I held Him, I would not let Him go.'—THE SONG OF SOLOMON iii. 4.

IN all literature there are but a few books that have that remarkable and rare character of being almost emancipated from the conditions of time and place, and being able to speak to men of every age, country, and temperament. Such books are sure to be intensely human and personal. Human nature in all ages is very much alike, and there are to be found here and there in the world's history a few of so marked a personality and so large a humanity, that, in giving their own expérience, they give and interpret that of a multitude.

But the recorded experiences of such men will be concerned mostly with the interior life. The accident of time, place, and circumstance is of little importance. It is the great drama of the soul that interests them and arrests us. The setting of their lives, the age in which they lived, the people amongst whom they moved, the events that stirred them, the shifting scenes that passed before their eyes, the things that tried and tempted them, all these melt into the distance before the intense reality, the living and vivid picture of that which takes place within.

[1] This sermon was preached at the English convent in Bruges on October 7, 1909.

THE CLOTHING OF A NUN

The bond that unites the centuries and brings us into close and sympathetic relationship with these men is the bond of their intense humanity. And this gives to the writer almost the character of universality. There is no secret of the human heart that he does not seem to know, he has sounded its depths and shallows. As we read we feel as if he were describing our own experiences. The heart beats quick and the tears spring to our eyes, as he analyses and reveals us to ourselves. We enter with almost painful intensity into what he felt and suffered; the light and shade, the storm and calm, the hope and despair, the bitterness of defeat and the joy of success, drawn by a master hand trembling with nervous tension, move the reader to the depth of his being, as he hears this voice speaking out of the far past, and telling him that another has suffered and fought and felt and sinned as he has.

And of all such human documents there are few that can be compared with the 'Confessions of St. Augustine.' It is one of the most remarkable instances of a person writing exclusively about himself without a trace of egotism. The Presence of God enfolds all with a hallowing atmosphere. It is all bathed in the freshness and light of a spring morning, radiant with hope and youth. There is throughout an entire absence of violence or anger against himself for his sins, however clear his appreciation of their gravity. There is no faintest trace of morbidness in his searching self-analysis or in his retrospect over the lost years of his youth. All is mellowed and softened in the tender light of the love of God. He might almost be writing of the failures of another whom he loved, rather than of himself. He throws the deepest secrets of his inmost soul before the world: his passions, his waywardness, his self-deception. He hides nothing, excuses nothing, but in language unsurpassed for its purity of style, simplicity, and reverence he tells the story of the struggles of his soul and its search for God, and its final and complete surrender to Christ. His triumph recalls the despairing words of the Apostate: 'Thou hast conquered, O Galilean!' And he sums it up in those words which are the epitome of the life of man on earth: 'Thou hast made me for Thyself, O Lord, and my heart is restless till it finds its rest in Thee.'

His life had indeed been restless and dissatisfied. He didn't know what he wanted, and he plunged blindly into the seething vortex. He had great gifts for which he found no satisfactory outlet. The pent-up streams of his energies broke out on this side and on that, and threw him back upon himself exhausted and dissatisfied. For a time he entangled and almost lost himself in the pleasure of the senses; indeed, for years this man, who had in him the power to be a great saint and one of the greatest teachers the Church has ever known, was held bound to earth by his passions. None who knew him then could have told what he might be if only he could gain his liberty, what powers of mind and heart were being wasted. He could not master himself. He longed for freedom, and yet loved his chains.

And then he tells us how our Lord came to him, spoke to him through those well known words of St. Paul, and set him free. There was, as he stood on the threshold of that new life, one last momentous struggle. The past and the future met in deadly conflict. The habits and associations of years, the entanglements in which he had involved himself, the pleasures so sweet and yet so bitter, they sprang to the front and claimed him, and told him of his weakness; they gathered around the door that was opening, and tried to silence the Voice that was calling. The future, with all its possibilities, hung for one moment in the balance. And then with one supreme act of the will he broke away and passed into the new life, and surrendered himself without reserve and with all the generosity of his nature to our Lord. And in the love of our Lord he found the rest and satisfaction of his whole nature —his restless heart had found its true home. Doubtless he had many a hard struggle afterwards, but none like that. The will that he surrendered never turned back, for soon it was held in the firm and tender grasp of love that endowed it with a new energy. And as the love of his new-found Master deepened, it opened up fresh springs within him: his intelligence expanded under its influence, his heart was enlarged. The clouds that hung over his soul rolled away, and the Sun of Righteousness shone down upon him with healing in its rays. It was like a new spring. Germs of powers lying buried within him burst into life, things half-dead gained new vigour; love that he had used amiss and that had well-nigh been his ruin, love purified and renovated at its source bathed him in its cleansing and life-giving energy, pierced into the depths of his soul, and chased away every lurking shadow. He awakened as one out of sleep and like a giant refreshed with wine. And there was put a New Song into his mouth, even a song of praise and thanksgiving.

There had been nothing in the world strong enough to call out all those plenteous gifts which God had given him, save the Love of God Himself. We see him before his conversion and after. Who would have ever heard of him or known him if he had lived on as he had been living ? One of the greatest minds and tenderest hearts would have been lost to the world ; one of the greatest champions of Truth, who could make the truth clear to many, and bring a vast multitude to the feet of Christ, would have lived and died cramped and buried under the stifling influences of the little world in which he lived. It was God Who found this wanderer and disclosed him to himself and set his feet upon a rock and ordered his going in His way, and showed the world that the greatest powers of heart and mind can only find their full development in Him : ' Thou hast made me, O Lord, for Thyself, and my heart is restless till it finds its rest in Thee.'

For love is the strongest force on earth. It breaks through every barrier and draws out every power. There is nothing that can stand out against it. It makes the weakest strong. What will not a weak woman dare for one whom she loves ? What will not a mother do or suffer for her child ? It transforms the character of the person whom it possesses, and makes the humblest and most commonplace interesting under its influence. Even though the object of love be unworthy, yet the love that is awakened in the soul transforms it and invigorates it. It enlists every power and faculty in its service, and develops them as nothing else can. It shrinks from no service, rejoices in sacrifice. Faith, hope, courage, daring, spring to life at its call. Secret springs that have never been opened break forth under its influence. The frozen streams melt and flow. The inmost depths of the soul are stirred. It awakens something of the poet in the dullest, and is the source of all idealism. It quickens the intelligence, sets fire to the imagination, gives infinite strength to the will, arouses and makes alert the whole man. There is nothing that has such power over every part of man's nature to unify and rally all to its service, as this central furnace of the soul's life. Everything that is in us seems made for its use. The whole complicated machinery of our nature will never find its unity and the perfect co-operation of all its parts save under its command. It resists all that would stand in its way. Anger is the sword which God has placed in the hand of love to fight everything that would oppose it. And with this sharp-edged sword in its hand, love will fight the world and the spiritual powers of the unseen world till it attains the object of its affections.

But love has also the power of narrowing life down to the poorest dimensions, for it can become a blind and unreasoning passion. It becomes a passion when it breaks away from the control of reason, and isolates itself from the checks and restraints, the guidance and promptings of the rest of one's nature. When it takes all into its own masterful hands it leads to the impoverishment and weakening of the person who becomes its slave. Yet even then there is a beauty in it : it bears, in its violence and degradation, the stamp of its royal origin, and of its omnipotence. But if it does not call to its aid all the noblest qualities of the soul, it does not even then stand alone ; it stirs up the baser passions and rallies all the powers of evil that it can enlist in its service— jealousy, intrigue, untruth. If it is not the source of moral unity, it becomes the source of moral disintegration, wounding and maiming every faculty that resists its tyranny.

For weal or woe, for development or destruction, love is the central furnace of the life of man.

For man is made in the image of God, and God is Love. The more true man is to his nature, the more he is ruled by love. God is also Wisdom and Power, but these are ever controlled by Love. They are the Wisdom and Power of One Who is Love. The Wisdom and Power of God are penetrated and flushed with Love.

So that we may say, all love in man is some faint spark of the fire of eternal Love burning within him ; and all that ever draws out the love of man is some reflection of the beauty or love of God. It is the veiled beauty of God that we see and love in nature ; it is some pale and ghostlike likeness to God that kindles our love to man. All that moves the heart and draws it is the vision of God, known or unknown. Sometimes the Divine beauty so penetrates through created things that men cling to them for their very beauty and lose sight of Him Who is its source.

And thus the history of the soul is the history of its search for God. The history of the wayward human heart is the story of love in search of its true object, the divine spark in man seeking for its origin. And that soul which is endowed by God with the rich gift of strong affections, clings to what it loves

THE CLOTHING OF A NUN

with a tenacity that has something of the infinite about it. What can loosen the grasp? Nothing but a clearer vision of the infinite beauty and love of that Person Whose presence radiates forth on all around Him.

And if the soul finds the veil between God and His creatures become transparent, and sees and feels the presence of God Himself, what then? Then other things do not lose their value, nay, the value becomes rather enhanced, because it sees and knows the reason of all their charm; but it is set free from the thraldom of the finite in the love of the Infinite. It cries, 'I have found Him Whom my soul loveth.' I have found Him Whom, unknowing, I have always been in search of. Love turns to and finds its rest in its true home, the Heart of God. The love of all created things and persons becomes purified and transformed, and they slip into their place. 'Thou hast made me for Thyself, O Lord, and my heart is restless till it finds its rest in Thee.' 'And Jesus rebuked the wind and the waves' of the restless, stormy nature, 'and there was a great calm.'

And then there is but one desire in the soul, to give itself wholly and without reserve to Him Whom it has found. It cries, 'Lord, what wilt Thou have me to do?' And who but the soul itself can tell what the answer is? Some are bidden: Go back home and show to them at home what great things God hath done unto thee. Others are called, 'Go sell all that thou hast, take up thy cross and follow Me.' It is not a question of choice, of like or dislike, of natural aptitude or inclination, it is what God wills. Only the ear that hears can understand. The soldiers that stood around Saul of Tarsus on the road to Damascus heard the Voice that spoke to him, but they did not hear the words. How could they? They were spoken to the ear of the one who alone had seen the vision that revealed to him all the mistakes of his life, and that changed the narrow, bigoted Pharisee into the Apostle of the world. Most of those who were with him, and later on his friends, must have thought this acute thinker, this man of the world, had suddenly lost his reason. There was no reasonable way of accounting for his action. Suddenly he joins the sect he was in the very act of persecuting, throws up a career that was full of promise, and for something like nine years disappears from sight. His own account of it is summed up in the simple words, ' I was not disobedient to the heavenly Vision.' What God wills for one whose eyes and ears have been opened to see and hear Him as a living Person claiming his life is a matter between the soul and God alone. Most of those who have found Him Whom all unknowing they were always seeking, are no doubt sent back to their places and duties in life to fulfil them better, seeing with wiser eyes and loving with purer and more unselfish love, bringing the power and love of God to sanctify all the relations of life. But not all. Some, a comparative few, from the time when our Lord Himself was upon earth, have been called to give up all for His sake; to help the world, not directly by ministering to it, but none the less really by offering themselves for it in a life of prayer and sacrifice. Such lives must be their own justification. None

THE CLOTHING OF A NUN

can prove to another that God has called him to live after a certain manner. To many it seems a waste of power and influence to shut oneself out from a world in which one is needed. Some characterise it as pure selfishness and cowardice. There can be no arguing with such criticisms. It can only be answered that we find our Lord in the Gospels legislating for such a form of life, and promising to it great blessings both in this world and in the next. And, moreover, that the idea embodied in what is technically called the religious life, lies deeply rooted in the fundamental principles of Christianity.

And it is a good thing for men and women, in the strain and pressure of life, who believe in the power of prayer but have little time to give to it, to know that there are those whose hands are ever stretched out in prayer to God for them. It is good in this age of luxury and self-indulgence, for those who deny themselves little or nothing to know that there are those of their own flesh and blood, brought up in the same ease and comfort as they, who have felt the attraction of the Cross, and have had the courage and the love to give up the harmless pleasures of the world, and all but the barest necessities of life, not because they despise these things or think them wrong, but that they may conform their lives more perfectly to His example, who ' being rich, for our sakes became poor,' and when on earth had not where to lay His head. These things appeal to people more than they know. There is a mysterious attraction in a voluntary life of hiddenness and sacrifice. What our Lord said of Himself—' I, if I be lifted up, will draw all men unto Me '—has been proved abundantly true, and it is true in its degree of all who follow closely in His footsteps. The fact that others are living far more strict and hard lives than themselves, taking the teaching of the Sermon on the Mount as the law of their lives, and striving to obey it literally, acts upon many in a way they scarcely recognise : not at once, perhaps, but this memory follows them about, irritating them at first, and then by degrees compelling them to be less selfish, less self-indulgent. We like and we don't like to think that there are higher standards than our own, that those who seem to be as weak as we are outstrip us. It disturbs our peace and interferes with our self-complacency, and undermines our contentment. It intrudes upon us in unexpected ways ; appeals to something in us that we do not understand and do not like to acknowledge. It brings before us in concrete form the sterner side of our Lord's teaching, and at once repels and attracts.

For it proves to men who doubt it, that amidst the changing ages and in the new conditions of the modern world the love of our Lord lives on unchanged and undying in its compelling power over the souls of men. In a world so wholly different in thought, aim, and activity from that in which He lived 2000 years ago, He still moves about ; and as of old He called Matthew from the receipt of custom, and James and John from their father's boat, and said to one, ' Go, sell all that thou hast and follow Me,' and to another, ' Return to thine own house and show how great things God hath done unto thee ' ; so now He still goes in and out amongst us, and the attraction of His presence and the spell of His words have lost nothing of their power. And there are not wanting, amongst people who boast of being the most practical and the least imaginative in the world, those who at His word arise, leave all and follow Him. Amidst the wrangle of controversy about the Person of Christ, while His doctrines are being explained away to suit the exigencies of the times, those thus called, who live true to their vocation, and separated from the world, are amongst its greatest teachers. They preach more convincing sermons than can be uttered by the lips of men. They preach by their lives. They are the very light of the world, the salt of the earth.

But, after all, earnestness and sincerity of purpose and even passionate devotion to the Person of our Lord are not, unfortunately, in themselves a warrant of wisdom. Many have striven earnestly after a life of devotion and sacrifice, but not wisely. Religious enthusiasm, if not under proper control and wisely guided, has often begotten eccentricity and led to the wildest fanaticism, and has made wreck of the overstrained physical organism, and unbalanced the mind and caused scandal to religion.

It is therefore a great security for one who would dedicate her life to the service of God and man in the cloister, to know that she is entering upon a path well beaten by the feet of many. She places herself under a rule drawn up by a master mind whose wisdom and holiness are known to the world, a rule that has had some 1,500 years of testing, under which many types of character and temperament have lived and grown and developed. You do not, my sister, enter upon a life surrounded with difficulties, merely with a good heart and a firm purpose. You do not step out into that most difficult path of prayer alone and unguided, where many have lost their way and found, not God, but their own morbid selves, overstrained, excited, fantastic. No, voices from the far past call you, holy lives beckon you on all sides, warn you of the dangers, encourage you when faint, support you with gentle hands when weary. The landmarks are well defined. Those who have gone before have left the path strewn with the marks of their journey. Here you can trace the firm footsteps of some strong soul that never faltered, but walked straight forward to the end, firm and brave even as she stood at the gate of death; there the trembling marks of one weak and timid who, if she had to find the path alone would doubtless have lost her way or turned backward, upheld by the strength of her rule, the support of loving companionship, and the knowledge that others had gone that way before her. It is no tentative effort that you are about to make upon an unknown, lonely path that may lead to perfection or may end in disaster. It is not a voyage of discovery. It is a path discovered long ago, tested and proved. You go amongst a great company, many of whom are with you to encourage you by their example, and to sustain you by their loving fellowship. And a vast multitude look down upon you as they stand in the vision of God and watch you tread the path they trod so long ago. Looked at from outside, the life seems harsh, severe, inhuman. The convent walls and gates and *grille* seem only meant to repel. Silence, austerity, mystery brood over all and fill the passer-by with pity that people should sacrifice a healthy life amongst their fellow creatures for one so unnatural. But within, there is one power that transforms and enlarges all, and that is love. Love alone compels each who enters and love alone holds them. Each new comer may enter as a perfect stranger, but she comes with an assurance of a lasting welcome that she could not have upon entering into any society of people gathered together for any earthly purpose. For the love of God necessitates the love of our fellows. 'He that loveth not his brother whom he hath seen, how can he love God whom he hath not seen?' 'This commandment have we from Him that he that loveth God love his brother also.' And love is the bond of unity, the one true source of lasting happiness. It is not sorrow or suffering or poverty or trouble that breaks in upon family life to hurt it: all these do but bind the members of a family more closely together. There is but one thing that relaxes its bonds, and that is the death of love: then it becomes disintegrated and scattered. And so with the Christian family of a religious community—it could not exist for a year if love were not the controlling force, the bond that cements together all who are in it. 'He that loveth,' says St. Paul, 'is free from law.' He is above law; he does what law would compel him to do by its cold command, under the warm compulsion of love. The human weaknesses and pettinesses that go so far to mar the happiness of life—individualism, rivalry, jealousy, cliques—have no place amongst those who are ruled by love; where they enter love soon dies. What better assurance, therefore, can a stranger have, entering a life to be lived amongst strangers, than the certainty that each and all are drawn together by the love of God, which wages relentless war against everything that could mar the reign of perfect charity? For charity is universal.

To love all but one is to lose charity altogether—it makes no exceptions, it enfolds all, even the most unlovable, in its large embrace. And the narrowness of outward circumstances yields and opens its doors to the largeness and greatness of the soul. There are people that are narrow, however wide the range of their life. There are people who are broad, however narrow their external limitations. But there is something greater than mere intellectual breadth—breadth of character. And this is the breadth that can develop only in the atmosphere of love. Any lack of love cramps the soul; perfect love enlarges, expands, dilates it. And the love of Him Who so loved the world that He died for it, makes the soul a partaker in the interests of the whole human race, and gives to its love something of the character of the Redemptive love of Christ. One who had but a few years before been a hard, intolerant persecutor, under the influence of this love cries : ' Who is weak and I am not weak, who is offended and I burn not.' The outward limitations of the cloister do but intensify, they cannot narrow, the love of those who live close to the Heart of the world's Redeemer. Such love is infinitely tender, broadly tolerant, intensely humanising. ' A heart of steel towards self, a heart of flesh towards men, a heart of fire towards God.' It purges the soul of all thought of self, and opens on all sides the outgoings of its sympathies. The narrowing tendencies of the cloister are counteracted by the constant intercourse with Him without Whose presence it would shrivel into insignificance.

And now, my sister, you are about to be clothed in the habit of the Order into which you are to be admitted as a novice, a habit bearing upon it the marks of its antiquity, worn and stained by the ages. It has witnessed many a spiritual conflict, seen many a victory and doubtless not a few defeats. It is sanctified by the holiest and most sacred associations, the most intimate relations between the soul and God. It has been worn in the centuries that are gone by some who differed from you, perhaps, in most things, but are bound to you by the bonds of the same humanity, the same religion, and the same desires for perfection. It has clothed many wearied in body but indomitable in spirit, beneath it many a heart like yours has fought hard to free itself from all that would hold it back, and through darkness has struggled to the light. Frayed and worn by the journey, it bears witness to the victory of spirit over flesh, of fragile human nature made indomitable by the power of God. It is the livery of the soldier who has volunteered for the very front of the battle, and dared to face all the powers of darkness. It has witnessed to unseen, unknown, unrecorded acts of heroism. Many have worn it whose names, though not enrolled in the Church's calendar, and known only to the few amongst whom they lived, were yet martyrs in will if not in deed. Now you enter amongst the ranks of this goodly company, choose the very best as your model; listen only to those who tell you that all things are possible to them that believe. Set no limit to what God can do in you. There is but one limit, and that is the limit of your own correspondence to His grace. It is a generous act to turn your back upon a world that is very beautiful and that has dealt kindly with you; but that act involves a daily and hourly testing. The surrender that it implied has to go through a long probation, but be sure of it, the more generous you are, the more God will take you at your word, that He may first fit you for and then endow you with a peace that passeth all understanding, a power of loving to which all you have ever experienced in the past is but as the ripple upon the shore compared with the heavings of the great ocean : ' I have found Thee, O Thou whom my soul loveth ; henceforth I will hold Thee and will not let Thee go till the day break and the shadows flee away.'

CHRISTIANITY AND THE MODERN WORLD [1]

'Ye are the salt of the earth. Ye are the light of the world.'
                                ST. MATTHEW v. 13 and 14.

IT is, my brethren, with a strange note of discord that the Sermon on the Mount breaks in upon the luxury, and culture, and sensuality of the world of this nineteenth century. As they come down to us, changeless and unchanging, across the ages, they seem words of warning and rebuke. There is one thing that has never changed, one great principle that has never altered, through all changing passions and constant fluctuations of human opinions and motives. Above the clamour and the din of human passions and sophistries ring out the grand, clear words of Jesus Christ, like some great trumpet notes in an orchestra, or like some great bell on a summer's evening making itself heard above the noise and din of the busy city life below. There they are: take them and make of them what you will; you can never alter them; they are the words of the Eternal uttered in time. And strange, indeed, they seem as they speak to our human life as we live it to-day. The sum and substance of the teaching of Jesus Christ, as given in the Sermon on the Mount, seems to be this—absolute and entire surrender to God of life and of

[1] This sermon was preached in St. Paul's Cathedral, May 3, 1891.

everything besides. Man is God's, and God claims man as His own—time and talents, power and wealth, powers of mind and powers of body. So says the Lord: all, all are His. Man has no right to use anything he has, save in the service of the Lord. So Christ seems to say in the teaching that He uttered to man when He appeared among us in human guise, and first began to live and to teach by the double force of words that were strong, nervous, true, sincere, and of an example that always was in vigorous and exact conformity to the tenor of His words. And they come down upon us, and seem to clasp us tight, and to ask what manner of men we are and what we are doing with our powers and gifts, for all are His.

Ever and always, brethren, as revelation progresses, so the claim of God upon man's nature progresses and deepens with it. In the times of man's ignorance God winked at and tolerated much. Because man did not know the closeness of his relationship to God, God allowed him to live some part of His life away from Him. But as life went on, and revelation became clearer and clearer, there was one distinct manifestation that the light of revelation brought to him, and that was, 'My son, give Me thine heart.' I will not have half-gifts, but all or nothing. There are many stern and terrible sayings of Christ in the Sermon on the Mount and elsewhere, such as 'Whosoever will save his life shall lose it'; 'Take no thought for the morrow, what ye shall eat and what ye shall drink'; 'If thy right hand offend thee, cut it off and cast it from thee, for it is profitable for thee that one of thy members perish and not that thy whole body be cast into hell'; 'Resist not evil; but

CHRISTIANITY AND MODERN WORLD

whosoever shall smite thee on thy right cheek, turn to him the other also'; and 'If any man will sue thee at law, and take away thy coat, let him have thy cloak also.' We turn from these nervous, strong, clear, exacting notes of a great and terrible Teacher, and we look at life as we see it lived to-day, and we ask ourselves: is it indeed the same religion that is being lived to-day, whose principles were laid down in the Sermon on the Mount?

If there were one word that would sum up all the teachings of Christ on human life it was this, unworldliness, self-oblation; but if there were one word that sums up the modern conception of it it is, intense appreciation of life and all that it has to offer. In the great struggle to exist, where the law of the survival of the fittest is the only rule, where a man can only survive by the trampling down of others, where all is one great competition and push for place, the language and the teaching of Jesus seem to be diametrically opposed to the principles, the methods, and maxims of modern life, and to tell a man that he cannot be a Christian if he is to live in modern society. And yet, strange as it may seem, we find Christians everywhere; the Christian is the leader everywhere, in the forum, on the bench, in the market-place. Yea, more than that, there has never been a step upwards made in the development of human and modern life but Christianity has taken the lead. It was Christianity, when no one else had thought of it, that struck the first blow for religious liberty and freedom of conscience when St. Stephen died rather than forego the rights of conscience. There is not, however it may be denied, one of our modern individual and personal rights but have been won for us by Christianity. Christianity, in the darkest days of the world's history since the coming of Christ, preserved literature and the arts and sciences; Christianity was the leader in civilising and taming savage nations. Certainly, whatever may be said of the civilisation of Rome and the culture of Greece, we Englishmen owe everything we have to the faith of Christ. And, more than that, there is not a single empire or country whose thought and life is worth considering in modern politics but are members of the Christian Church. Take the races that know not Christ, and you will find that they are not worth considering in modern politics. Christianity owns all the nations that have been leaders in the progress and the development of life. And yet Christ lays down for our guidance principles that seem to be altogether in opposition to our modern ideas of culture, of development, of luxury, and of refinement. For Christianity bids us be indifferent, and modern life bids us be intense. Christianity bids us look away, and modern life bids us look on. So that it has been said that the Christian Church stands blocking the way to all true progress, and that if a man is to be a leader to-day, or at least in the near future, he must forego his faith in Christ; for, it is said, the principles of Christ are distinctly opposed to the principles that instigate mankind to push forward. Every new intellectual development has been instantly brought to subserve human happiness, every new discovery instantly made the servant and minister of human luxury and comfort, and we are told that Christ will have none of it.

Therefore, brethren, we have to ask, is it true that

CHRISTIANITY AND MODERN WORLD

Christianity and Jesus Christ, as its Divine Founder, are to stand out of the great concourse and rush of modern life, and that Christianity can have nothing to say as to the material and intellectual development of the human race ? Are we to look up and not down ? Are we to say to ourselves : I am a member of the heavenly city, and am not of the earth, I have my mind, my thoughts, my aims, all settled on the world beyond, and all that is of this world must sink into insignificance in the mind and heart that is consecrated to Christ. I know that there are those who will tell you that it is so, and that consequently Christianity must be placed among the religions that have done their work and be relegated to the limbo of things that have had their effect on human life and then died out.

Now such a theory of Christianity, that it stands in the way of progress, is most emphatically and distinctly in direct opposition and antagonism to much that we find in Holy Scripture. Our Lord tells us 'there is nothing hidden but that it may be revealed,' and there He gives the impulse to the development of the human intellect. Our Lord laid down principles other than those which seem in such flat contradiction to the spirit of our modern life. He laid down the basis of the married life, and consequently of social life, and by living amongst men He gave the standard of life for all time. And yet we cannot for one moment deny that a vast deal of the teaching of Jesus seems to be in distinct opposition to the principles that are being lived out to-day. I know that Christianity will not let a man live for mere money-making, for mere fame, for mere earthliness and worldliness. And yet I am certain that there will be no man, whatever be his position, who will be such an ornament to society, as the man with Christian principles. I am convinced that there will be no judge on the bench, no man in the Stock market, that will be so true a man as the follower of Jesus Christ.

Now let us see for one moment if we can find any clue to the apparent contradiction between the words of our Lord—such words as 'Take no thought for the morrow'; 'Whosoever shall smite thee on thy right cheek, turn to him the other also'; 'If any man sue thee at law and take away thy coat, let him have thy cloak also'—and the life that we are living in the world to-day with so much pleasure and enjoyment. And I would suggest to you merely a line of thought which will bring it into the sphere of your practical lives rather than into the sphere of theory.

It seems to me that we get at least some clue to the answer to the question, how can a man be true to Christ and true to his position in the social world, in the language of my text : ' Ye are the salt of the earth : ye are the light of the world.' You will remember that these words came immediately after our Lord had uttered the eight Beatitudes, wherein He laid down the principles that were to guide the life of the Christian saint ; and then turning to the representatives of that Church which He was founding, He said : you have two offices to fulfil. ' Ye are the light of the world ; ye are the salt of the earth.' In these words I see two distinct offices, two distinct functions, that the Church of God in every age and in every country has to fulfil. The Church of God

CHRISTIANITY AND MODERN WORLD 137

must always and everywhere be the light of the world, and the Church of God must always and everywhere be the salt of the earth. If there be any place where the Church is not the light of the world, there the Church has failed; and if there be any place where the Church is not the salt of the earth, there also the Church has failed.

Now you will notice that not only are these functions distinct but they seem to be the converse the one of the other. The light stands upwards and apart. As our Lord says, men do not 'light a candle and put it under a bushel, but on a candlestick, and it giveth light unto all that are in the house.' The Church therefore has one office, to stand apart from the world, to hold up the standard of absolute consecration, of absolute devotion; and when I say the Church, I mean the Church in its members, for the Church has no abstract existence apart from those who constitute its living reality. In every age and in every country there are men and women whom the Lord calls apart to live true to the very letter of the Sermon on the Mount; living devout and consecrated lives, taking no thought for the morrow, and turning the other cheek to the smiter.

My brethren, you look back over the ancient world, and you see times when sanctity seemed to take strange forms, when Simon Stylites could stand on his pillar, and live there alone up and above the world. I believe that such a life as that in such an age appealed to the savage men and women around him. They gazed upon that man and said: here is one who can live for Christ alone, who cares nothing for all that the world has to give him. His answer to the enigma of existence is Jesus the First and the Last. And so in other ages, in the twelfth century, for instance, when the Church had sunk into sloth and dreariness, St. Francis of Assisi came forward and espoused holy poverty; and the villages and towns of Italy looked upon a man who cared for nothing that the world had to give him; and the fire was stirred anew, and men felt that Christianity was not dead; and long before St. Francis died he could count his members and followers, not by hundreds but by thousands.

And so it must be to-day. There are those whom God calls out from among their own people to live true to the letter of the Sermon on the Mount; and in so doing men do not profess to be better than their neighbours, far from it; but they feel they cannot stand the power of the world's attractions, and they turn to their Lord, and give themselves up to Him, and then they turn back again towards the world and bless it by lives of consecration and devotion. We have heard a great deal about Brotherhoods of late. My brethren, the real meaning of a Brotherhood is not a mere instrument for utilitarian purposes, but it is for the life of consecration, it is to hold up a candle to the world that the world may feel the power of Christianity; and any such system that is started on utilitarian grounds will fail in the very work that it is meant to do, unless it is based on those grand words of Jesus Christ, 'I, if I be lifted up, will draw all men unto Me.' Every man or woman that is lifted up on the cross of sacrifice will, like the steel that touches the magnet, himself or herself become touched with magnetic power, and men will know that Christ is in the ship, though the storm be raging round the Church and men's hearts are sinking with fear. And thus as the Church ever holds up the candle of the pure doctrine of revealed truth, and will not allow it to be tampered with by human sophistries, so also the Church holds up the candle of the consecrated life of sacrifice and devotion ; and he who is called to it must follow and obey, bending his head in lowly worship and adoration.

But, brethren, if this be the call to some, it is only to some. If this be one office of the Church, it is only one office. The Church has another and as great an office as this. If, on the one hand, it is the light of the world, on the other, it is the salt of the earth ; and if the light is to be kept alive, with its bright beams shining across the dreary waste, the Church has also to act as salt acts upon the earth. Salt is the fertilising and recuperative power. Take the world as you find it without the Church, and it is sinking down into ruin and decay ; place the Church in the world, and the Church fertilises it and gives it the power of recuperation. The great office of Christian men and women is to be the salt of the earth. Everyone is not called out of the world to live the consecrated life, but all are called to be the salt that fertilises and preserves the world from corruption. If you are not called to the consecrated life, you are called to live in the world to witness there for Truth, for Right, and for God. It is that same Christian spirit that makes an elect few stand aside as the light of the world, which also makes other followers of Christ mingle with the world and purify it—as the salt of the earth.

I have been asked again and again:—do you think it is wrong for me to go to theatres and generally to join in worldly pleasures? My answer is this. Any man or woman who mingles in the world's pleasures must do so bearing this in mind—that they are there first, not to uphold the world's morals, but the morals of Christ; that they are there to witness for another world, another life; that they are there to be the drag upon the downward drift of the degraded morals of fallen man. Mingle in innocent pleasures if you like, but remember this, God first, the principles of Christianity before the pleasures of the world. If in your place of business, when all around you is dishonesty, you refuse to be dishonest, you are the very salt of the earth; if in your pleasures, when all around is stained by impurity and sensuality, you refuse to take part in the low tone of life around you, you are the salt that keeps the world from decay. Every man and every woman in his place or in her place, in business or society, who thus lives and acts, is a witness for Christ. But if you take part in principles, in motives, in a code of morals distinctly in opposition to those laid down by Christ, then remember His words : ' If the salt have lost its savour, wherewith shall it be salted? It is thenceforth good for nothing but to be cast out and to be trodden under foot of men.' There is the man who professes to be a Christian and who is negativing in his life the profession of his lips; he is doing harm, not good; he is taking a leading part in the world's decay, not in its recuperation, though calling himself a follower of Him who died to save it.

Let us remember this. If God has committed to

man the keys of the kingdom of heaven, God has committed to woman the keys of the kingdom of earth. You, my sisters, have the power of binding and loosing in the social world. A legislature that is fast ceasing to be Christian may pass laws that are in the teeth of the doctrines of Christ ; but they can never be generally accepted till they pass the bar of the judgment of women. An unchristian world may allow men to live in legalised adultery, a legislature may allow divorce, but if women bind themselves together to protect society against that most grievous wound, the law will fast become a dead letter. Whenever there is anything that tampers with the code of morals laid down by Jesus Christ, every Christian man and woman living in the world and enjoying its pleasures must remember that if he is to be true to Christ he must stand out in antagonism to the evil and bear witness for the truth, and refuse to surrender the standard of Christian morality into the hands of the world.

And with this I would leave these thoughts for you to work out for yourselves. We are called into one or other of these two positions, each of them strong, each of them holy, yea, each of them perfect. Some are called to the married state, to support the fabric of the social world, some are called to the single state, to come out to live for God. Thus the Church mingling with the world is the world's savour, and the Church standing apart from the world is the world's instructor. Choose which it is to be. And be sure of it, no man can live in the world where He Who witnessed for the truth with His life left His last footprints stained with blood, and expect to have it always easy. There are times when you have to go in the face of public opinion, when, like your Master, you have to stand alone ; and then you say: now I am doing the very thing I was baptised for—I am witnessing for the truth of Christ, for the rule of life He laid down for men to live by. And if there be any here that feel that they cannot rest here, that they cannot take the pleasures the world has to offer, that they must give up all and follow Him, oh, your reward and blessing will be great indeed ! The barren shall bring forth, and she that hath no children shall rear a family in the nurture and fear of God. Living for Christ, you will be a blessing to men, and on the world's darkness the beacon light of holy lives will throw down its radiance, warning against the rocks on which the ship might be wrecked, guiding men across the darkness to the haven where they would be at rest. The light of the world has guided them, the salt of the earth has healed them ; and Christ in the nineteenth century is as strong and as real as when Peter left his fishing-nets and Matthew the receipt of custom, and followed the magnetic power of that mysterious Personality Who drew around Him men of all sorts and condition, and held them under the spell of His presence and gave them the blessing of His peace.

SIN [1]

'Thy will be done in earth, as it is in Heaven.'
ST. MATTHEW vi. 10.

THERE are, my brothers, two ways in which we may speak of religion. Whatever form of religion it may be, it must appeal to man on his moral side : it must waken up his conscience, and rouse him to a sense of his own imperfection. But there is another side of religion which will always appeal to men, and that is the intellectual side ; it may appeal purely to reason and imagination and the intellectual faculties, leaving altogether out of question the affections, the emotions, or the conscience. A man may come away from some sermons not only not better, but even worse. He may have a great passion for listening to and discussing some of the deepest religious questions, and he may be heartily convinced, many and many a time, that the position taken up by the preacher is a right and a true one, and yet the sermon may have no effect on his life ; it may be purely an intellectual study. Religion can never be brought to men so that it will really reach them in a way that appeals simply to the intellect ; there must always be the undercurrent of thought to appeal to the moral sense, to appeal to the conscience.

[1] Preached at St. Columba's Church, December 13, 1895, and reported in the *Church Times*.

There is a danger now, as there has been many times before, of presenting religion to certain classes of men clad only in garments of the intellect. Many a man believes that the only thing which keeps him back from being a good man is some intellectual difficulty. If he knew himself better perhaps he would find it is not so. Many a man wastes himself in a higher region of intellectual pursuit whilst he leaves the moral affections and the emotions untouched. He wastes himself in intellectual subtleties, and thinks he is a good man or kept from being a good man by intellectual difficulties. There is, consequently, a danger, never perhaps more felt than in our own day, of trying to lay hold of the intellect alone, trying to present what we have to say in such a form as will convince.

And you will agree with me when I say that there are two dangers which every religious preacher on any great question has to guard against. On the one hand there is the danger of refusing to acknowledge difficulties where difficulties exist, trying to shirk, trying to turn aside from great questions, great difficulties. I am speaking now of the apologist, the teacher. Some man comes to argue with a person absolute and complete in his own conviction. Such a person cannot understand, he can scarcely know the difficulties that present themselves to other men's minds ; and he is so earnestly anxious to win that man round that he will pretend there are no difficulties where they truly exist. Such a position as that is an utterly false one. The man will go away with some sense of unreality, and perhaps come to feel that the teacher only wished to satisfy him on certain questions, but all the time knew there was a difficulty and did not tell him. I have no hesitation, my brothers, in saying there are difficulties, very grave and deep, that we have no right to evade, and which, on the other hand, we cannot answer.

There is another danger which besets another class, when the teacher will defend the truth at the expense of perfect truth. You will sometimes find an argument brought up that will be an *ad captandum* argument; the more you look into it, the more you will feel its unsoundness. If you over-harshly state the case of an antagonist, there is bound to be a revolt in favour of the antagonist. Perhaps the strongest feeling in men's minds, in the matter of religious doctrine, is the earnest struggle to get at what they believe to be the truth at all costs. And if ever you detect a teacher in what seems to you to be untruth, there is bound to be a revolt, and you turn from him: you feel as if Christianity were a cause to be defended at all costs, as if Christian priests were persons paid for being apologists for a poor cause, and your whole nature will revolt against the cause he has to defend. Truth and sincerity are the absolute conditions for any teacher on any question. You may feel that a man believes a thing himself. But that is not enough. You must also feel that the method of his defence is true and sincere too. And yet we all know how hard it is, from the many points of view from which many questions can be regarded, to be perfectly true and perfectly simple.

Again, we must remember, on the other hand, that it is not a question, as many seem to think, between the difficulties of Christianity and the getting rid of all these difficulties by throwing over Christianity, you hear certain classes of men talk as if in giving up Christianity they get rid of all the difficulties of life. You will not escape a shade of the difficulty of God's foreknowledge and man's free will by doing that. What are you going to do about it ? Any Theist has the same difficulties. As long as you believe in God you must feel that He foreknows, and as long as you believe in yourself you must feel that you are free.

Then again, it is said : who can believe in a just God, and yet believe in such a law as the law of heredity ? That poor, wretched man, the slave of sins that his father passed on to him—what do you think of a God that is going to punish that man for his father's sins ? Well, what are you going to think if you give up Christianity ? Is the law of heredity the creation of Christianity ? But it is a fact. There it stands, no matter what your creed, or if you have none. Many a man, having given up faith in Christ, has given up the whole thing. Some of the greatest difficulties now are charged on Christianity. But they existed before Christianity and they still face men when they have given it up. They exist in places where the name of Christ is not known ; and you have to face them, and get out of the difficulties somehow. Believing in the Lord Jesus Christ does not add one jot or tittle to the seeming injustice or the difficulties of the question. The man who says he believes in God has all these difficulties to face. If he adds belief in our Lord Jesus Christ, he does not add one bit to the difficulty.

The other thing to remember is this : that you must not turn your back on Christ because you don't get a satisfactory answer to all questions presented. Suppose you are a Christian teacher, and a man says: what do you make of God's love and the existence of sin? or God's justice and the existence of sin and suffering? You answer: I don't know whether it makes any difference to me whether I believe in Jesus Christ or not about that matter; but what do you make of it if you are a Theist? You are bound, as a Theist, to believe that God is just, and it does not add to the difficulties to say that God became incarnate to try to help sinful man.

Christianity does not profess to be the solvent of every question that comes into men's minds. Christianity herself says to many of the greatest difficulties: I have not any answer to them at all; I don't know. She professes to know nothing more about God's foreknowledge and man's free will than Theism. Similarly, Christianity does not face the question of God's justice and the law of heredity. Christianity professes to bring men into a moral relation with God which makes them say: I don't care now to have many of these questions answered, because I have a complete trust in the goodness of God.

Every man in this church to-night knows about sin from his own personal experience. It does not need that you should read any books as to what is the meaning of sin, for you say: God help me— I have felt its scourge, its burn, its poison. From the first and most patent point of view sin is not a question simply of religion or of philosophy, but a practical question. Whatever a man's religion may be, or if he has none at all, still anyone that has to do with his fellow men, anyone that has a couple of hundred men in his employment, any foreman dealing with men in the same works has to ask himself, how am I to deal with men who are constantly breaking some or all of the last six commandments of the Decalogue? He may not believe that these commandments come from God, but he has the matter forced upon him, and has to deal with it just as a Christian does. See a judge, for instance, in his private room, when he has laid aside with the robes of office the duties he has been engaged on during the day, and ask him what he thinks of the mystery of human life. Perhaps he may propound the theory that he does not believe in free will; but in this public life he deals with men exactly as if they were free. On the bench he spoke words of contempt to that poor culprit, and said: I wish I could give you a severer punishment; and yet in his own private room he says: I don't believe he is guilty at all, because he could not help it. Thus, the moment you come to practical life you have to deal with a man as if he were free, as if he had brought upon himself the guilt for which he deserved punishment.

You will hear very often that sin, after all, is only one of a number of the same kind of phenomena in different orders and forms of life; that it is, in fact, the same kind of thing as ignorance. But the more we look into it the more we find that it stands absolutely alone. It stands out from everything else, challenging our minds to find a solution for it. It puzzles us. The whole nature can grow and develop. That man's mind unfolds; his intellect becomes sharp and clear, his reason more keen, his imagination more powerful ; his power of dealing with men shows a larger and more vigorous grasp of things. And alongside this there is growing a deterioration vile and gross. We look back to the ancient world—Greece with its wonders of art, Rome with its wonders of government. Here were men developing intellectually, and alongside of that development, the other side of man was growing more and more corrupt, till at last, in dismay and despair, he looked for some one to help him, for he had no power to help himself. Can you find anything like that in the animal creation ? Can you, as a reasonable man, find anything whatever in the vegetable world of which you can say, That corresponds to sin in the moral world ?

You say : look at that poor wretched cripple ; look at him hampered in every step of his life. But see how the misery of his body has made him great ; everybody respects him. Look at that man with all the intellect and power of his moral nature becoming more and more corrupt till, in spite of all his intellectual endowments, everyone despises him. Is there anything anywhere else corresponding to that ?

You notice this, that in every relationship of life sin comes in to destroy it. No one can doubt that there are forces in our nature for drawing men together, and man is at his best in his social life. Civilisation and development and all that belongs to progress is impossible for man alone in a solitary life. Yet no sooner do men come together in vast multitudes—say in a great city like this—than instantly there are other forces which begin to operate for the dissolution of all social life. A man's property, his good name, are not safe in his brother's keeping. Man has something within him, that as soon as he gets among others, comes in to destroy social life. What is it ? It is sin.

The history of the ancient world shows man's thirst for God. Men were always in search after God, and yet when they knew Him they hated Him. The history of the human race shows that man was ever searching after God, and no sooner did he find Him than there were powers within him which led him to hate Him, till at last sin broke out in all its fury, and men, having found God, killed Him ! And this happens in the story of the individual as in the story of the race.

Again, the instinct of self-preservation is the strongest in our nature, and yet there are powers in us that will throw it on one side, and for a passion, for the enjoyment of a moment, man will ruin health and prospects, and all self-preservation be set aside. Is it not an extraordinary thing, that instinct of self-preservation ? Is it not a more extraordinary thing still that man is the only being on the face of God's earth that will destroy himself ?

Looked at from those points of view, we must say that sin is not like anything else. It stands alone. It is not like disease. It stands on an entirely different platform. In its effects, its results, its whole operation it is quite different. Disease can make a man morally great ; I never knew of sin making any man great. A man may be great, and there may be one flaw ; he was untrue, he was insincere, he was impure, he was intemperate ; few men of his time were so capable of high position and exalted power, but there was one thing that grew alongside of his power, and that was passion, and passion took the crown from off his head and laid his honour in the dust. Will you tell me that disease will do that ? You know it does not.

Now, Christianity has given her own definition and analysis of sin, and her own remedy for sin. That remedy stands absolutely alone ; every other plan deals with sin by punishment, but Christianity deals with it in her own way. The State puts a bad man in prison ; Christianity does something quite different. Christianity has given her definition long, long before the time of science, before all the new ideas of late times. Can you imagine anything more different from the past than the new conception of life in the last century ? Everything is changed. And yet Christianity has the same analysis, the same definition of sin, that she had eighteen hundred years ago. Christianity has never altered her remedies for sin ; and to-day, amid all the changes and progress of the age, stands by the old remedies. Of all systems that ever existed, hers alone has proved itself capable of taking a man with the most rooted fiendish habits, and breaking them by turning round the whole drift and current of the man's will, changing the heart that loved vice to be a heart that loved virtue, and changing a nature corrupt to the very heart's core to be pure like the clear water springing from the mountain side. Look at Augustine before and after his coming to Christ. Look at the Magdalene before and after her coming to Christ. There is no sin so great that Christianity has not a remedy for it, and this not by punishment but mercy. Christianity brings a new element into life, an element that heals the wound, and turns round the whole current of the life.

Certainly the language of Christianity stands alone. She does not use mild names for bad things. She speaks of sin in language peculiarly her own, and of the thought as well as of the act of sin : of every idle word you will have to give account. The first of sins named by Christ Himself is the sin of evil thoughts. The State can only deal with evil acts. Christianity will tell you that not only is it wrong to commit adultery and fornication, but that the lustful look has evil in it, and is a sin to be repented of. Christianity will tell you that sin is death, and that the sting of death is sin, and that sin is a slavery from which the man seeks to get free and cannot. 'He that doth sin becomes the slave of sin,' and that is infinitely more true to experience than any of the more light and airy definitions in our own day by men who seem to put aside all experience, and to theorise in their studies. Whatever answer our Blessed Lord and the Christian Church may give to questions on the meaning of sin, and whatever answer other systems and philosophies may give, you will find that the answer of Christianity on this, and on all questions on which she has an answer, will not be in the teeth of reason, experience, or the moral sense, as most of the answers given by other systems are. If you believe some of the theories of our own day you have to put your own experience altogether aside. In some cases you will have to refuse to follow out the workings of your own reason, and I know there are some answers against which the conscience of the human race rises up and says they are immoral.

SIN

Now, there are three views that we will find contending together in our own day as to what is the meaning, cause, and remedy of sin.

First of all, there is the answer that we may call the philosophical one. It is an answer that has carried a vast deal before it in our time. It was given at the beginning of the century. It appealed to man's pride, to man's self-sufficiency. The answer is this (practically) : most of the evils in life—and the chiefest of them, sin—are to be traced, not to the individual heart or the individual will, but to bad institutions, based upon bad education and ignorance ; and if only you could make a clean sweep of all those old corrupt institutions that hang over old civilisations like a pest-house, and sufficiently educate the human race, sin would come to an end. That is, the cause is not in the man, but in his circumstances : and if you could only get an ideal condition of things (which is said to be arriving more and more), then we shall make a paradise on earth.

I perfectly grant you anything based on any untruth is bad. In so far as any man is living under a system, or under a principle that is not true, he will suffer for it. We cannot doubt that the old idea of the divine right of kings was wrong and bad, and produced evils. The sovereignty of the people would have produced just as much evil in its way. Our whole system about labour and capital as we are working it to-day is fraught with evils, crimes. When that is set right, in God's good providence many of those evils will be removed.

But is it true to your own experience to say that you get morally better as the institutions in your country improve? I lived for some years in America. Anyone who knows American politics knows that they are about as corrupt as they can be. Was I conscious of any moral improvement when I came to England? I lived under the Turkish government, but it did not affect my own moral life. Do you find that the institutions of your country have any effect upon your own passions and desires? Liberty and justice to the race outside do not affect the inner heart of man. He must get the conquest in himself, altogether apart from what is going on outside him. We are told these bad institutions grow out of false ideas, and that the great remedy is education: that a man should know more of himself, of his physical life, of his moral life, of his intellectual life, and of the political world, and so forth. Is that true to your experience? Do you find that a man's knowing the results of sins of the flesh emancipates him from the power of the flesh? I once went into a hospital, and behind the screen I heard a man breathing heavily. There was a man in there dying of drink. The doctor had told him that if ever he tasted a drop of brandy again, it was bound to bring him to his death; and he did it. Knowledge did not stop him. Are the most educated the most free from sin, and the poor the greatest sinners? Not so. Knowledge has nothing whatever to do with it. The seat of sin is not in the intellect, but in the will.

There is the answer of science: that the whole principle of life is the struggle for life and the principle of the survival of the fittest; and that in the struggle for life, as we are progressing, there are certain elements in our nature that will be beaten out and destroyed as we go on. Man, we are told, has fought his way upward, and what he is to-day is only an earnest of what he will be to-morrow. The elements of the lower nature are still in him, what some people will call sin, but that cannot be helped; they are parts of the animal nature still left in him. In other words, this answer is that sin is only imperfection on the way to perfection.

Is it true? Your own feeling in regard to sin, is it the same as your feeling in regard to imperfection? Do you feel towards it in the same way that you do about failing in your ideal of work? The cold, callous wickedness of the man who will lay himself out to seduce some innocent girl—is that simple failure to reach the highest ideal? Is he not on a downward plane? Take the case of a man struggling towards purity, and yet guilty of many an act of impurity whilst he is trying to conquer. But the other case is not like this; it is not merely failing to reach what is higher, but developing upon another plane, the downward plane of vice. Is the man who constantly yields to bad desires, towards sins of intemperance, only failing to reach the ideal of self-control, or has he not altogether abandoned it and taken another ideal, the ideal of self-indulgence? Will he gradually raise himself up till he becomes more and more temperate, or does not all experience show that the longer he lives the more he will give up all efforts of discipline and yield himself to self-indulgence.

We ask again, and what is the answer which Christianity gives? First of all, it tells us quite clearly that sin is not an evil substance that is in us. There is nothing in you that you have to destroy. Sin is simply the misapplication of powers that in themselves are good. You are to find out the true life of all your faculties, and see that not by death, but by life we live.

And mortification, self-discipline, is moral restraint of these powers of our nature ready to go in a wrong direction. You are to discipline the heart, to turn it to worthy objects. You are not to destroy all power of hate—' O ye that love the Lord, see that ye hate the thing that is evil.' It is the power of abuse which is sin, and the power of use is virtue. The noblest man is living the fullest life. The sinner is taking these powers, and turning them to ends that can never satisfy, and consequently his life is an utter failure. Ask him, ask the drunkard if he has found happiness. Every man is looking for it. In one word, the Bible ' sense of sin ' is ' missing the aim.' We are to try for happiness. The sinner tries in the wrong way. The man who tries to conquer himself turns all the faculties in the right direction, and finds it in the end. You never can destroy the forces ; you can combine and change them, but you cannot destroy them. It would be a hopeless task. Who made that flesh that is bad ? God made everything. If so, it must be good, therefore I must develop and purify it. If sin springs from some evil substance in us, that shows God must be wrong. It is not that. It is directing the faculties in a wrong way. There is that man loving with all the passions of his manly heart the thing that is dragging him to the very depths ; give up that false life and find a worthy life in its place. There is the man who thinks these powers are only to work out some little scheme, and he has cramped all his faculties for that little thing. Give up that narrowness, and throw your nature into the width of His expansiveness, and you will live and love good.

Christianity tells us—we see ourselves—that all other lives are a unity. The seed springs out; there is nothing to hinder it in itself. You educate a man, and he works himself out, and there are a multitude of opposing forces, one part striving to get at this, and another at that. ' I cannot do the thing that I would.' As an Apostle says, analysing himself with perfect skill, I find different forces warring in my members. So we look into ourselves, and say : I am not at one with myself. If only I could gather together all my whole nature, and direct it to one end ! But no sooner do I try to live the intellectual life, no sooner do I try to turn myself to God, than a multitude of passions rise up to drag me down. My nature is not a unity.

And Christianity tells us why. It is because it has lost its controlling force ; you were not made as you are now. Oh, what a life that was of man's before he lost the crown of his manhood by original sin ; when there was one great master-force that held every power in one, and all the powers crowded round the will, so that every movement of the whole nature was a unity, and whatever he did he did with all the powers of his being ; the body helped the soul and the soul the body. The reason, the passions, the emotions, everything went on in one movement towards what is best. When man sinned in the Garden of Eden, man forfeited that mighty gift, the life controlling gift of the Presence of God ; then all the powers of his nature drooped ; he forfeited and lost the single force that held it all together. So if you look into yourselves, you find there is a split in our nature, a division. On the one side stand the reason and the conscience, on the other the passions, the feelings, the affections. Now, a man will say, on the one hand, I know what is right, I long to do it ; and, on the other hand, I yet deliberately go and do exactly the opposite. The fault is not in my intellect, my reason, my conscience. I know I told a lie ; I made up my mind but this instant that I would not do it. I could not help it. I love truth ; my ideal of the men I most respect are the men absolutely true. Well, I say, is not this an extraordinary thing—a man's ideal is truth, and he deliberately goes and lies. What would you think of a man saying : I understand art ; I know a good picture, but when I buy a picture I buy the ugliest daub I can get ? A man bent on success in business faces his difficulties and answers them. He does not say: I ought to go to the bank, or to my office, and then fail to go. But the man in moral life is always doing that. A man says : I love purity ; my ideal is purity, and yet I live an impure life, and I cannot help it.

More than that, there is only one sphere where your will plays such pranks as that. It seems as if I had two wills—one which I use in my daily life, and one in my moral life. How is it I face the difficulties of life and conquer them and stand in the teeth of opposition, and yet, before the first little temptation to sin, I break down ? My will in moral things is utterly unreliable ; in other things it is reliable. I have said to men again and again : you feel that domineering temper is destroying the happiness of your home, or that miserable selfishness that takes from your wife and children, to spend on yourself, what you ought to spend on them. You know that utter sluggishness that can never rise up to meet the difficulties of life, and passes them on to some one else. You loathe yourself for it, as you sit there now you say you will stop it; and before you are five minutes in your home it all breaks out again. You said: I have yielded to the sin of intemperance again and again, but now, with the help of God, the thing is at an end. But you pass by that public-house, you fall in with an old comrade, and you will prostrate yourself before the god that is ruining you; you will say to-morrow morning you did not want to do it, but you could not help it. 'I cannot do the thing that I would.' You can in ninety-nine things out of a hundred; in things not moral you are as safe as can be, your will can be trusted, but in moral questions it will play the very devil with you.

This is the reason: in other things there is sufficient to stimulate you; you have your gold, or your pride or whatever it may be, but in moral things the conscience has no chance against the claims of passion. The conscience is not strong enough. It speaks with the voice of the judge, with the warning of a far-off penalty. Passion promises immediate enjoyment. The craving of your passion is almighty against the claim of conscience. You say: I know what that is; I know I shall suffer; but it will be a long time hence, and I can repent. Here is passion calling me to an immediate pleasure. And the claim of passion with its immediate rewards of pleasure, and excitement, and enjoyment, and intense delight, bears down the whisper of conscience, though you know that conscience is right and passion wrong.

What is the remedy? When you find a good man do you find a man passionless and emasculated? Do you say: You are chaste, pure, temperate; true, but you are cold; you have paid a price for your chastity, and the price is you have given up passion. You paid a price for your truth; the price is one I would not pay, for all that passionate richness of a strong life is gone.

My friends, that is not true. A great French writer says, 'No act of the will is a strong, complete act unless it is a passionate act.' When Christ comes to the soul He does more than say: kill passion and obey conscience. He says to you: I want you to range those passions on the side of conscience; I want you to be as passionate in the cause of truth as you were once in the cause of untruth; I want you to be as passionate in purity as once in impurity; as passionate a servant of Christ's as once a passionate enemy of His.

How is it to be done? A young man said to me once, 'I have been living a very bad life, but I hope to marry a pure, good Christian girl; and before I venture to do so, I think I ought to slay the life I have been living; I feel her influence upon me strengthening me to do right.' He had suggested the type of what Christianity is, only he did not know it. When he was tempted, his passionate love for that Christian maid made him for the moment a passionate lover of purity, and won passion from the side of impurity to the side of purity. What can that power do which has won the hearts of the human race, which has led men with passionate joy to the stake, and made them cry out to their persecutors : come on, put me to more pain for love of Him ! Let passion be moved to the side of truth and religion ; that is the way to conquer sin.

Don't think you can give sin up, loving it and keeping back from it. As you love the Law-giver, you will hate to break His laws ; and all the passion that made you the rebel against His cause, will make you the faithful warrior, ready to die in His service. And so Christianity comes with her definition of sin :— and her remedy the life of Jesus Christ our Lord ; the life of Christ given you in the Sacraments of the Church, will make your conscience so strong that it will win all passion to its side, and in the power of Jesus Christ our Lord, you shall be more than conqueror.

THE LORD'S PRAYER [1]

'Thy will be done in earth, as it is in Heaven.'
ST. MATTHEW vi. 10.

OUR Lord's Prayer takes us outside ourselves. It lays a great and solid foundation—the Kingdom of God—in the first place. You must first turn away from yourself, and lay the foundation of the spiritual life in the Being of God. Say what we like, Christian life cannot get on without theology; man's true knowledge of himself is rooted in a true knowledge of God. A false idea of God may lead to a life absolutely devoid of a true conception of life; it may lead to a life confined to some form of fatalism. Anything that touches the nature of God touches the character of man.

There was a man, of whom our Blessed Lord speaks in the Gospel, who wrapped up the talent of his life in a napkin, because he thought God was an exacting Being. With such a thought, what else could he do? No man who had an idea of that kind about God could really serve Him. If we thought God demanded more than we have power to do, we should be right to say: I cannot respect Him, and therefore I will not worship, pray to, or serve Him. And so the

[1] A Lenten Sermon preached at St. Paul's, Great Portland Street, 1896.

Lord's Prayer says to begin life by directing our looks away from ourselves to God Himself.

We have many things to ask for. There are three great things which every one needs: forgiveness, protection from temptation, and deliverance from the power of evil. That means a great deal, about all we need so far as the spiritual life is concerned—the past forgiven, present protection, and deliverance from the power of evil for the future. And for you and me this comes in one way, the pouring into our souls of our Lord's own Divine-human nature. We have to ask for that. That is what we come to God for, most of us, at the beginning.

Many of us have been driven to Him by a sense of our own spiritual needs. Perhaps we should not have come to Him at all if we could have got on without Him. We may have tried many things, but did not become better, but rather grew worse; and have felt that if we could but touch the hem of His garment it would do more for us than all the rest. Now, there are these great needs in the background of our souls, but you must not begin by bringing up these needs before Him. We must be able to ask for forgiveness of sins and protection from temptation; still, if you begin with that, you may go altogether wrong. There is some trouble, some temptation injuring and wounding your whole nature; but when you come to God, feeling all these needs and perplexities, drop them for the moment and begin: ' Hallowed be Thy name; Thy Kingdom come; Thy will be done in earth, as it is in heaven.' In other words, if you want something from God, don't begin by asking for it; you must begin by setting yourself right with God before you can get it.

Why is it (one says) that I have asked God so often to deliver me from this or that, and He will not do it? Because if He did it in the way I want it I should never come again to Him. Why is it that God throws back my prayers again and again on myself? I know I am in earnest; I cry day and night before Him, I am worn and wasted away with longing for some help. Why is it? Because He sees we are doing it all wrong. Go on with those prayers. Yes; those very prayers will drive you at last to see the mistakes and that there is only one way to pray: 'Hallowed be Thy name; Thy Kingdom come; Thy will be done.'

For you want a thing from God, and He wants to give it you; but He does not want simply to give a thing you want. He wants above all things your spiritual and moral development; He wants that you may be fit for it. You may have to wait till you are fit for it. And it will be better, because there is then the preparation of heart. If you got it at first it might be a curse. There is something that touches on your present life. It may be some physical ailment or some great sorrow that crushes you down, and you cry to God that He may deliver you, and you have been taught to believe that He will hear the needy, and yet you get no help. There is nothing but the void, the echo of your own voice thrown back upon your own despairing heart. Then thought begins to wake up. Am I doing this thing in the right way? Is there something that must be cleared out of my life before I can get that thing? Then I look up, and begin: 'Hallowed be Thy name: Thy Kingdom come; Thy will be done.'

'Deliver us from evil'—that comes last. Before

I come to that I have been able to say, I glory in infirmities, if it be His will. I began by asking that He might remove some thorn in the flesh, but, as I went on, I got such a deep and clear insight into the whole relation with God that I said : I don't care about that thorn in the flesh, for God will give me grace and spiritual strength.

There are three petitions with regard to ourselves. We have got nearly half-way through the Lord's Prayer before we reach them ; before they come, we must be right with God. So says the Lord's Prayer. We so often forget that. We have a kind of rude, impertinent way of pressing ourselves into the presence of God, as if with the idea that He will be glad that His creatures are at His knees at all. He does not want you to believe that He is a great machine that you can 'turn on' at any moment and get what you like. Therefore, He will rather hold back your gift than give it when it would not be a blessing. There is only one order and one principle : the principle and order of the Lord's Prayer. There is a reasonableness in all God's dealings with us. And the closer we get to God the more we can understand the reason of God's dealings with us. At the earliest stages He seems to deal with us according to that saying, 'With the froward Thou shalt shew Thyself froward,' and we being froward, it seems as if He were froward to us. As we go on we see the reason. The Lord's Prayer lays down the lines of the spiritual life. You may almost guess what the next would be from what went before. Having taken for your motto, not yourself but the glory of God, you are driven into many other things. Finding the combinations of earth to be always upset by failure, containing forces indeed that almost ensure that they must go to pieces, at last the soul understands what is meant by the Kingdom of God against the kingdom of earth. Swayed by one great motive, the Christian life is a necessary outcome of that; the Christian cannot say 'Thy kingdom come' except as a citizen of the heavenly kingdom.

Then, as a consequence, 'Thy will be done.' In the heavenly kingdom itself the glorious spirits that never had a taint of evil and the ninefold choir of angels dwell. When you have come into the outskirts of that kingdom here on earth, the first thing you feel is: if I carry out my own way I have the power of almost destroying, as it were, this kingdom. It is a building, a foundation no man can destroy; but there is that which, if it will not destroy the kingdom, will spoil the unity. I mean egoism. Many coming into this kingdom want to carry out their own plans in the kingdom of God. But that would destroy the unity of the kingdom. Thy will be done on earth as in the higher regions of that kingdom, where they see Thee face to face and serve Thee; all swayed and governed by one great comprehensive will, the Will of God. That is the true ideal:—unity in diversity, and that diversity never interfering with perfect unity. Each life is complete in the development of its own powers—I do everything I want, and I never want to do wrong; I have the full swing and sway of my being, and I never clash against another life, all only adding splendour to that kingdom, and glory to God. For even here there dwells the mighty power of that heavenly kingdom, all held together in the mystical body of Christ. These sanctified saints had once their own petty designs, some of them thinking they could manage the kingdom of heaven on their own plans. They had to be beaten down. Many of them found it was only by throwing themselves on the will of God they could understand. It is only in the crash and discord of life that we have to come to saying : O my God, may Thy will be done here in that kingdom of heaven on earth as it is in heaven, that we may be all one in the mystical body of Christ our Lord.

It was necessary you should fail in that good work ! Time has gone by, and all the sore feeling is beginning to be healed. Yes ; it was necessary you should fail. It was all selfishness. You see it now quite clearly. But it took you a long time to see it. There was the time for many a year when you said: I will never do another hand's turn for God or man ! Everything is misunderstood ; one is always misrepresented ; bickering, and party spirit, and jealousy are all around. And you drew yourself off in scorn and bitterness. And then you took up that habit some have of abusing good people. Then you found it was all soreness, all selfishness ; not devotion for God's glory you cried, but my own glory ; if I had succeeded I should have lost my soul. Only at last taught, perhaps worn out, by failure you said, ' Thy will be done, Thy kingdom come.'

You may look back at a time in life when you thought of other people when you were praying ; if God would but make people know His will and give in to me ! I cannot give in, because I am working on principle, but I know they are not working on principle. Often you had some crushing failure. Praying for others, you sinned yourself. You felt your whole life slipping away from beneath you. You thought: I will give up praying for other people, till at last you said: don't do Thy will in that other person, but in me; Thy will be done.

If you have realised that; if in the midst of multitudinous forms of character you don't want to carry out your own little plans and designs, but try to feel: I must beat myself down under the complete sway and dominion of the will of God; I must lose that selfishness which is the curse of personality, not the blessing; then you bring yourself down under the dominion and the will of God. Then, when you know the will of God is being done, when troubles come and difficulties, you will say, ' If it be possible let this cup pass from me,' and then you check yourself and add, ' Nevertheless not my will but Thine be done.' Let this design be carried out; yet if failure is better, let it be. Let me spring to the front; but if it be for the interest of others that I should be in the background, let my failure be the way to forward the movements of Thy kingdom. Rising up from some bed of sickness, perhaps, you have feelings of jealousy and utter moroseness; but at last you thus pray; and then you go out to do work as you never did before, with that prayer rising up, ' Not my will, but Thine be done.' Do it in Thy way; succeed as Thou seest; not as I see it.

We can see it at last, that that spirit is an absolute necessity in the kingdom of Heaven. It certainly is in the kingdom of earth. If everyone in England had their own way it would be chaos. Think of what chaos would come to-morrow, if everyone could do as he liked with the criminal law. There is a widespread system of law that says you must not do a thing; you will be put in prison; you must sacrifice yourself to other people. Everyone has in himself the power of protecting himself from everyone else; but the State comes in, and says, I will rob you of that liberty. You have no right to take a man's money, to take his place, to go into his house. Human life must be protected from that gross selfishness, so that it may be possible to live at all. Remove the criminal code from England to-day, and we know what would be the result. There would be murder, adultery, theft—the breach of all the last six of the Ten Commandments. And so every man, even of the sinful world, feels they can only govern men by insisting on six, at any rate, of the Ten Commandments.

And in the kingdom of Heaven, where all want to work for the glory of another Person, to keep the glory of that other Person constantly before them, there must be a more and more complete self-surrender, so that each individual—you or I—should feel that we might get on in perfect harmony together, because no one wants simply his own way, but each has a passion for the Will of God. As my arm surrenders to my will, if it is to do my work; as the whole body is under the sway of the will; so the government of the kingdom of Heaven is to accept the Will of God.

We go one step further. There are two ways in which our life may fail. First, by deliberate sin. Whatever that sin is, it is bound to make itself felt. It is going directly against the will of God. It is lawlessness (*anomia*), as St. John tells us. And no one ever did grievous wrong that rested with himself, it is bound to go out ; a certain atmosphere exhales from each one. No man or woman can have a good influence and themselves be bad. We may take that for granted. We may think no one knows of this or that sin, but one moment the veil is lifted and the true self comes out, and in that moment more harm is done than the good we thought to do. Think of a person to whom people look up, and he breaks down. People see there has been badness ; it undoes the good influence, and shakes many a person's faith. And so in sin, in deliberate evil, be quite sure that your life has been a failure, and one day the cancer at the heart of your life will show itself and destroy the whole thing.

Secondly : thank God I don't suppose many of us here are under the dominion of grievous mortal sins. And yet many, when looking back from the mature years of life, when no longer what they were, will still say : I feel this one thing, that it has been a failure from first to last : I had power within me that I never really used ; I should have made more of my life ; I have been selfish, self-seeking, fond of pleasure, and I have not developed myself, and my life is passing away.

God has posted on the pathway of life ten preachers, signposts : do not turn this way or you will hurt yourself—the Ten Commandments. But people who obey all these may narrow within their confines the life God has laid down for them ; they may say, I have never broken deliberately any of the Ten Commandments, but here is the full

THE LORD'S PRAYER

power of my life undeveloped all the same. Why? No life can reach its own full development unless it has the right aim and goal in view. An aimless life is a miserable life—none more so—the life that is lived (as it were) from hand to mouth, from day to day. There the forces that God gives are tending to no relation between the good thing to-day and yesterday; a rushing after something here and there, but no progress onward to a goal that is seen. If you want to know that man, you must know where he is going. If I want to know the meaning of your life, I must know what your aim is.

Now, a person living without any purpose in life may be complete. A person going for noble ends is bound to have inconsistencies. How dare you find fault with that person for inconsistencies when you have never gone out of your own little path where you cannot go wrong? The life of that person is beyond your reach. Here is a young man who succeeds, and goes about criticising the life of other men. I don't profess, he says, to be a Christian or a philanthropist, and I never fail. You insect, I say, for shame! What do you know about failure; you never tried to aspire; you have enclosed your own life in narrow confines, and you can succeed there. Let any man go for noble things, and he is bound to fail. There is that man, and from the fit of his gloves to the tone of his conversation there is nothing to find fault with, within his own little lines he is perfect. And here is a strong man blundering over things which this other man would not soil his hands by meddling with; and I say even this strong man's blunders are successes. The present moment is not the criterion, but what a man is doing, what he is aiming at. Some one goes and sees a man at work. He is spending year after year that he may go forth with greater power. It is the aim that accounts for this. He lives by faith. He is living for something he sees in the far-off future.

'Thou hast made me for Thyself, O God, and my heart is restless till it finds rest in Thee!' So said St. Augustine. But no, says some one, I think life a very pleasant thing, and nothing infinite or eternal about it; I can bring all the powers of my soul into that pleasure, and then throw it away and get another to-morrow. When you hear a person speaking thus you look with the greatest pity upon him. That man's aimless life is sadder than another's failure.

Then there is the life that has had an aim, but has missed it. I aimed at happiness and I missed. I thought I would get happiness by self-indulgence. I thought I would find it in some profession. I threw the whole forces of my life into that, I missed, and I am wretched. How many a man and woman with all they have got that is so good and great, yet, as you think of them, you say they aimed and missed; now old age comes on, and there comes, with times of darkness, that deeper darkness—the consciousness of utter failure. They have only one thing to say: try and do better than I; I failed.

But why have you failed? Were you bound to fail? Was it that the aim was too high, too great, too noble? No; no one ever failed from that. But why did you fail? Why do you look back on a life that failed only with a feeling of lost opportunities, wasted days, powers paralysed and weak? Did

THE LORD'S PRAYER

you set before yourself a goal you have not the power to reach? If so, it was not because it was too high. It was not high enough; it was not great enough. Is it not wonderful? I can take any one of you by chance, any one I have never seen before, and I can say to you, you fail because you are not aiming high enough. Aim at the highest, and you must succeed; aim at anything short of it, and you fail. Like the life of the flower, only living as it thrives in the bosom of the sun, so God has made you in such a way that you can only develop freely as your nature grows towards God. With anything short of that you will fail. I want to be like some other person; I try, and it is only a caricature. I try to make myself God-like, and I find the powers of God unfolding within me. I can go on and on with this for ever. There is no end to it, infinite possibility. O my God, let me see Thy glory; I have no rest till I see Thee face to face. That is the never-failing aim; that it is which has within itself the assurance of its own success, which, if a man takes up, he is sure to have the promise of success, and in any other the promise of failure.

It is not that I will choose to go through this door or that. It is not that I will choose for myself to take up such and such a pursuit because I like it. We look back and forward—back to training and school days, and to the various currents of life moving within ourselves; and then, as one door after another opens, voices keep calling us to go this way and that, and promise us great things. Oh, what is going to influence you, young man, young woman, as you stand and turn from door to door, and through these open doors bright light, fair scenes, pour in upon you ? Are you to keep the passion for a noble and great ideal ? Listen as these voices call you. Which of these doors will you pass ? Will you choose ? These hands were made to work, so I will go and work ; these eyes to look, so I will seek all pleasant sights ; this heart for love, so I will give myself to that, to the passion of the senses. There is a better and higher and a nobler way. As you stand upon the threshold of life where a false step may mean so much —God forbid it may mean utter failure ; in all these many appeals through those open doors, what did God mean ? What is the will of God ? That is the key to success. Let the command of God point to us, saying, this is the way, walk ye in it ; turn neither to the right hand nor to the left. Some of us have made false steps and recovered ; Moses did, Paul of Tarsus did—you may make a false step, but get back again to the right path.

If there be one thing of which I am more and more assured every day, it is that the intelligent Creator made me for a purpose. No one member of the human race has come here by chance. Not one single member has been put here for nothing. Not one single child of man has ever gone through the doorway of birth, to go on through the doorway of death, that he might find merely a place of amusement, and pleasure-seeking. God, Who put you here, put you for a purpose ; if you fulfil that purpose, you succeed ; if you don't, you fail. Think of a reasonable man, looking out on the world of nature, and seeing marks of intelligence, seeing the same in his own nature ; does it never

THE LORD'S PRAYER

occur to him to say that God, who made him, had some purpose; does it never occur to him to ask what did He do it for? Why did He give me these gifts and withhold those? Why was I born in England and not elsewhere? Why in the nineteenth century and not in another? Why in that home and not in another? Why so strangely brought up or not brought up at all, making shift for myself from the first, and yet others so well brought up? Why was it that in the early days of my life it seems to me I was thrown amongst companions that did me no good, and with some one else it was so different, living under a protecting Providence watching over him? Why, why, why? Must it not have some meaning? Is all quite haphazard and by chance, all a blind freak of nature? Is that what has produced me and framed and fashioned the circumstances of my life? I will not believe it, I as a Christian do not believe it; but I know that every portion of my bodily and spiritual and mental nature was made with design, and if I can get into the right course I get into the place that suits, and if I get into the wrong course God knows what may happen. There is a right and a wrong. There is a purpose. There is an acknowledgment of the purpose, and a denial of it. If you don't want to know God's will you won't know it. You must keep it before you that there is a plan and purpose and a thing that, if it is to be done, God means it should be done by you.

If we believe that, then this follows: if God made me, He knew what He was doing, and gave me everything necessary for carrying out His work. Not everything necessary for carrying out my own ambitions.

Not everything necessary for that brilliant position which my friend has got, and which I envy him with all my heart and soul. But, if I say to myself that God made me for something, then I see also, of course, that He has given me what is necessary for carrying it out. His wisdom and power and love are all equal. His wisdom saw what was wanted; His power was able to make what was wanted; and His love wanted nothing that was not good.

I have no patience with people who, in false humility, are always running themselves down:—Get some other person to do it; I can do nothing. It sounds very humble, for instance, to say this, but it really means intense pride and intense sloth—pride that would shield one's self by throwing the blame on God, and sloth that keeps you from rising up to do the work God gave you. Therefore I look into myself, not with pride, but with true humility (which always has the spirit of self-respect) and say, there never was a man created on this earth so fit to do this work as I am; or, there never was a woman so fit to do it. God, who made the work, made the man. Look at him; see him at his work; it draws out every power of the man; there is that strange power over that work that it seems to understand the man; he is suited to it, and it is suited to him. When the man realises that there is a purpose and aim and object, then he feels that he must do it, and says he will do it like a man.

There are multitudes of people who have come face to face with their work, and said: you think I am going to do it; thank you. They are too proud to do God's work. They go through life bitter and make other people bitter. They have lost faith in themselves; and the key to the whole situation is absolute pride.

In one word, the will of God for each one of us, is *vocation*. Everyone has a vocation. Each one is put here, and that mysterious voice which whispers in your ear at your birth, and more articulately as you grow up, gradually becomes clearer and clearer till in the stillness of the night you rise up like Samuel, saying, ' Speak, Lord, for Thy servant heareth.' You feel that you have got into the right place and have the right thing to do. I spoiled, you say, various things I took in hand, because it had never occurred to me to take the true key to life and see what God wanted. Then I found what God wanted, and I tried to do it. I found I was not so popular, not so outwardly successful; but my whole inner life was suffused with a consciousness that I was doing the right thing, that the development of a person was going on, and not the development of a fragment.

One word in conclusion. Vocation—that is the real meaning in the kingdom of heaven of 'Thy will be done.' Thy will be done on the largest scale of all, and by me as God wishes me to do it; I have the power of choice and correspondence.

It is true to say that some vocations are more marked than others. Such and such a man, you can see, was meant to be a missionary; another to be a priest. Here is a person meant to be a sister of mercy, another to be a nurse, another a teacher; and so on. You can see at once everything corresponds with these vocations. Such cases are marked vocations. Other vocations are very much less marked, and yet they are just as true. My good woman, you have as true a vocation to be a mother as St. Paul had to be the Apostle of the Gentiles; as true a vocation to stay at home, and do your work there. There is that young Christian woman, out from her own quiet home, and gone to see some work that everyone is talking about. She goes over a great institution with the Sister in charge of it, and sees a great number of people under that Sister, and a great work developing all her powers; and the young woman goes home with a strong sense upon her: here I am as truly where God means me to be as she is where God meant *her* to be. That may keep down personal ambition; but there is a deeper current of joy running through the whole character, which says: I would not change at present, for 'I had rather be a door-keeper,' so long as it is the will of God.

Again, brethren, there are some vocations that are very hard to understand. I have not the least doubt that there are some people whose vocation— the highest of all—is to suffer. To many seems to be given that great vocation of Jesus Christ our Lord, to suffer for themselves and others. God knows what the world would do without the hospitals; and few people know what some young man is doing in intercessory prayer to God; every pain he suffers, he offers up prayers for the Church of God. I knew a woman once—she was then seventy years of age— who had been on her back for fifty years; her room was the brightest in the whole house, and when anything happened people came and gathered round that bed to get some cheer and joy from one always suffering.

If that be a vocation, there is another, perhaps, equally difficult to understand. It is this: 'Thy will be done on earth,' so says that poor soul—and I believe if it were physical or mental suffering, I could do that; but I have no place of my own to fill, no special domestic duties; I believe I might drop out of the world, and no one would miss me. Such a life seems to be all broken into scraps. That is quite true. But if you could grasp in your imagination what the world would be without these lives, you would find what a vocation they are. How would it be with many homes if there was no kind friend to drop in sometimes and take the place of over-worked hands and brains, and help to make things bright and cheerful? What would it mean to many if there was not a person who could constantly be looked to? These persons thus surrender themselves because they feel there is nothing else for them to do, and they do it well. Take these people out of the world and you will find what a loss they are. Rouse up, then, and realise—this may be the very thing that God made me to do.

There is that man in his place of business—a successful artist; see him at his work. See how people crowd to purchase the work of his hands. And there is also the poor girl who sweeps out his office; he could not get on without her. Did God make the artist and some one else make the poor sweeper? God made them both. So the artist and the poor sweeper are equally dear in my eyes. And any life is great that rises up through the strain and stress of circumstance and is strong, that says: here is where God has put me; Thy will be done.

SERMON NOTES LEFT IN MS. BY THE
LATE FATHER MATURIN

NOTES OF A SERMON FOR THE RENOVATION OF VOWS. March 4, 1909

'I bear in my body the marks of the Lord Jesus.'—GALATIANS vi. 17.

'To serve is to reign,' when we crave to be our own masters we crave for the cruellest master that ever lived. St. Paul was scourged, imprisoned, ill-treated in every way, and yet the wretch who held the scourge thought only of the chastisement he had been ordered to give and had no thought of imprinting the name of Jesus on his victim. It was St. Paul himself who turned the blows and scars into his Master's Name and glorified in being signed with the Name of Him Whose slave he loved to be. You have to bear many things you do not like. Now, on the one hand, they may embitter you and cast you down and be mere painful wounds against which you fight and repine; or, on the other hand, the *will* may rise up and say: I will bear them for my Master Christ, and they will then become the glorious marks of His slave. The marks may be given by anybody, but it rests with you what those marks are to become, you have the magic power of turning them into the name of the Master Whose slave you are.

St. Paul learnt this lesson from his Master scourged, crowned with thorns—one wound from the crown of His head to the soles of His feet—wounds which came from senseless people drunken with party spirit, envy. ' Crucify Him—crucify Him ! ' was the cry. No sign of love here. But in the midst of it all there is *One* who can turn it into a *sacrifice*, into a suffering that can *redeem*. That human Will takes every blow that strikes His hands and feet and side and changes the angry blow into redeeming love. There was nothing there with any beauty or comeliness, and yet it became the centre of the greatest act of worship and love the world has ever seen. What was it that made it so ? *The will of the Bearer*. . . The bad thief, self-contained, rebelled against every blow—and the blows of Jesus, meekly accepted, made His the greatest sacrifice ever known. His wounds in His hands, the feet, the side, live on after His Resurrection. They are the wounds of One Who has been a wanderer, misunderstood amongst His own creatures. Does He want them to be removed ? Oh no ! for we love them. They were made in hatred by us, but He has turned them into the Wounds of Love.

The Hands. Poverty. — His hands had been stretched out in doing good. He left no one unaided, and now the world has left Him and He is taken and hung upon a Cross. The hands are the instruments of action. He could do nothing henceforth. He is hampered and cannot stretch them out to do one good deed. What does He do ? He offers up His useless Hands and they redeem the world. The mighty power of His love *transforms that transfixion into a mighty blessing* for the multitude.

Those who ' follow the Lamb whithersoever He goeth ' bind their hands in *poverty* to the Cross that they may never deliberately minister to their own comforts. Many kindly acts you cannot do—relieving the wants and miseries of the world, for those hands are bound; *turn all that restraint into the blessing and prayer of sacrifice*—they can reach far further and do more good than ever you could were you free. Your inability generously sacrificed may become a redemptive act, a blessing to the multitude, but this depends upon the *will*. Union with Him Who gave up His liberty for our sakes. When sometimes those who are striving to serve God find themselves hampered, then those hands may do nothing, or they may get a great blessing by their very uselessness.

The Feet. Obedience.—The feet represent the power of motion, or ordering one's life, going where we will. 'He went about doing good.' Now the feet are tied, the great nail has passed and He can move no further. Behold again the power of His transforming love. He cannot move, but He can lie there upon the Cross and draw all the world to Him. At those transfixed feet the sinner finds hope and peace, whilst the fountain of the redeeming Blood flows upon his head from the outstretched and nailed hands.

Again, in those who follow Him: the nun's feet are nailed by Holy Obedience—she can no longer carry herself about hither and thither, and it depends upon *herself* if that nail will burn and tear or be a blessing.

The Vow is the protector of the Virtue and the virtue is that fastening of the feet to the Cross, so that you do *not* regulate your own life. The devil says: you had better get down. No! I made up my mind that I would not choose my path and therefore

I shall be able to minister in places my feet could never have reached.

The Heart. Chastity.—As long as love lives, life lives. The heart had had many wounds 'in the house of His friends' and now it is broken; yet, as He lies dead upon the Cross it bursts and the Water and Blood pour forth from it for our Redemption. The dead heart does more than the living. My vow of chastity pledges me to discipline of the heart, to the restraint of that which is a mighty power for good when it is trained and turned in the right direction. It must be with us as with Jesus; in her measure and degree each religious must find some mark of the stigmata upon her, hampered—the heart *must* be wounded, misunderstood—the hands not always free to do just what they like, nor the feet, nor the heart to pour out its love, for it would not be received. Everyone of you, my sisters, must have the stigmata marked deeply upon your heart, for you cannot do your work perfectly if the marks are not there, for what are your Vows but the marks of Our Lord Jesus Christ which you carry in your body? It is often easy to read on your face or body whose slave you have been—what master you have had—pride, anger, &c. &c., but the wilful slavery and the loving bearing of the marks of Jesus Christ will in time wipe out the lines and scars of old slavery and you will be transformed:—no man on earth, no devil from Hell can trouble me, for am I not crucified with Christ? and I shall be a partaker of His joy as I have been of His sufferings.

SORROW TURNED INTO JOY

THERE is a tendency in a great deal that we hear to separate between this world and the next, to make them more or less independent. Anything that tends to relax the conception of continuity, and of the development of the life of the soul from here on into Heaven, must have this effect. The considering Heaven a place of external rewards with its golden streets and its pearly gates and its sweet music and leaving out the condition of the person who is there, has this effect. No amount of external splendour will make the discontented soul happy, no amount of spiritual privilege will make the sensual soul spiritual—the Heaven must be within as well as without. The love within is satisfied by the vision of the object of its love, the peace without is in harmony with the peace within.

Again, there is a way of setting Heaven and earth in contrast which has the same result. We will bear the miseries of life and look forward to the mercies of Heaven. We will bear suffering and sorrow with the thought of that Land where there is no more sorrow, &c. All of which is true no doubt to a certain extent, but it is very far from the whole truth or the perfect truth, and can only lead the soul on a very limited and measured distance, and it tends in many minds to make rather a contrast than a continuity of the life here and the life of eternity.

Now there are contrasts between earth and Heaven. In Heaven there will be no suffering, no sorrow, no sin; and most certainly every sorrow well borne, every temptation resisted will make our Heaven more glorious and more joyous. But how? Is it because of the infinite contrast? Is it the joy of the just saved crew at last in port and recalling the dangers of the storm? of the weary and footsore traveller who has reached his home at last? or of the hunted and disturbed soul, tempted almost beyond endurance, free at last from temptation and safe.

It is all this indeed, but infinitely more; this in a sense is but an accident, it is not the essential blessing and joy of Heaven. The well-borne troubles, the well-fought battles of life make in a measure the contrast between Heaven and earth rather less than more, inasmuch as they help to give to man here on earth some foretaste of Heaven.

This idea of contrasts between Heaven and earth and the looking forward to Heaven as the place of compensations tend to lessen the idea of what God is to do for us here and now. All the rewards are by no means in the next world; we are to look for, and to expect, and not to be content without many a reward here. The reality of our life here and of its experiences, the present mitigation of many of our greatest trials is a thing that the true Christian must never forget. Indeed our capacity for receiving the blessings of eternity will be largely measured by our capacity for receiving them here.

The knowledge of God, for instance, changes everything in life. The man who knows God has a power of happiness amidst everything, that is unknown to the man who does not know Him.

Thus there are two theories of the meaning of life's troubles and trials in relation to the joys of Heaven.

1. One is the theory that we are to bear all that comes to us in life looking up to the compensations which will make up for them in Heaven. I bear this suffering and clench my teeth and brace myself with the thought it will soon be over and there will be no more pain. I bear this sorrow with the thought of the great reunion beyond the grave where there are to be no more partings, and this thought will give a man of strong faith a certain power no doubt, but how poor and thin and superficial can be its effects. To many Heaven and earth stand out in this contrast of a great compensation. They cry to one another: hold out a little longer and you will get your reward; and certainly many places in Holy Scripture give support to this view and certainly so far as it goes it is true. But it goes a very little way and its results are very limited in the maturing of character. They can never produce the perfection of Christian virtues.

2. Now there is another and a nobler, the essentially Christian theory of life's sorrows and troubles, and it is that not merely of compensation but of transformation. I do not want to bear as much as I have to bear here that I may have the joy of nothing to bear through eternity. I will not work and labour by the thought of an eternal holiday. No, I want to get out of these trials and difficulties here on earth, an immediate and present blessing. I feel sure the

highest lessons and the deepest joys come to me in forms that cause me pain. I know the lips conquered and controlled can utter words more weighty than lips undisciplined. I know a heart that has bled, has sympathies unknown to others. I know the joy that creeps over the soul like the joy of morning after a night of suffering, when some great sacrifice has been made, and therefore I seek not merely a Heaven of compensations, but a Heaven that crowns and completes the great moral joys of earth. This is the theory of transformation—your sorrow shall be turned into joy, not succeeded by joy, but the sorrow is the substance out of which the joy is extracted.

This changes the whole view of life and the whole of a man's bearing in life. What a difference between the man who says: I'll work hard now and enjoy a good rest after dinner, and the man who says: I'll work hard now and get out of this work some knowledge that makes the hard work worth while. How different the bearing of a person who says: I'll try and bear poverty with the thought of the riches of Heaven which I shall one day possess, and the man who says: this poverty has some power in it of bringing here and now a blessing to my soul. Blessed are the poor, for theirs is the Kingdom of Heaven. One looks far off to a distant reward, the other finds plenteous foretaste even now. He says: if these sacrifices bring such blessing in time what will be their reward in Eternity. What different consolation would be ministered to one suffering in sickness by one who told him: bear up, keep patient a little longer, soon you'll pass into the land where there is no suffering, and by him who said: wrestle with that sickness till through it you get the blessing wrapped up in it.

This then is the true idea of life's troubles and sorrows, they are given us that we may turn them into joys. The Apostles as they went through the dark night of Good Friday were laying hold of the substance of their sorrow and transmuting it. Their faith was being purified, the structure of their spiritual life was being made firm, and when the Easter light came it was not merely a contrast, but they found the sorrow turned into joy.

THREE PARADOXES

I

'As dying, and, behold, we live.'—2 CORINTHIANS vi. 9.

THERE are two words that underlie all our experiences here on earth. One is life and the other is death. Every hour of the day a new life is beginning and a life is ending. At this moment probably a child has been born into the world with all its possibilities of success or failure yet untried, and at this moment someone is passing out of this world to give an account of the things done in the flesh. Between these two moments of life and death lies the history of the world. Some page of unwritten history is waiting to be written by one yet unborn or just born, just as another fills his last page and closes the book of his life. They are both solemn moments. A new-born child coming into the world to show what he can do; another leaving the world with his last deed done, his last word uttered. It is a solemn thing to see a newcomer enter upon the beginning of his life's work, a solemn and awful responsibility to be the instrument through which such a life began, and it is a solemn thing to see one go forth from the world to his last account.

Life and death are always in deadly antagonism. The two extremes, they are always at war. Looked

THREE PARADOXES—I

at from one point of view life is a hand-to-hand struggle to keep death away. Every act, every effort to think brings exhaustion of the physical frame which is the warning of the presence of death. Every breath we draw in feeds life, every breath we exhale is laden with death. Every throb of the heart that sends the blood through the arteries bears life through its channels. The blood returns through the veins exhausted and dying. We can do nothing here on earth save at the cost of a struggle between life and death. When death finally comes, it comes triumphant, having conquered life. Every day we live it is because life has gained the victory over death.

We know this too well, this struggle to live. Many old men feel it as they drag their exhausted limbs about. It cannot be therefore in any such sense as this that St. Paul uses the expression 'as dying behold we live.' Every man can bid people look at him, and see how in dying behold he lives. St. Paul's words are stronger. They mean that the act of dying seems to result in life. In the order of nature the dying is remedied and defeated by fresh supplies of life. The act of life and the act of death are antagonists. In St. Paul the two acts are brought into correspondence. The two antagonists have been reconciled and death is made the servant of life.

So far as we see one another in an earthly life we can say: behold me as living and behold I die. Life the path to death, the wasting of the energies, the weakening of the powers, the dimming of the eye till life is exhausted in death. Whatever life I seem to have I use at the cost of death. Death is the enemy of life. St. Paul reverses it. Look at me, he says, a poor, dying, wearied, suffering man; but this is only the price of the richness of my life.

The normal process is inverted in him—not living into death, but dying daily into a fuller life. Death is conquered. I have faced it and robbed it of its terror and made it the servant of life.

To be able to do this is indeed to know how to live. All through life the gate of death stands before us as the end to which we are hastening. Each year we have to say, one year less to live. Can we seize upon this enemy of life and tame him into submission, and make him not the enemy but the friend?

I think we can. What is death? It is a disintegration, the loosening of those wonderful combinations, the unlocking of those forces, which holding together in unity form life. Every living thing is composed of the blending together of a multitude of different forms of matter into one whole. Life takes a number of minerals lying disconnected in the earth and binds them into a mysterious unity. The human body, so much carbon, hydrogen, oxygen, nitrogen, &c. Let life depart and these combinations are destroyed; as long as I can keep death off I preserve them. When it comes the bonds are broken and they are scattered. But a human being is more than so many chemicals combined. He is a combination of spirit and matter; he has a soul and a body and a mind. And these three bound together make a man. I have a body and a soul and a spiritual life and a mental life. But this unity has been disturbed and we are not at one with ourselves. Some live the life of the mind, some of the spirit, some of the flesh. No matter how carnal, you can't get rid

THREE PARADOXES—I

of the cravings of mind and spirit. No matter how spiritual, you are never free from the demands of the flesh. This inner conflict goes on from the first awakening of consciousness till it is lost in death. The conflict itself is a dying, it is an effort of death to intrude and break up the combinations of life. No one as our dying nature is constituted can live the full life of body, soul and spirit. What then is the nearest approach to life ? It is to follow the order of reason. First spirit, then mind, then body. To keep the different compartments of our nature in their place. To subdue body and mind to spirit, to make them servants not masters. To realise what the life of a man really is and to live it.

But how can this be done ? Only in one way, by starving the other parts of our nature into submission. The body has wants that are deadly to the spirit. The mind has thoughts that are poisonous to all that is the highest life of mind and soul. Death comes to man at the beginning of this life and begins to force an entrance. It says : I have to be dealt with, you must use me or I will make havoc of you. I will treat you as I will, I will be master if I am not servant. And so many a young man, living, as he says, just as he likes, to enjoy that side of his nature which is strongest in him, never considers how every moment of his life is a submission to the tyranny of death. He is living for enjoyment and for work, &c., but one part of his nature is dying. The life of the flesh kills the spirit or leaves it in a state of death agony. As he says, he knows death must come, and his motto is ' Let us eat and drink, for to-morrow we die.' But he doesn't realise that *it is not to-morrow but to-day*. He is letting death have its own way and kill all that is noblest and best in him. 'If ye live of the flesh ye shall die.'

Which is the highest, to let death choose and kill what it wills in us, or to triumph over death by making it the minister of life?

There have always, amongst the noblest of our race, been men here and there who did not indeed understand the full meaning of this but who strove in a blind way to do it. There are those outside of Christianity who strive after it to-day. In the East silent forms sit by the sacred river gazing out into the dim unseen world, striving to die to everything that they may live. Some perhaps reach to life, many are but living corpses—death is too strong for them, they don't understand its power or how it can be tamed and used in man's service. One alone understood, and He realised and revealed it. Mohammed looked at man's nature and said: what he desires strongly is not wrong. Let him live and indulge himself. Buddha said: man's nature is bad, the desire to live is the root of all evil, let him die. Christ said: man's nature is sick unto death, I will come and heal him. 'I am come that he may have life and may have it more abundantly.' The longing to live is good not bad, but man must live by dying or die in living. And St. Paul seizing upon this great paradox, the conflict between life and death, brings the two together and cries, 'By dying behold I live.'

Look at him, worn and emaciated, covered with the blows, seamed and marked by the conflict with death. Look at that brilliant mind that might have made him the first in the *forum* or a great teacher in

THREE PARADOXES—I

the schools of philosophy. The mind is disciplined and brought into the service of Christ. 'We have the mind of Christ,' read the epistles, we see his mind has brought all his knowledge into his master's service thus. Those who saw him said, 'his presence is weak and sickly.' Verily no one could look at him and not feel that externally he was a dying man, a man who was always dying to the flesh and to men. But look deeper and you say :—behold he lives. The power of the spirit is supreme. He drags his half-paralysed body wherever his spirit would lead it, he can use his great gifts to see deeper and deeper into the obscurity of life. He was a man who made terms with death, and became its master, and as the last act of death—the opening doors to heaven—draws near he cries : 'I am ready to be offered, the time of my departure is at hand. I have fought the good fight,' &c.

The Church of Corinth was a great trial to St. Paul. It was torn with schism and contaminated with heathen immorality. St. Paul had already written excommunicating a man who had married his own heathen stepmother, delivering his body to Satan that his soul might be saved in the day of the Lord. Then he had waited. He sent first Timothy and then Titus to deal with them. He had made up his mind to go to Corinth himself, but had hesitated lest his presence should do more harm than good. He had started from Ephesus and gone to Troas, but though he had there great missionary opportunities he had no strength or heart for the work. A restless and feverish anxiety consumed him, he returned to Macedonia, probably to Philippi; there after a time of anxiety Titus came to him. He was able to report to him the effect of the first Epistle and this was, in part at least, full of comfort. The majority had acted towards the incestuous offender as he had bidden them. They had endeavoured to clear themselves from the charge of contamination and had shown warm feelings of attachment to St. Paul. But Titus told him more. There were two parties who at opposite extremes agreed in resisting St. Paul. The party of license had given no proof of repentance. There was also a Jewish party claiming to belong to Christ in a sense in which St. Paul didn't, boasting their Hebrew descent, arrogating especial apostolic authority, lording it over their abject followers. And from either or both had come taunts and sneers. They accused St. Paul of weakness in his change of plan. His personal appearance, feeble and infirm, did not match the authoritative tone of his letters, his speech had nothing to command admiration. He threatened supernatural punishment, but he didn't dare to put his threats to proof. What right had he to claim the authority of an Apostle when he had never seen Christ in the flesh. They reproached him for having worked at a trade and yet received gifts at Macedonia as if he had favourites. They insinuated dishonesty in regard to these collections for the poor. Who was this Paul who came without credentials and expected to be received on the strength of his everlasting self-assertions? Was there not a touch of madness in his visions and revelations? These were the reports of Titus piercing the sensitive heart of St. Paul, passionately craving for affection and feeling the bitterness of living without love.

THREE PARADOXES—I

We may imagine something of the whirl and storm of emotion with which St. Paul dictates the answer.

He tells them of the acuteness of his sufferings before Titus came, he defends himself against the charge of fickleness in changing his plans, he is glad he waited to give time for repentance. He absolves the offender. He tells of the fitness and unfitness of their own weakness and Christ's strength, the hope of immortality, the fear of judgment. Will those to whom he writes receive his message in vain? He pleads for a place in their affections on the score of all he had done and suffered. He speaks of his credentials as a minister of Christ.

'In all things approving ourselves as the ministers of God, in much patience, in tribulation, in necessities, in distresses.

'In stripes, in imprisonments, in tumults, in labours, in watchings, in fastings.

'By pureness, by knowledge, by long-suffering, by kindness, by the Holy Ghost, by love unfeigned.

'By the word of truth, by the power of God: by the armour of righteousness on the right hand and on the left:

'By honour and dishonour, by evil report and good report: as deceivers and yet true: as unknown and yet well known:

'As dying, and behold, we live.'

THREE PARADOXES

II

> 'Peace I leave with you.'—St. John xiv. 27.
> 'I came not to send peace.'—St. Matthew x. 34.

One of the results of the ever increasing knowledge that is spreading on all sides, is that this becomes an age of specialists. It is impossible for one person to master all the subjects that press before the mind, and therefore one person takes up one and another the other. And the result is that knowledge becomes more extended and more exact. But all such specialising necessitates also the narrowing of the mind. A man who limits his studies to one subject or one small detail of the subject will be the first to confess that he has to be always on the watch to prevent his mind from getting narrowed. There is then a danger in our day of narrow-mindedness, while it is an age that boasts of its breadth. It is the glory of the City of God and of its citizens that the length and breadth and depth and height are all equal. One part is not sacrificed for the development of another. For remember, it is with the mind we see and know all we come in contact with; as is the mind so is the vision. And the mind has its influence upon religious subjects. The Catholic Church is a very large thing, some minds make it a very small thing indeed. To many the moral attributes of God are little more than those of a man somewhat enlarged. Indeed, except perhaps a confused and inaccurate or a dishonest mind, few do more grievous harm than a small mind. For God is infinite and all that He touches has something of His greatness about it, and this must escape the view of one whose mind is narrowed. Now nothing so helps to open and enlarge the mind as variety of experience. A person of observation who travels much and sees many men and many things almost unconsciously gets his mind enlarged. The tendency of a great many people, the natural tendency of ordinary people is to settle down into a groove. Most of us have a very limited circle of friends and acquaintances, and the large majority of people have their roots so deeply in their native soil that they know little or nothing of other lands and people. We have often to fight our way out of our grooves, to try to see some new faces, to hear some new point of view. In some small valley shut in by the mountains men talk and think of the great world much as if it were a magnified village of their own. And then things of very little importance get magnified and out of all proportion. Narrowness has generally as its consequence very serious moral defects.

And nature is always stirring to bring us out of our grooves and enlarge the mind. Nothing has a greater tendency to produce this enlargement than passing through different experiences, through striking contrasts of mental states. Even externally nature necessitates this; the most monotonous lives have their changes from day to night, summer and winter, sorrow to joy, health to sickness, labour to rest. And then external changes are reflected like the sunshine and shadow upon the sensitive mirror of the mind; there is an inner response as men pass from light to darkness, from summer to winter. We all know what it is to feel of certain people that they have never had the enlarging experience of sorrow. I doubt if there's anyone, however dull and unimaginative, who doesn't have duller and more exciting days, and who is not more or less conscious of those rapid mental passages from surface to depth and depth to surface. We all have to deal with the eternities and immensities and with the very trifles of the passing hour. A man is troubled because his child is dead and because his dinner is not properly cooked; gradually as our minds become enlarged and deepened the power of being troubled is deepened in the one case and weakened in the other. Then again, we pass from the rack of pain to the repose of health. It would not be good for anyone to have his mind always kept on the strain by the stirring of the depths of his soul, still less for him only to have the surface moved. Life plunges us into the depths and lifts us to the surface. And we have within ourselves the elements from which these contrasts are produced. They are often altogether independent of outward things. The life of a solitary peasant in his cottage knows them as truly as the man of the world. One moment we are face to face with the deepest things in life, the next we are chattering and laughing as if we were the most superficial beings upon earth.

Now one of these contrasts is the change from

THREE PARADOXES—II

peace to battle. He who never knows peace has certainly failed in an experience which has a great power for enlarging the mind. The whole view of life and men and things is changed, as though it were a different world to a man who passes from struggle and conflict to peace. Remember, we only can see things in the mirror of the mind. If the world be reflected in a soul at perfect peace, it will look a very different thing from what it looks to one who views it in the turbid medium of a strong and restless nature. Take for instance the one very superficial matter of money. A man who has to fight for his daily bread, whose life is lived under the conditions of ceaseless competition, knows a truth about life that the man of wealth can never know. We need both experiences if we are to widen our view and get out of our ruts. He whose life is one ceaseless battle loses the knowledge gained in times of peace, and he whose life is always in undisturbed peace is shut out from the knowledge gained by struggle and warfare. We need both. A tumult of temptation sweeps over the soul, its very depths are stirred, the waves are mighty and rage horribly— we are stirred to the naked foundations of our being, everything in us is thrown up to the surface. We understand men as we never did before. We understand ourselves. The whole world at such a moment looks different. We look into the faces of others and wonder what they are going through. Our sympathies become enlarged, our trite judgments become merciful. We wonder at our hardness in judging others. And then the waters calm down and there is a great peace. Again the world looks different. We see the quiet peaceful faces and we begin to learn that this peace may have been fought for and purchased at a great price.

Each of these states has its own lessons to teach, its own development to bring to the mind, its own widening view of the world of men which I think we could not otherwise gain.

I have seen a picture of an Angel touching, with a look of wonder, one of the thorns of the Crown of Thorns—the symbol of the most terrible battle that ever was fought, the battle between good and evil. He cannot understand it. He touches it with a delicate finger and wonders. In the peace of that calm harbour he knows nothing of the storm, in the unruffled peace of Heaven he cannot understand the tumult of the conflict upon the earth. These things he desires to look upon. He sees them from the high place of his dwelling, but he is not like his Master and Lord a sympathising High Priest who can enter into the feeling of our infirmities for that he himself suffered being tempted. He knows the peace, he knows nothing of the struggle. All the revelation of that side of life is shut out from his view. Has he lost more or gained more we wonder. At any rate we should not seek the sympathy and perfect understanding for our troubles from an angel that we would from Our Lord. In the midst of struggle we envy the peace of an angel's life. But we feel the peace of the Prince of Peace, the King of Angels, is a more wonderful thing, and the only kind that we can have.

And we find that Our Lord's teaching on the subject was for man not for angels: it is to be won by man,

THREE PARADOXES—II

completed in Heaven, but we are to have deep experiences of it on earth.

His teaching on the subject is a paradox. 'Peace I leave with you, My Peace I give unto you'; and again, 'I am not come to send Peace but the sword.' And St. Paul following His teaching says, 'Be content with what ye have,' 'Covet earnestly the best gifts.' How can I be content with what I have and covet better things? How can I be the follower of the Prince of Peace when He puts into my hands a sword and bids me fight? War is the very antithesis, the contradiction of peace. Contentment forbids coveting something better.

We have two feelings corresponding to these two commands. You live in the quiet country and go your daily round of peaceful employment, nothing disturbs the routine of your life, there are no rough intruders, like the measured sequence of the seasons with their rhythmic tread you pursue your course. Hard by is the strenuous liver in some great tumultuous city. He goes down to the country to see you and breathes and bathes himself in your calm. He says: what a contrast, how I envy you. But soon he gets restless. He says: this life would kill me, I should soon become a vegetable. It was the momentary contrast that attracted him. Both views have an element of truth in them, but neither have the whole truth. The world would soon cease to move if all men lived that quiet life. And the world would lose something if none did.

A brilliant lover of paradox once said to me, 'There is no more fatal thing than to preach to the working classes the teaching of St. Paul, " be content with your ways." It is discontent that sets the world moving and keeps it awake.' Is a man, born among the working classes and feeling powers stir within him which are capable of greater things, to be content where he is ? Is he not to use his powers and rise ? Is not competition the key to progress ? Is it not one of the laws of nature ? What has set men to work to better their condition and to rise out of obscurity into positions of prominence but discontent ? May not such men say : I am following the very words of St. Paul, who rose from a little local celebrity into the position of a world-wide Apostle, I am coveting earnestly the best gifts. And when a Christian priest preaches contentment and peace, he feels if there be amongst his audience a man of gifts and ambitions he must be preaching to deaf ears. For he is not preaching the whole truth. 'Seek peace and ensue it,' yet he knows there is the other side, 'I am not come to send peace but a sword.' For in the midst of the struggle men crave for peace, and in the dead calm of quiet men long for the struggle.

THREE PARADOXES

III

'Who coverest Thyself with light as with a garment.'
PSALM civ. 2.

'Clouds and darkness are round about Him.'—PSALM xcvii. 2.

THROUGH the passing ages the general aspect of things remains pretty much the same. The heavens spread their changeless arch over the great expanse of earth and sea. The mountains with their snow-capped peaks look down in grim silence upon the passing seasons, and see but little change. Here and there man intrudes and turns a silent place into a great city. But his presence might be removed from the earth and little change would be seen. Yet man is in fact always changing. Every few score of years a generation disappears and a new generation takes its place. The race moves onward, memory holds all gains of the past in its treasure-house, the savage becomes civilised; the mind develops. Every age and country has its own tone of mind and that changes rapidly. You have but to read the works of fiction of half a century ago to see how quickly that subtle change creeps over the mind.

And every age has its special tendency and its special shibboleths that meet with the approval of the many and the stern condemnation of the few.

Amidst the influence of these new ideas on popular sentiment there are always to be found those who are passionate adherents of the past.

These adherents include some of the wisest men. But I think mere dull conservatism, holding on to things because they have been, will not win many of the younger minds. There is a better way. In every change that comes over the popular mind, however startling, there is an element of truth. In the successive changes there is a gradual revelation of truth, a passage from darkness to light. It is the wisest though the hardest thing to find out that truth and try to emancipate it from the admixture of error. We must ever remember that the mind was made for truth, not falsehood, as the heart was made for love, not hate, and the will to choose right, not wrong.

Now it is a curious thing that so critical and dogmatic an age makes one exception to this principle that our minds are made for truth, and that is in regard to religion. The fashion of the day about religious truth is to repudiate dogma, to assert that no religion can claim to have a monopoly of the truth, that the Catholic Church is really not one body guarding religious truths but a combination of all creeds. And the reason is this.

1. Different minds get different aspects of the same truth, people do not keep clear the distinction between the mind that thinks and the truth.

2. As we study any great truth that touches deeply either upon God or man we become conscious that the deeper we go the more we are aware of another set of facts or considerations that gradually diverge till they seem to stand in direct opposition. Every

THREE PARADOXES—III

heresy has been an effort to assert a truth or a part of a truth. The history of the fourth, fifth and sixth centuries is a history of the effort of the mind to grasp the two sides of the doctrine of the Incarnation. Calvinism expresses a part of a truth and so does Pelagianism. No one can be even a Theist who does not say: God cannot suffer, God cannot die. No one can be a Christian who does not believe that God suffered and died upon the Cross. All the great truths of life are composed of two apparently conflicting elements. Thus to guard religious truth is not to make all things clear, but to treasure a revelation which must ever remain full of mystery.

There are minds that will not grasp this, that want to have everything clear, everything labelled and pigeon-holed, and that is just the kind of mind which falls into heresy.

Now it is the same in these words of the Psalmist about God. 'Clouds and darkness are round about Him.' 'He covereth Himself with light as with a garment.' Here are two statements that at first sight seem to be directly in contradiction. Darkness and light, the two opposites that divide the world, the two foes in perpetual warfare, which never can come to terms. Where light comes darkness flies before it, when darkness comes the light must go.

Now when we try to reach the ideas which are included in these two pictures so as to hold them both in the mind at once, we notice that the difference between them is the difference, not between mystery and no mystery, but between two kinds of mystery. It is not that the figure of darkness represents to us a being all obscure and hidden and the figure of light throws open all closed doors of His being so that we can see everything clear and distinct and without a shadow. This indeed is what people want about many of the things in life, but they can't get it. Man is a mystery to himself, he can't understand himself. If he could ever wholly understand God so that all the mystery of His being was gone for ever, there would be no further progress; he himself would have attained to the infinite.

What then do we mean when we speak of God at one moment as clothed in darkness and at another as clothed in light? There are two kinds of mysteries, the mystery of darkness and of light. We know something of the mystery of darkness: some object which we would study is hidden in obscurity, we can't make it out, what it is, its shape or colour; we strain our eyes but it eludes us still, we know that it may really be very different from what in its faint and undefined outline it seems to us. The darkness can wrap the simplest thing in mystery which the first ray of sunshine dispels. Many things have nothing mysterious about them but the darkness which shrouds them. You and I can remember many things that used to seem strange and perplexing and full of wonder to us in our childhood because we did not understand them; the mystery sprang solely from the darkness of our ignorance. When the light of knowledge came the mystery disappeared. We all know the mystery of darkness.

But there is even a greater mystery of light. Suppose that the thing that perplexes us in the darkness is a mysterious thing, no mere trifle. Suppose it is a great personage about whom you have heard much, but whom you scarcely know. You have seen him, perhaps said a few words to him, but that is all. He stands before you shrouded in the mystery of darkness. But now he steps out of the darkness into the light : you have got to know something of this remarkable personality, to see some tokens of the brilliancy of his genius, and the strength of his will, and the power of his influence. So far as you are concerned he is clothed with light as with a garment. But is the mystery lessened or deepened ? Is it not infinitely deeper ? A mystery that fascinates and leads you on, but never ceases to be a mystery. The mystery of darkness bewilders, misleads and often frightens. The mystery of light fills us with awe.

Or the mystery of darkness has another effect. It blinds the eyes to the fact of there being a mystery at all, but when light comes the mystery discloses itself.

To the ignorant and superficial the darkness is often so dense that they don't see even the fact of mysteries all about them moving in the darkness and taking obscure and shapeless forms. They only see what they think they see clearly and the rest they close their eyes to.

How many look up to the starlit heavens and they are in such darkness that they see no mystery at all. Others have looked up and felt the mystery of darkness that filled them with superstitious fear. But to the astronomer who knows the laws of those gigantic worlds as they swing along on their mighty course through the heavens, the whole is bathed in a far deeper mystery — the mystery of light.

So it is with everything—everything that can be seen at all with the eyes of the mind, everything that to the person who sees it is more than a dumb physical fact, passes with the deepening of knowledge from mystery to deeper mystery. It is good to remember this, because a great deal of the knowledge we gain seems to superficial people to make things clearer. To know that a great tree springs from a small seed only fills me with deeper wonder. To know—if it be true—that all life has been a development from a single cell is no explanation, it's a mystery clad in light. Gravitation, ether, all the deeper things of life become more mysterious in light than in darkness. The shallow things are capable only of the mystery of darkness; the charlatan, the trickster, the humbug wins his victories in the dark. The profounder things clothe themselves with light to disclose their full mysteriousness.

But every growth in knowledge of whatever kind is a constant passage from the mystery of darkness. And this is especially so with people. Everyone who will trace out the growth of a friendship or of a great love for another will recall days of darkness and days of light—times of misunderstanding and anxiety, when things were said and done that only so perplexed you and put you to suffering, and days when the whole personality seemed clothed with the light of self-revelation—passages from times of alienation to times of closer friendship. Yet they were both of them, as you see now, revelations of the person. The mystery of darkness and light, both of them mysteries and both helping you to a deeper knowledge of the mystery of personality.

THREE PARADOXES—III

And it must be even more with God. The law which we have been tracing finds in Him its consummation. He reveals Himself in the darkness and in the light. Clouds and darkness are round about Him, and He clothes Himself with light as with a garment. But be sure of it, we shall never know the Creator better than we know the created. The deeper our knowledge the deeper our wonder at the mystery of His Being.

Revelation is not an unveiling of God, but a changing of the veil that covers Him. Not the dissipation of mystery, but the transformation of the mystery of darkness into the mystery of light. Behind the veil of darkness God stood for ages before the world. There He was, men felt and knew His presence, but what manner of being He was they knew not. Clouds and darkness were round about Him. Then He came forth and revealed Himself—revealed His nature as the Trinity, but in that mystery of light the mystery grew deeper ; revealed His character in Jesus Christ who is the Brightness of the Father's Face, &c., but the mystery only grew deeper as it became more and more luminous.

And in His dealing with each one of us there is something corresponding to this. God reveals Himself sometimes by clothing Himself with darkness and sometimes with light.

And is it not true that when we pass into the dark our feeling is that God is not there—darkness in prayer, sacraments, in the struggle with temptation, darkness and solitude. What can we do but wait for the light. Spiritual writers tell us to hold on to our prayers and rules, &c., but is that all ? Can we do nothing but fight on in the dark till the light returns? Does it not change everything if we can realise that this darkness is itself a revelation of God? that it isn't a mere testing of the soul to see what it will do; but that it is a method of revealing Himself and teaching man something about Him that he could learn no other way than by passing from darkness to light.

1. I think it is. We measure God very often by human standards—how can we help it—I only know of love as human, justice, &c. And this is true as far as it goes, but not the whole truth. God's ways are not our ways. The elements that go to make up the idea of love exist alike, I suppose, in God and man. But there is this difference, human love is limited by its ignorance and its weakness. The love of one who sees the effect of temporal things upon eternal must be different from the love of one who can only judge by their immediate effects.

Is it not true? You pass into a time of spiritual darkness, clouds sweep across the clear vision of faith and obscure it. Every emotion is dredged out of faith. You have entreated God for something and He turns a deaf ear, you grope with outstretched hand and feeble steps along the way. You are left in blank and desolate solitude. You say: I would not treat a friend like this; God cannot love me. And then there gradually dawns upon the mind a new vision of yourself—you are unconsciously learning something. You are learning that the love of God is stronger, different from yours; it sees further, it will often withhold many things—good things—for your eternal welfare. If a temporal blessing be weighed against an eternal blessing the temporal will not be given. There dawns upon your soul the love that is strong enough to endure through misunderstanding and querulousness. Through all that time of darkness God is speaking, though for a long time you do not hear Him, for your ears are not attuned to a voice so superhumanly patient and tender; and afterwards, as the light breaks in upon your soul, you say: O Lord, Thou hast done well. Thou hast revealed Thyself in clouds and darkness and taught me what I would never have learnt in the light. 'Heaviness endures for the night, but joy cometh in the morning.'

2. There is yet another thing we have to learn from the gradual revelation of God, and that is holiness. We have never seen it untarnished, our nature is vulgarised by sin. The better we become the more deeply we are conscious of the ramifications of sin. It has spread as a subtle poison through our whole being. None were more conscious of their sinfulness than the Saints. The whole modern tone about God's holiness is shallow and sentimental. How shall we ever learn to realise it as it is revealed. We sometimes think we can only see it as God reveals it to us. But if He did, if He let its light shine down piercing and scorching upon you, you could not stand it. No, it needs a preparation, and I think it is undoubtedly true that the chief way we learn it is in darkness rather than light. The light blinds us, the darkness prepares us and helps us to understand it. For the hindrance to the knowledge of holiness is sin; only as we ourselves become purified can we in any way realise the holiness of God. Now it is under the same condition that

we learn sin and holiness :—temptation. A man plunged into the darkness of temptation realises his own sinfulness and something of God's holiness. Buffeted and tormented by temptation we become conscious of our own terrible weakness and we long, as never before, for purity. It reveals what sin is, and spiritual contrasts stand out in relief. You were fairly satisfied with yourself, you had no idea of the capacity for evil within you till you were swept into the dark tornado of sin. Why were you ever allowed to be so tempted ? Why when you cried out for deliverance did not deliverance come ? Because you were passing through the conditions necessary for a great revelation. Perhaps there was something you could only learn by failure under temptation. Your pride and self-reliance needed to be broken, and as you lay in the dust for the first time you realised something of God's holiness and looked up to Him who dwelleth in the Heavens.

So, my Brethren, we pass constantly from light to darkness and from darkness to a clearer light. The evening and morning make the day. The revelation of darkness and light lead us onward to the sabbath of our eternal rest in the endless sunshine of eternity.

PERSONALITY

THE chief discipline of our character, that which has the power of making or marring our life, lies in our relationship with others.

(*a*) Those who have to do with a great many people show at once a difference in their whole bearing and character from those who live more or less alone. People affect us more deeply than all the things in the world.

(*b*) We may ignore things, we can't ignore people. We may not notice many things around us. You may be absorbed in thought and not notice a thing in the room; but you can't ignore the presence of another human being. You may enjoy the silence and quiet of your room, a perfect stranger enters and you feel at once a difference—a disturbing element has entered, whether pleasant or unpleasant, your silent thought is disquieted, currents begin to pass from the person to you which challenge you. They call out feelings and questionings. I think you'd feel it if you were blind and deaf. Everyone we come in contact with, if only a fellow-traveller in the train, has this curious power of awakening our consciousness of his presence and disturbing our calm. God brought to Adam the animals, &c., but they were not his helpmates, a great part of his nature remained dormant or untouched. It needed a fellow-creature, another human being, Eve, to arouse his whole nature and to move it to its depths.

(c) And people can do this. Things may and do help to develop the intellect, to awaken the imagination, to arouse the æsthetic sense. But persons appeal to the whole person, and can in a short time draw out capacities and characteristics you never knew or dreamed of. There's nothing in the world that can call out love or hate, sympathy or antagonism, joy or sorrow, as a person. You may be able to bear with exemplary patience many of the trials that come to you through circumstances, loss of money, health, position; and while in all these cases you are almost heroic, you may find it impossible to keep patience with some personal characteristic of one who lives with you and who, you know, loves you. You will never feel as angry with the opposition of all the circumstances of life as with a person. Everything is against you, and you bear it well; one person enters into these opposing circumstances and criticises you or is unjust to you, and you are filled with bitterness.

It is a person that can draw out all that's best and noblest and all that's basest and most ignoble in others. Many a woman has been guilty of viciousness towards a rival, or one of whom she was jealous, of which she ought to be ashamed. And what is more beautiful than the unselfish devotion and sacrifice which many a person that seemed silly and empty has shown to husband or child that nothing else could call out?

A human voice can set all one's nerves on edge, or soothe us as nothing else can. And the meanest can be led for a moment to feel and say noble things, and sometimes the noblest to do ignoble things by a fellow creature. A person can in a moment ransack the soul of another and bring to light lurking faults or unknown virtues as nothing else can. One who has borne well a heavy cross, has found an unknown depth of bitterness brought out by the unkindness or neglect of another that poisoned all the springs of life.

(*d*) There are people who have never had a chance of bringing out the treasures of a rich and sympathetic nature, because they have been always crushed by the presence of another who cowed and frightened them and made them shrink within themselves. There are streams of sympathy that have been clogged or frozen in an atmosphere of criticism or narrow intolerance. There are women who have thus been made weak and characterless, and men who have been driven to other women for the sympathy they should have had at home, but which was refused them.

(*e*) Again, you can do with *things* pretty much as you please without much effect upon yourself. You can carve a stone into a statue or a door-step —you can bend or break a sapling—but you can't bend or shape personality as you will, or injure or develop it without leaving the marks deep upon yourself. When you come in contact with men or women the strongest will is often baffled, God Himself has set human personality as a limit to His own omnipotence.

For a person who has always had her own way, who swept out of her path everything that obstructed it, to find herself brought in contact with a human will she can neither bend nor break but only win, is to find herself in a situation in which she has to restrain herself and set herself to develop other moral qualities perhaps never used before. She learns that there are things in life which will not yield to force, and that victory can only be won by gentleness and sympathy and love, and she must stoop to conquer.

(People draw out our pride and humility—duty to equals.

Persons and subconsciousness.

Three roots of charity—pure heart—good conscience—faith unfeigned.

Charity and likes and dislikes. Friendship with those who have violated social laws—cutting.

Charity superficial.) [1]

[1] Unfinished.

INTRODUCTION TO A RETREAT FOR PERSONS LIVING IN THE WORLD

WE are all apt to feel that the difficulties of our own lives are especially great—how gladly I would change places with you. We feel the difficulties of our own character and our own position, we don't feel those of others.

There are those whose lives are crowded from morning till night. The world rushes in upon one person almost before he leaves his room, and one thing treads upon the heels of another all day long.

Another has too much time. Nothing that is really necessary to do from morning till night. One lives in the midst of a large family and a wide circle of friends, the other almost alone.

There are advantages, great advantages, in a full life. Widening of interests, enlarging of sympathies, testing one's own by others' experiences.

Advantages also in a life lived in comparative solitude with plenty of time, self-culture, prayer, &c. But there are also disadvantages in both.

Disadvantages in a full social life. The danger of being swamped, of neglect of oneself, all the doors of one's nature thrown open to everyone, never drawing the line between duty and fussy self-importance.

Disadvantages in a solitary life. The danger of

becoming eccentric, self-absorbed, brooding, exaggerating the importance of the few things that enter in and lay their hold upon it, clinging to the one or two friends it has with a fierce tenacity and becoming morbid. Social schism.

And is it not often true that the very busy person is always talking about the longing for time to pray, &c., and the person who has plenty of time to pray doesn't say so much about prayer nor pray as much as he or she might? We all imagine that we would be different if only we had the opportunity.

(a) Here let me notice that there is a way of talking about the will of God which is a kind of fatalism. People accept situations as the will of God which He never intends. God expects and demands our co-operation even in the arranging of our lives. It is possible, it may be very probable that you are where God means you to be, and are doing what God wills you to do; but it is not necessarily so. Moses was brought up in Pharaoh's palace. The rich man is given his riches. 'Why cry ye unto Me—speak unto the Children of Israel that they go forward.' The Lord ordereth a good man's goings. If you are where God means you to be, be sure all can co-operate for good—but don't put down the difficulties you bring upon yourself as God's doing. You should make an effort to get out of them if your difficulties are too great for you; if you can't, then accept them as the will of God for you, at any rate for the time.

(b) And again about ourselves. There are some people that take a kind of fierce delight in heaping contempt and abuse upon themselves, they call themselves bad names and delight in putting down everything to their own miserable selves:—what can you expect of such a miserable person as I am? I think they are sincere, but this state of mind is very often a subtle pride—it engenders and defends their sloth, and they are very sensitive if anyone else tells them that what they say is true. There is a certain inhuman pleasure but no possible advantage in degrading yourself in your own eyes. There are two attitudes of man before God in Holy Scripture; one prostrate and the other where the command comes, 'stand upon thy feet and I will speak unto thee.' One which speaks of man's dignity, the other of his nothingness. Whatever I am I am God's creature, made in His likeness. When Ezekiel was bid to stand upon his feet, was it not a declaration of the truth that man might lose the words of God because of a low and grovelling estimate of himself as well as because of a conceited one? We are often told of the pride of self-esteem, but there is the other truth, unless you honour your life you cannot get God's best and fullest wisdom. It is not nice to hear a conceited, blatant man boasting vulgarly of what he can do, hating to feel the need of help from God or man; but it is almost less nice to hear a man spluttering about his feebleness as he grovels on the earth. The latest and favourite philosophy of to-day is that which under the name of Pessimism declares deliberately that human life is a woe and a curse, and that the will to live is the fiend which persecutes humanity. And either in the soft way of sentimental whimperings, or in the hard way of hard, rude defiance, men are saying that life is miserable and that they are worms. Man is on his face. It seems to me he must hear

God's Voice—' Son of man, stand upon thy feet and I will speak unto thee.'

Now wherever you are and whatever your circumstances everyone has an inner life and an outer. Behind all nature there is the hidden life of thought. Nature is the clothing of the Will of God. So in a country institutions represent ideas—a revolution is first a conflict of ideas, these institutions fall and new arise. So with man; he stands between two worlds, the world of nature and of spirit.

We live among things we touch and taste and see, the body is in contact with the solid earth, but that is not all; there is the life of the soul. It mingles with all these—lives amongst them, is affected by and affects them.

The outer life has its value as the discipline of the inner life; that is all its real value. Not the things which go into a man, but the things which come out of him defile a man. Two people draw from the same things, one good the other bad. We can't neglect the outer life, if we do the body cries out by its demands and recalls us. But the demands of the inner life are not so pressingly felt, and we can if we please ignore them; but if ignored the inner life takes things into its own hands.

The life of the body is under law—we have to feed and sleep, &c.; if we violate any of these the result is physical pain. Many of them we can't break, they aren't under the control of the will. But the laws of the inner life all depend upon the will, yet they are just as stringent and if violated bring their vengeance; their laws, subtle and inevitable, work with the most accurate precision. The ablest mind unless controlled by will may become delusive, fantastic, enfeebled. The inner life is a life of thought drawn from external things whether of Heaven or earth, built up by reason, imagination, memory.

Now as in nature there comes first the mind and thought of God, then its form in outer things; as in a country first ideas then institutions which are their outcome; so in the ordering of the life of man the inner life should always take the lead. Living in the same set of circumstances, doing day by day the same deeds, we can rise to Heaven or sink to Hell, merely by the motive and inspiration of the inner life. In proportion as the inner life rules, due order is preserved and character developed on the right lines. This inner life is twofold.

1. Of the mind. Getting to see deeper into the meaning of things, but judging by experience not by theory, getting to know what is good for us and what is bad.

2. Of the will. The power of choosing.

But on the other hand there are two alternatives if the inner life is not ruling.

(a) Separation between the two lives, and an inner life of unreal dreams and the outer less and less connected with it.

(b) Outer life ruling, and the man drifting along while the inner life becomes one of shifting and compromise.

Therefore we come into Retreat to examine where we may have failed and to set things right.

1. We get entangled in our surroundings and don't see the line of demarcation between inner and outer.

2. Habits grow rapidly.

Examine your temper of mind.

(*a*) Is God gaining more or less power over your soul? Do you feel more or less need of prayer, &c.

(*b*) Are your outer or inner wants more on the increase?

(*c*) Do you find that the inner and outer are more closely bound together, or getting more apart?

New beginnings. All nature renews itself yearly.

1. The possibility of a new beginning.
2. Something definite to do.
3. Our Lord the Healer.

INTRODUCTION TO A RETREAT FOR A RELIGIOUS ORDER

A LIFE full of activities has its advantages; it tends to develop many interests, to fill the mind and distract it from itself, to broaden it and widen it on many sides, to round off its proportions, and to bring it amongst different kinds of people, which opens sympathy in many directions and helps people to test their own experiences by others, and in a measure to be humble. A life lived alone tends to become eccentric, to exaggerate the importance of the few things that enter it and lay their hold upon it—it loses all sense of proportion. It will cling to the one or two friends it has with a fierce tenacity and become morbid. Social schism is not unlike ecclesiastical schism—a religious community shut off from the religious world becomes narrow, exaggerated, fantastic. There are dangers in a life that is very full, but there are great advantages. Now these advantages are abandoned in the religious life. The surrender of oneself to the religious life is a risking of all in the belief that God has called you, and that He will make up to you for everything that you have abandoned for Him. It is in reality in no sense like that social schism in which one cuts oneself off or allows oneself to be cut off from one's fellow-creatures, but on the contrary a surrender of all those joys and helps to give the world a blessing and to get all the advantages and more in God Himself. In a life in the world men find God in their work and through creatures. In religion one makes direct for God Himself. In proportion as one fails to do this we see at once the same kind of narrowness and eccentricity as we see in those who cut themselves off from their fellow-creatures. The little things, the few people become of exaggerated importance. The love that might spread over a number becomes concentrated in one or two. A little slight or neglect from a superior becomes a heart-breaking trial enfolding one like a dark cloud. All the disadvantages of a narrowed life display themselves in exaggerated forms. The give and take of a full and active life is lost, the rubbing off of corners by contact with others, the distractions that keep the mind from morbid concentration—all these are lost. (A great block of stone rests upon the earth in many points, the sphere rests in one, but the whole weight presses on that one point.) These are the dangers of the religious life. I suppose most have to face them and fight them. The one thing that protects and gives far greater advantages, breadth and largeness of sympathy, is the effort to live true to the Religious vocation, which is the centring of the soul upon the Person of Christ; bringing the small things of one's surroundings into the infinite light of God's Presence; seeing the little things, the little crosses, the details of Rule, &c., not as so many details but in their relation to the Eternal.

Thus God is the Alpha and Omega, the centre of the soul's life for whom it has sacrificed all.

But when anyone has centred their whole existence

upon any one object, the failure or success of that object becomes the source of all its trials, sorrows and joys. A man concentrates all his energies on business, political success, &c., that frees him from a hundred worries, but this single object gathers into itself all the power he has in life of pleasure or pain. The things that amuse others don't amuse him, what pains others is powerless to give pain to him. The one thing becomes everything—it frees him from other cares, it becomes the source of all his cares. And this is infinitely more true if the object of his life is a person. A person can give to another more pain and more pleasure than the whole world put together. One friend dedicates her life to care for another; a smile, a kindly word, responsiveness and sympathy is the source of all her happiness, and the lack of it the keenest misery. A doubt as to whether her love is returned is Hell, a certainty that it is, Heaven.

And it is the same with God. The source of suffering and of joy to the Religious, in proportion as she is true, is God. God can make her suffer as none else can, and He can make her rejoice with joy unspeakable.

(*a*) But there is this difference between the relations with God and with a fellow-creature. We can see our friend, we can watch his face, hear the tones of the voice, draw conclusions from a hundred sources besides his actions—the act may seem unkind, but the look, the voice shows us that he is kind.

(*b*) Again, the human being can understand the motives and objects of another pretty well, he can gauge them by his own; but God's ways are not our ways, &c. God's dealings with us puzzle us, His love is wiser than human love and acts in a way that cannot be measured by the love of a creature. It is a training, a disciplining love, its object is to purge the heart and to fit it for the love of the infinite. It is based upon and altogether dependent upon a blind trust and confidence in Him. We do not understand what He means. His voice is often indistinct. With the best desire to please Him we often do not understand what He is saying, and with the best intentions make blunders and mistakes.

And this especially in the beginning, when we are getting to know Him and judging, as all must at first, His character by His actions. Later on, we judge His actions by His character. We know Him and can say, 'Though He slay me yet will I trust Him.' But that is only as the soul progresses.

Consequently the Religious whose life is cut off from the healthy and manifold discipline and occupations of a full and arduous life and all concentrated on its relations to one Person, finds that her relations with God and God's dealings with her become the absorbing interest of her life, the source of all her trials, sufferings, joys and hopes. If she knows that she is pleasing God she is happy; if not, she is miserable. If she feels God's love, all she has given up seems nothing; if she does not, she asks: was what I have gained worth the sacrifice? There must therefore be to the devout Religious dark days of misery and anguish of heart, of bitter solitude and harrowing doubts. She has given up everything for God, stripped her life bare, and God does not seem to accept her. And other days of exultation and expansion of soul when she feels it was worth all her sacrifices, and more if she could make them, to gain this glimpse and foretaste of Heaven. In fact her relations with God have become her purgatory. The life is concentrated, narrowed if you like, upon one point, and yet at the same time with all this inner tumult of the soul there is the daily routine to be gone through, the monotonous round of prayer and work and recreation and intercourse with the few others out of all the world who have become her world. If she could break out and get relief in something which could absorb her, if she could meet some new people, amuse herself, distract herself for a moment, she might forget her fears and hopes and anxiety; but she looks round, the convent walls are high, and her vows are even more formidable barriers, there she is locked up with those few people till death relieves her. Is it to be wondered that there are moments of revolt and repugnance that seem beyond endurance, when every voice jars and every duty becomes intolerable, and the world outside calls with alluring voice and says: you have made a great mistake. Yet it is good at such times to remember three things.

1. Remember past moments of insight, when you knew and felt the nearness of God and had a certainty that was founded upon your experience.

2. Remember that cry of the perfect Man in the moment of His consummated sacrifice, when He was doing the greatest work for God that ever had been done. 'My God, my God,' &c. It seems therefore that human nature cannot enter into perfect union with God without such times of anguish. Love has

to be tested on the basis of trust: 'Though He slay me, yet will I trust Him.'

3. The deepest love may not have any conscious element of emotion, it rests in the will. Emotion belongs to the earliest stages of love, but as love grows deeper it penetrates to the centre of personality, which is the will.

In such a life therefore among the most difficult things to face are those times when God is silent. We often think of the different tones which may belong to the same words. We don't think so often of the way silence may be understood. A man stands silent in my presence and I ask what does he mean, why doesn't he speak? Silence is as various as speech. Silence is what the silent man is. A silence of concealment and one of completer revelation than speech. Silence of condemnation and of praise. The completest joy and sorrow are silent. Silence of snow. The silence of the snake in the grass, of the cattle, of the regiment preparing for a charge.

1. Apparent silence. We want some special thing; we need other things we do not know, more. God is supplying them but we do not know it, for we don't know our need. The soul does not dream what God is doing, blessings come into it of which it is quite unconscious; later it recognises the need in the supply. Children come to know their parents' care while they are asking for something else.

2. Not answered because we can do the things for ourselves. You ask Him to show you what your sorrow means—to show you in a flash what He wants you to do.

THE MANGER AND THE CROSS.
I. ST. STEPHEN

'Let this mind be in you.'—PHILIPPIANS ii. 5.

THE feast of Epiphany is the completing of the Christmas Festival. The recording of that fact to the world outside. Now the Festival of Christmas stands alone in this. It is surrounded by three other Feasts. The day after Christmas we find our thoughts turned away from the Manger.

It is not so with Easter or Pentecost. The whole octave is given to each. We are bid to dwell upon the great mystery for eight days. Even so with Epiphany.

But no sooner do we commemorate the Birth of Our Lord than our minds are driven off to think of St. Stephen, St. John, and the Holy Innocents.

Christmas Day is the beginning of the Life of Him who came to change men's whole idea of life; to bring in those ideas and principles which, however some like to dwell upon their failure, have still such powers.

The Birth of Christ is the birth of a new religion, a new idea of God, of life, of man, and of the world in which we live. What we have to get at is to keep before us the mind of Christ.

No sooner have we dwelt in humble devotion upon the Birth of Christ than we are hurried on to get renewed the impression of His mind.

There are three feasts around the Cradle of Bethlehem. There is the Birth of Christ and Christianity, and here is what it means and involves. This is the mind of Christ caught afresh and aflame and put into practice—childhood, youth, old age, suffering in His cause, laying down their life for Him. Blood streams forth around the Cradle at Bethlehem; the blood of innocent infants, of a young man in his prime. The life of an old man who couldn't shed his blood but could live on a sacrifice and witness to the end.

Christianity has now developed and spread over the world and brought its own civilisation and impregnated the world with some of its principles. But it is always hostile to the lower tendencies of human life in ourselves and in organised society. There is an element in it that may at any moment spring to the front and bid us face opposition—stand alone—make great sacrifices in its cause. To be swamped in the ordinary tendencies of our own nature and of life is the constant danger.

The Christian religion has always been at its best when it is surrounded by antagonism and persecution. When at any time that passes away and things settle down the spirit of worldliness may enter into it corporately and individually, and that is its emasculation. There is something so grand and great about the Church that we can't but feel proud of it—its great history, its marvellous organisation, its solemn ritual. Many a person takes this for the spirit of the true Catholic; it isn't. The true spirit is the mind of Christ and that is the martyr spirit, the readiness to make sacrifices when called for.

So St. Stephen stands guard over the Cradle. St.

John, worn out with sacrifice and suffering in the cause of Christ. The mothers with their slaughtered children. Think of Stephen with his great popular and personal gifts, who in a few moments made a name that has lasted for 2,000 years. How little we know of him and how much. Was there ever so beautiful a death? The young man with an angel's face surrounded, hooted down, done to death, by an infuriated mob. The stones flying and crushing the life out of him, bruised and wounded beyond recognition, dying in slow agony.

What beauty is there in it? Only his courage and his love.

This is the Epiphany. The manifestation of the mind of Christ. The candle of Christ's life set in the candlestick of a faithful servant to give light to the whole house of the Church.

II. ST. JOHN

'If I will that he tarry till I come, what is that to thee?'
ST. JOHN xxi. 22.

LAST Sunday we considered the first of those three Feasts which stand round the cradle of Bethlehem revealing and protecting the religion of Christ in its infancy. It was not a religion to be sentimental over because of the beauty of its ideals, nor to be emasculated of its sternness in a self-indulgent age. St. Stephen grasps its fundamental idea. The religion of the Manger and the Cross has great things to give, but the best is only given to those who are ready to make sacrifices in proportion to what they want to get. St. John wants the very best and he is prepared without a harsh word or thought to give his life. Next to Christ he is the first of His followers to transform a scene of revolting cruelty into one of beauty by his love. He is the candlestick in which the light of the Epiphany is placed to give light to the whole house.

But, brethren, if the pathos and romance of that scene springs largely from the attractiveness of his personality and the strength of his faith to die for an untried cause, it has the added beauty of youth. A young man who was ready to let his life be cut short in the noonday of his powers.

Yes, there is the beauty of youth; but there is

THE MANGER AND THE CROSS

also, if there is the beauty, there is the daring of youth. You can do many things before mid-life settles down upon you that are harder to do after—sometimes perhaps impossible. Nature endows youth with the gifts that enable it to meet the difficulties of a new person in a world beset with difficulties.

What of middle life ; what of old age ? Many a person doesn't awaken to the real responsibilities of life till youth is passed, with its dauntless courage, its glorious belief in its powers of doing what others have failed to do. What has the Manger, the Infant Saviour to tell us about that. First comes Stephen the young man, first in the natural and moral order. But next comes extreme old age, the withered and shrunken form of an old man weighted with years, suffering and disappointment. John too had been with Christ in his youth. He had heard His words, drunk deeply of His doctrine and built his hopes as he had given up his life to spreading the Faith that he believed. He had seen the invincible power that was in his Master pass on into His disciples. He had felt it like the breath of spring flow into his veins at Pentecost, filling him with His spirit and uplifting him with its unfailing energy. And he had, as everyone must have had, his hopes for the world when men should understand its meaning and believe. What a world it would be, when the kingdoms of this world should have become the Kingdom of God. A renewed, re-invigorated humanity held in the bond of a loving brotherhood of men, when the grosser forms of evil would have passed away. The wise men from the East were the first fruits of that general coming of the nations to the footstool of Christ. And then he saw what happened. A deadly and irreconcilable opposition; all the brutal force of the heathen world arrayed against them. One after another brought into the arena and slaughtered. That Kingdom from which he had expected so much having to all appearances the life crushed out of it. And just as he remembered the life of the Baptist bartered to a dancing girl, so the best of the Christian community was sacrificed to the lowest passions of greed, jealousy, &c., and he himself living on while the years passed to see, as it seemed, the wreck of all his hopes. And still he lived on. What was the use of a life so old and worn past the power of working or helping anyone? And we are told he used in his extreme old age to be carried into the Church amidst the younger generations—this old man who had seen Christ and leant upon His bosom, the friend of Peter, the guardian of Mary—and stretch his hands over them and say, 'Little children, love one another.' Why did he linger on? He had faced death at Rome years ago, but had come forth from the boiling oil with renewed youth; was it true indeed that the saying of the disciples was to be verified that he should never die?

And then the surviving Apostle did what no other living man could have done. He took up his pen and with all the wisdom and experience of that long life, he wrote the Christian Gospel. *The* great work of his life was done when he was long past the years of most men. The Son of Thunder had not let his spiritual energy die out; it was all there, and with a Voice of Thunder he uttered to the world what he had seen and heard.

III. THE HOLY INNOCENTS.

'In Rama was there a voice heard, lamentation, and weeping, and great mourning, Rachel weeping for her children, and would not be comforted, because they are not.'—St. Matthew ii. 18.

St. Stephen in his strong young hands holds up the light of Christian life as he saw it, and shows us the sacrifices it demands. St. John in his trembling hands holds up the light of a life lived out to the last dregs in Christ's service, and kept in all its powers so as to do the best of all in extreme old age.

But to-day there stand around the crib a crowd of weeping women with bared breasts and empty hands, whose children have been torn from them and slaughtered before their eyes. Rachel weeping for her children who will not be comforted. For that Infant in the crib has been born in a welter of blood, and Mary bending over Him knows that these mothers' children have been slaughtered that her child might escape. The Angels sang 'on earth peace'—these poor women cry: He has not come to send peace but the sword. These are the first to feel that the coming of Christ upon earth means the rising of the powers of the world against Him.

St. Stephen offered his own youth to die in the service of one whom he loved. St. John did the harder task of living on for Him in the midst of fading hopes and disappointments. We reverence and honour them as martyrs, the one in deed, the other in will. They had the power of doing with their lives what they pleased and they did the very best, without a murmur or word of complaint. But there are cries of indignation and protest from the lips of these women. They did not offer their children. The children were snatched from their breasts. They fought for them, they cried to Heaven against their fate. They gave their children because they could no longer keep them. What can they witness, what light from the Incarnation do they throw upon the world? What was the cause of their sufferings? It was the savage jealousy of a cruel and godless profligate awakened by the Birth of the Child of Bethlehem. It was the murder of a multitude of innocent infants, the anguish of mothers made childless by a cruel monster who for the moment held power in his hands.

These desolate women with the mangled and bleeding remains of their children gather around the Manger. What light does this show?

It shows this, that a great deal of the meaningless suffering on earth may have a meaning which we can't see at the time.

The suffering of the innocent—of innocent children, their suffering through others' sins—the vice and neglect of parents, or of self-indulgent people—children brought into the world as the mere result of indulged passion to live with a stigma on their names; all this Our Lord gathers round Himself and makes them hallowed. We could never have guessed that the innocent sufferers for others' brutal sins could be looked upon as the sweet flower of martyrdom. Yet the Holy Innocents were the first martyrs for Christ.

The trivial and worthless enemies that triumph and seem to defeat God's purpose. (Herod and a dancing girl.) But they work good instead of evil.

So Herod tried to trample the life out of the King of the Jews. These mothers knew nothing about it, the infants had no knowledge, yet these women were the proud mothers of the first martyrs for the Incarnation.

THE TEMPTATIONS OF OUR LORD

I

'Man shall not live by bread alone, but by every word that proceedeth out of the mouth of God.'—ST. MATTHEW iv. 4.

THE need of bread, which has had such a power over men, leading them to violate duty and commit crimes, which has been such a force working for their development, Our Lord is feeling. This need is one of the primary forces that control men's lives.

He was hungry after the forty days of fast and strenuous conflict. That was one thing.

Another thing. He was God the Creator. He could turn stones into bread or create it out of nothing.

The human nature was faint with hunger. He could by His Divine power feed it in a moment. But in doing so He would have broken with the conditions and limitations of our humanity. It was an essential part of the Divine plan of the Incarnation that He was to live under those conditions. Would He when the pangs of hunger were upon Him still abide by them? Would He obey the deep wants of His lower nature, or sacrifice them to the higher claims of His mission? He couldn't do both. He must choose and do one or the other. Here are the essential elements of moral trial in their most elemental and violent form. The conflict between desire and law. Those desires were perfectly harmless in themselves.

Our Lord could have no temptation to do anything against the moral law, but being human He could feel hunger, and He could feel the barrier of law opposing its gratification.

It is essentially the first and most elemental temptation of every man. My lower nature wants what my higher nature forbids, wants to the very verge of dying for need of it, and can secure it without any trouble.

Which will He do? If He turns the stones into bread we can only say that if He couldn't get on without bread at any cost neither can we. If He can't keep the conditions of our humanity under the pressure of bodily hunger, we may be pardoned if we too sacrifice higher obligations to the paramount claims of our lower necessities.

1. The devil said, 'If Thou be the Son of God.' Our Lord's answer ignored the taunt, the implied disbelief in His Divine Sonship. He said: man shall not live by bread alone. I am not living here and now as God but as man. I am under the conditions of human life when I must sacrifice the lower to the higher or the higher to the lower, and I don't hesitate. He asserted that there are higher needs than can be satisfied by food, money, raiment, any external thing, and that he who sacrifices those higher interests for these will not be satisfied. It was the clear assertion that man is more than an animal with his animal wants, that he is an idealist and is haunted and tormented by these unsatisfied ideals.

2. He said more. It is written—written in the history of human life—in the history of those who sacrifice their faith for place and power, their religious obligations for passion or earthly affection. For the

moment the hunger is satisfied, only to feel the pangs in the other nature that is starving. It's written in the history of those men all the world over who do not hesitate when some great national crisis comes to sacrifice home for country, when a personal crisis comes, to sacrifice comfort for duty. Happier is the man who spends his life in the quest of truth, than one who settles down satisfied without it. Happier he who spends his life struggling against passion than he who gives up the fight for higher things and accepts the lower.

3. This is what Our Lord asserts for man. It is the assertion of his dignity, his true nature. It is a protest against the baser pessimism that makes the worst of human life. Say what you like, Our Lord seems to say, those who live for bread alone do but half live, and the other half cries out in revenge.

It's impossible to go through life without having times when the question is put, not in words but acts, and you have to make your choice—the idea of fasting is meant to train people in this, to be ready to give up the lower for the higher.

This is the first temptation. Just at the outset of life we are led into some solitude, where we realise our own individuality and the temptation is that of Christ, the assurance given in some form or other that bread is all man needs, that everything else is a delusion, that to live a life of physical and natural comfort is the only solid wish for a man's soul. A wrong business—abandonment of others for self—hiding convictions—the giving up of ambitions for comfort.

If He had yielded, the famished body had become vigorous, but the price was a heavy one.

THE TEMPTATIONS OF OUR LORD

II

'If Thou be the Son of God, cast Thyself down': etc.
St. Matthew iv. 6.

The first temptation is in the wilderness, the second is in the Temple. The first is the ordinary temptation that comes shrouded in whatever garments to every one of us, to sacrifice the higher nature to the lower.

That test is upon the broad basis of human nature, the fact of being a man exposes us to it.

The second temptation is in the Temple. It's the temptation that comes to people who are more or less religious. It comes within the Temple precincts, it has to do with a person who knows and cares about the influences of religion.

It would be strange if we had no temptation that came from the religious side. Temptation will come through anything that interests us, or which we believe to be a source of power.

Our Lord's first temptation came to Him as a man, the second as a man to whom religion was not merely an interest but a great interest, who knew its power and wanted other people to realise it.

In a moment the silence of the desert gave place to the centre of religious worship. The City of Zion the joy of the whole earth; that fair vision of gold and snow shining in the light of the eastern sun, with the crowd of worshippers gathered perhaps for the evening sacrifice, rose before the eyes of Christ.

Everything in that Temple was typical of Himself. It was His own design for leading the people on to recognise Him when He came. The smoke of the sacrifice ascended up. Upon the thirteen steps leading from the court of the people to the court of the priests stood the choir of priests singing the Psalms in alternate verses. Upon the great brazen altar under the open canopy of the Heavens the smoke of the sacrifices ascended and the great crowd were prostrate in worship.

Above them and unseen stood the two strangers. Him whom they all expected and that other who tried to impede and wreck His work. Messianic hopes were in the air, coming events had cast their shadows over the people, and there was expectation that the time of the coming of Christ was at hand. Down in the crowd were perhaps Zacharias and Elizabeth, Simeon and Anna; perhaps that young man prostrate on the earth is John, who soon will be an Apostle; hard by that older man with his deep devotion and enthusiasm is Peter the Rock upon whom the Church is to be built.

And the song of the priests ascends. 'Whoso dwelleth under the defence of the Most High shall abide under the shadow of the Almighty—He shall give His angels charge over thee,' &c. And in the ear of Jesus is whispered the voice of the Tempter. Cast Thyself down—Take them by storm—Come, as they pray on that He would rend the Heavens—Come as the Messias straight from Heaven and appeal to their imagination and win the whole nation in a moment—Escape the Cross and win the Crown of Thy mission—and have a crowd of wondering followers ready to accept Thee. And our Lord's answer again: it is written, it's an old saying and an old experience, 'Thou shalt not tempt the Lord thy God.' As a man I should have no right to cast myself down and to look for Divine protection—that's not what the prophet meant.

In the wilderness the Son of Man stands confronted by physical dangers, by peril to life from circumstances beyond His control as man. On the summit of the Temple He stands safe from physical danger, master of circumstances, secured by the promise of supernatural protection. In the former it was to save life, here to risk it. In the former to save life at the expense of the higher side, in this to risk life in assertion of supernatural protection. There it was: command the stones — thou canst not live; here: cast Thyself down—thou canst not die. In the wilderness the temptation was mainly of the flesh, in the Temple it was of the spirit.

Had he yielded, and if angel ministers had borne Him safely to the ground in the sight of all Jerusalem, what would this be but the very sign of the Son of Man in the Heavens which they were always asking. The nation would have crowned Him, His kingdom established in Judea. It was a temptation to the Prophet and patriot:—men who would not look up to His spiritual claim, had accepted Him if He had descended to their earthly hopes.

It is the temptation that assails those who have resisted the other. A temptation not to the flesh but to the spirit, to the high-minded. What thoroughly spiritual man has not had to fight it?

1. It is one that must always assault the Church, to tamper with her spiritual and doctrinal standards and come down for the sake of saving those who are alienated—to trim, not to stand so high and so solitary.

2. It attacks the young Catholic just realising or thinking that people look askance at his ideals.

THE TEMPTATIONS OF OUR LORD

III

'All these things will I give Thee, if Thou wilt fall down and worship me.'—St. Matthew iv. 9.

We have seen Satan approach our Lord in the first two temptations. The first an appeal made through the flesh. The second a very much deeper and more subtle temptation to change the plan of man's salvation, appealing to what is highest in man, his religion. Then the third, he taketh Him to an exceeding high mountain. Now this temptation has been considered in two ways. It has been noticed here he leaves off the supposition, 'If Thou be the Son of God.' He began, some think, to doubt that He was—He showed no sign of power, His resistance was not active, it was passive: I won't do anything you ask me, for everything you ask has some deep-seated principle opposed to the Word of God. He had twice refused to work miracles, and so the devil addresses Him as man: I see Thou art not what I thought Thee, but Thou art something—what a power there is in that strong Will of Thine, what great results might be effected with so firm and unwavering a resolution. Bodily weakness cannot tame Thy spirit, nor can the prospect of vast results lead Thee to flinch from Thy resolve. Thou art a man; I have seen men and I know what is in man. I stood by the side of every man who has ever gained influence amongst mankind, good and bad. I stood near the throne of Solomon and David and Saul. I sat in the councils of Nebuchadnezzar, and I watched by the heart of Daniel. I know the minds that are meant to sway the wills of men; I have tried Thee, and Thou art such an one. Now look—all this will I give Thee if Thou wilt fall down and worship me. He did not mean perhaps actual worship such as was given to God, but pay me homage. Take it as from me, owning Thyself under obligation to me. It was a temptation to gain power, to do good, to help others, to lift up mankind, at the expense of His own integrity. It is a temptation that comes to all great souls. They find their power, they see their influence, and the temptation comes to take it as a gift, instead of earning it. There are two ways of succeeding—one by the fascination of brilliant gifts, the other by struggle, contest and difficulty. How often a man has withstood the other two trials and failed under this. Who can bear success? Who can sit with steady eye upon the throne of power and influence? 'All these will I give thee.' The young man starts in his course with sound principles, religious purpose, &c., and money comes pouring in; all he puts his hand to succeeds, his life is a wonder of success; gradually his high principles flag, his love dims, his philanthropy is a cloak for selfishness. 'All these will I give thee'—nay, it is a lie—all these will I sell thee; and what is the price? fall down, down from thy high purpose.

So with Christ. Satan saw His greatness, His human greatness, and he offered that which his wise experience had taught him so often proved a successful remedy to devout purpose. Beware, my brethren, when kingdoms of the world are shown to you and offered you—from the young girl in the ball-room to the young politician stepping forth into a world of promise that seems to yield to his genius and great schemes. Beware of the price, beware when you remember the vendor of those goods—political, social, religious, literary, æsthetic, material, the manifold fields of human power, the many kingdoms of the world.

See, too, the value of one great soul as estimated by Satan. I will let you do good, I will help you, you will raise up, you will save many—I don't care about them so that I can injure you.

But there is another aspect of this temptation. We may take it as some do, that Satan did still fear that this was the Son of God.

He had appealed to Him through His bodily weakness, to abandon His Passion. He had appealed through His love for His people. He had quoted scripture, sought to deceive Him. Now he comes with his last final grand assault.

He stands before Him as the prince of this world, with his great false boast of power: I know Thee who Thou art and wherefore Thou art come. Thou art the seed of the woman, to bruise my head. Thou art the Lion of the tribe of Judah, Shiloh to whom the gathering of the nations shall be, who art to wash Thy garments in wine, Thy clothes in the blood of grapes. Thou art the star who is to come out of Jacob and the sceptre that is to rise out of Israel, who is to smite the borders of Moab and destroy all the children of Sheth. Thou art He who is to have dominion from one sea to another and from the flood unto the world's end. They that dwell in the wilderness are to kneel before Thee and Thine enemies to lick the dust; all kings are to fall down before Thee, &c.

Now see my power—all this is mine; and it was indeed seemingly true. He showed the vast sway of idolatry, the mighty fabrics of empires, the great political and religious systems; his face brightened, his eye glittered as with pride he pointed out one kingdom after another, and the rebel creature boasted of the gifts which he was using to overthrow his creator, and then he threw off his mask—all this will I give Thee if Thou wilt not rob me of it, but take it as a gift.

(Second Version)

'All these things will I give Thee, if Thou wilt fall down and worship me.'—St. Matthew iv. 9.

The second Temptation was on the pinnacle of the Temple, amidst the scenes and sights of religion. Our Lord saw the worshipping crowds, He knew their expectation of the sign in Heaven and that in a moment He might win them, not by a great moral victory, but by an appeal to their sense of wonder. Cast Thyself down and win them in a moment. It is the temptation to come down from one's solitude and ideals and to win people by an appeal to their superstitious awe, rather than through their highest religious sense.

The third temptation is on the mountain top, the Scripture image of world power and dominion. There stood the Prince of this world and He who came to deliver the world from his hands. The Tempter saw the power of his enemy, he saw that He could not be moved by the ordinary temptations by which he had seduced so many. He could not understand Him. He felt that He had some plan which he could not solve. Was this indeed the enemy he had always feared, who was to conquer him? The seed of the woman—the Lion of the tribe of Judah—foreshadowed by so many types, foretold by so many prophets, the Virgin's Son, the Messias for whom the people of

God were waiting. If so he knew that He was to conquer. There was in man, he knew, a side that had always puzzled him, an idealism that lived on in spite of age-long failure. Was this young Prophet, so calm and gentle, yet so dauntless—was He whom he saw was man to the heart's core, was He to deliver them by an appeal to that element in man's nature which he never could analyse or fathom?

Satan will risk everything, if only he can keep men from that which he fears. And so he brings up before the eyes of the Prophet a vision before which he had known the greatest to fail. He showed Him all the kingdoms of the world, all that great heathendom which girded like some great mountain range the Holy Land and overtopped and overshadowed the highest pinnacle of the house of the Lord. All these lay before Him, glittering in the golden light of its civilisation, stained deep indeed in its crime, but with many a splendid endowment and many a gracious gift. He, the tempter, was manipulating it all, working upon man's ignorance and man's weakness to carry out his own ends, to separate it all completely from God. He had led these people to set up a false worship. He had put his own plans in the place of God. He had got many a people, many a noble teacher to sacrifice the higher side for the lower, tampered with many a religion that had noble guesses at truth, to cast itself down, to win and to hold men by superstition. Well, he will risk all on one last throw of the dice.

All these will I give Thee if Thou wilt fall down and worship me. What did it mean? Not surely that this lofty teacher should worship the enemy of man-

THE TEMPTATIONS OF OUR LORD

kind. No, it was this; you have come to deliver these people from moral evil, to emancipate them from these degrading vices that stain their civilisation, these savage lusts that feed upon their vitals like a cancer. I am their destroyer. I have instigated them to every national and personal degradation. I will stop all this on one condition. Make one act of homage to the world spirit, incorporate that into your religion, and I will leave them. Let your religion recognise and accept the world spirit and all shall be Thine. In other words it was this: I do not know what your plan is, but I can see something of it in the way you have dealt with me, refusing to tamper with conscience or to recognise the lower side of human nature. Mingle with your plans a homage to the spirit of the world and I'll leave you.

The spirit of the world is neither diabolical nor divine, it is that of fallen humanity; it is respectable, it is decent, it isn't vicious, but it ignores the supernatural. Let it be a grand religion of humanity with all that's left of what is noble in it, and all removed that is degrading and positively vicious. Let it be the religion of fallen man without the distinctively supernatural and I withdraw. The world would indeed be a fair place; it would not be the enemy of God, its principles would keep men from falling into the mire, but it would not lift them above themselves.

This was the offer—this it was which hung in the scales on that exceeding high mountain when these two leaders stood and bargained for its future.

And this is surely the temptation of the hour. Satan uses the same language to the leaders and teachers of religious thought to-day. What are good men striving to do to-day but to eliminate from Christianity the supernatural side; to take from it those elements which keep and bring before mankind the gravity of sin, the need of redemption; to measure religion solely by experience, not by the highest ideals of the human heart, or its deepest, albeit at some times unrecognised, needs.

The new Theology, the advanced criticism that emasculates the Bible, the turning of earth with its faults and imperfections into Heaven.

THE TEMPTATIONS OF OUR LORD

IV

'If Thou be the Son of God come down from the Cross.'
ST. MATTHEW xxvii. 40.

THE three great temptations of our Lord—in the desert, in the Temple, on the mountain top—were secret. They were the testing before He began His work. So far no gracious word had been spoken in public, no Apostle had been called. His life had been lived with His Mother in the quiet round of the village of Nazareth.

There, before He went forth, He faced things—in His inner hidden life—in solitude. We see this in the temptations. He faced things as Man, as the Redeemer and Example of true manhood.

1. Would He try to escape the difficulties that might assail His Life itself; would He for a moment, for any ends, use means that men couldn't use to avoid difficulties: that was His first temptation.

2. Would He come down to men's expectations when He saw that they couldn't understand His lofty teaching?

3. Would He, when He saw failure staring Him in the face and the multitude turning away, make an alliance with the world, adopt worldly methods when He saw the religion He offered misunderstood, scorned?

And His answer to all these was—no.

But it's one thing to make resolutions, it's another to live them out in the drab colour of daily life. It's one thing to dream of spiritual success, it's another thing to keep it before you, when it seems to mean supreme failure—no fruits apparent from the work to which you have devoted your life.

The model in the solitude of the desert is little use to us, if He be not the model in the crush and pressure of active life. Our Lord came forth from the desert into the crowded streets of Jerusalem and the stagnant backwater of the villages of Galilee. He had to face life as it is.

And one thing stands out clearly upon the page of His public life, and that is failure. At first the crowds were taken by storm, His teaching went home to their needs. Then His miracles were taken amiss; the crowds ran gaping after them, excited by them, but they did not consider them as signs of His mission. Then He withdrew more and more from the public gaze; then the tide swept up against Him. Public opinion turned and He was arrested, tried, condemned by Jew and Gentile, and His death-warrant was signed and sealed.

What will He do now?

Behind the scenes He sees the great enemy who would have made a compact with Him, who has played upon men's passions and blinded their intellect. Through the cries and voices of the crowd the voice of the tempter of the desert came to His ears: come down from the Cross and we will believe— win them by astonishing them. What's the use of preaching what the world rejects? The lash of the

THE TEMPTATIONS OF OUR LORD

scourge, the mob dancing round Him, buffeting Him, spitting upon Him, came to Him like the voice upon the mountain top: this is the outcome of your teaching, they don't want it, they ridicule it. Had He surrendered—' Wist ye not that I could pray to My Father,' &c. Had He done it the history of Christendom would have been different. It would have taught man that religion was to save him from suffering and failure, not that he was to triumph through it. They are going to kill Jesus. It was the last desperate act of the Prince of this world. It was a hideous blunder on his part, a failure to realise methods wholly different from his own. He thought he could vanquish and have done with this Prophet who came to deliver men from his power. He would hound Him out of the world in a blinding storm of antagonism, scorn and contempt. Jesus died the scorn of men and outcast of the people. And within seven weeks His triumph began.

He teaches us that fidelity to God, to Truth, to the high standards that men scorn and reject is the course of real and lasting success. Not by condescending to lower the standards or stoop to men's apparent weaknesses, but by a high belief in their real possibilities we win them.

The Church's greatest triumphs are when she is hated of all men, the Christians' often when everyone turns upon them. The Saviours of the world have been those whom it has rejected.

You won't violate the limitations of the Incarnation; very well, you shall die.

You won't cast yourself down to the level of men; very well, they'll lift you up in scorn on the Cross.

You refuse to bend the knee to the spirit of the world; very well, the world will turn its back upon you, and show you it cares nothing for nor believes in your religion.

All that followed was the working out of the temptations in the wilderness into facts, the apparent triumph of the Tempter all along the line.

THE LIGHT OF THE WORLD

Man's mind has been always sensitive to the power and beauty of nature. He is moved and stirred by it in a strange and unaccountable way. The feeling is to most minds a distinctly religious one ; even when it is not formulated it calms and it awes and inspires and overwhelms. It is strange that it should be so. So much light and shade, so many lines and curves. Great masses of rock climbing up into the sky, or a quiet evening landscape with the slanting rays of the sun casting the shadows long and deep, and as we gaze and drink in the scene our hearts beat quick and the tears spring to the eyes. This religious feeling has formulated itself in pantheism, and the truth in pantheism lies in the Christian doctrine that all Creation is, as it were, the vestment of Our Lord. We are gazing upon a picture which clothes and reveals something of the mind of the artist.

But when we turn from nature to man who is thus moved by it our feelings change. Certainly no one can look deeply at the mystery of human life unmoved, but the emotions are very different from those aroused by nature. We know that he would be unworthy the name of man who would hesitate to sacrifice material things to save the poorest and most ignorant of the human race ; and yet man does not move us as nature does—more deeply no doubt, more passionately, but always morally, with moral approbation and reverence or with moral disappointment. We never really in our hearts can separate off any department of human life and judge it alone. The greatest intellect, the greatest force will always be affected by the moral character of the person who uses it. The longer we live the deeper the conviction grows upon us that it is not the gifts, but the man who wields the gifts that has weight, and therefore the study of man is always disappointing, always surprising. Men have not the weight they ought to have in the world of art, letters, politics, religion, business, because they are not themselves all they might be. This shrewd business man lives upon his wits and cleverness, but he doesn't make the way in life he might because of his moral character. Now why is this, brethren? Why is it that try as we may we never can value a man merely by his powers but by his moral character?

It is because man is made in God's image. To be a true man therefore he must be Godlike. Let him ignore God, give up all effort to be Godlike and he fails, and men feel though they may not understand the reason of his failure. Like some splendid horse made for service he can never be used because of some vicious habit.

God made man with an extraordinary power of resembling Himself. He is but a speck upon the universe, God is infinite and man is finite, but as a light from the spark is essentially the same as the light from the sun, so is holiness and morality essentially the same for God and man. The lower forms of creation cannot choose but tell of God what He has given them to say—the mighty mountains, the heaving ocean, the wayside flower. But man can choose. He can show forth something of the character of God, or he can refuse to. This is the meaning of man's life, this is what he was made for. He is a lamp that can be kindled by the fire of God's Being and reveal Him, and as the fire glorifies the lamp, the lamp reveals the fire. Without this fire of God man is incomplete, like an unlit candle; we feel somehow that he might be more than he is, that he has failed though we may not understand the reason.

Man stands thus between a world in darkness and God who is light, that lighted by the fire of God he may show Him to the world. As we look back through the past we are struck by this fact; every ray of Heavenly light that God ever gave to man, He gave not directly but through other men. Watch through the history of Israel the growth in the knowledge of God and of truth and you will find it has been always the same. God gave the light to Israel through some great Israelite if there were any time of special darkness or of national apostasy. God takes one man, fills him with the knowledge He would give, sets his soul on fire and puts him in the darkening Temple of His people to pour out the light, and in His people we always find that mysterious quality in response, the power of being ignited. In the darkness of Egypt he led Moses apart into the solitude of Midian and set his heart on fire and sent him to his people. In the widespread apostasy after the settlement in Palestine He sent Samuel. In the dark days of Ahab, Elias. In the hopeless darkness of Babylon, Daniel. There they stand in the great halls of that ancient people, a splendid row of lamps pouring out their light and illuminating and igniting the chilled and darkening souls of His people.

Now what God did to Israel in the past was a type of the great illumination which He gave to the world in Christ. In those other cases God kindled His Divine fire in the hearts of individual men and through them He illuminated His people. Such kindlings were premonitions of what human nature was capable of, that it was capable of a mysterious union with God, of being made an instrument through which God could be revealed. His holiness and wisdom were felt; in the Incarnation this was seen in its fullness. There God set human nature on fire with His Godhead, ' to be a light to them that sit in darkness,' &c. Men saw what manner of Being God was and what they were capable of. That union like a lighted lamp revealed the light and revealed and glorified the lamp. What men needed was to know God, to know what manner of Being He was, and they saw the glory of the only Begotten in the face of Christ.

And what He was, we in our measure are to be. He was the light and we are to be the light of the world. We may be very small and feeble creatures, but as men we are the candles of God made to be ignited and give light and to set others on fire. It is to us God looks to remove false conceptions about Him and to show men the true meaning of life. Around that sacred name false ideas and bad traditions constantly gather. Men form their ideas as to how God ought to deal with them, and if He does otherwise they say He does not love. And as man is, so is his idea of God, as the image of God is obscured or marred in them so they form false ideas of Him. For the idea of man and God will always be closely linked, 'with the pure thou shalt be pure,' &c., and in our measure we are to remove these false ideas and we can, but it is not by argument but by life. 'The life was the light.' Now sometimes we feel when near others that we see objectively in them a glorious outstreaming of the light that shines within themselves. You may describe the glory of light to one in the dark. He cries: don't talk to me about it, show it to me. Every Christian should be a light to others. The saints are the great lights.

1. Believe in men—there is light in every man.

2. Believe in the power of the Christian life to attract.

3. Show it forth.

Then one thing more. The candle is put in the candlestick to give light—you have not to choose the place to shine, it will be given you. And once more, you haven't to think of lighting others you have but to burn and you must shine.

1. First as to ourselves. Christ is the light, the fire. We see the light play around us, we feel its glow. The Church is the mighty reservoir of that fire on earth. We, in God's Providence, are privileged to live in this City of Divine Light, the light of Heaven kindled on earth and illuminating it. It is the light of Heaven, it's the warm glow that makes glad the City of God. Yet we may live in all this light, rejoice in it, feel it around us, and not ourselves be ignited. If so the Church burns none the brighter for our presence. Many persons have an extraordinary reflective and refractive power. They catch the light that is around

them and break it up and throw it back in its wondrous prismatic colours, but they themselves are not lighted; that fire is around them, upon them, everything except burning in them. We see them as they pass from religious to worldly surroundings and we should scarcely know them. With the holy they are holy, and with the worldly they are worldly. Under the inspiration of their brilliant surroundings they seem capable of anything, but take them out of these surroundings, place them in the dark, put them with men and women of lower standards or of no standards and the glow dies out. These men and women are not a force to withstand evil, in the gusty and wind-swept world of passion and excitement they can send up no strong flame, a beacon light to guide or warn. They are dependent absolutely upon their surroundings. And they are conscious themselves of this. They say: I am so weak, I get carried away by the people I am with. Yes, but why? Why can't you show the high standard as well as speak of it; why can't you, when called upon, stand alone and pour out upon the darkness around you that light of which you speak so well. It's because you have never had that magic touch which enables you to appropriate the fire and be yourself a lamp. You are an unlighted lamp, reflecting upon your polished surface the light that shines from another source. Fire is always the same, but lamps may be large or small; no matter how small, how ungifted, the smallest candle can do something to dispel the darkness. On some great night of illumination when the whole city is jubilant in a great national fête every candle put in the window adds to the decoration and helps to make the city a city of light. So it may be with you and me. Till we have caught the light ourselves and are aflame we can never shed a glimmer in the darkness, we can never throw a beam upon another dark soul. We are like the darkness dependent upon light from without. We live in the city of light, rejoicing in its illumination but ourselves dependent upon the light around us.

For every lighted candle does two things, it glorifies and utters the great fountain of light from which it comes, and it is itself crowned and glorified by the light that burns upon it. The lamp was made to give light, it has no meaning however costly and however exquisitely chased till the fire touches it, but when it does the lamp gives forth the light and the light explains the meaning of the lamp. This, brethren, is the great truth of the Christian life, the perpetual revelation of God through the Christian. Men see the Christian life burning and shining and they get somehow to know more about God. You come to someone hardened and embittered against God, with some crude or false idea of His character, and he sees you, he feels your tender compassion, he feels the warm breath of Christian charity and he says: Ah, when I see you it makes me feel that God may love me. You may be ignorant, unable to argue, but never has anyone who has been standing in the cold doubted the warmth of the fire, or one who has been shuddering and haunted in the darkness doubted the light.

This is the office and place of the Catholic in the world. You know yourself to be poor, and ignorant, and uninfluential, and awkward, and dark,—so does the candle till it is glorified by the light. The flame touches it and it is transformed, it is a light bearer and a light giver, yet it knows that the light is not its own, yea it knows that it only gives it forth as it is itself consumed by it.

The candle and light were made for one another, and only a person can alter a person, only a character can reveal a character. This was the secret of Francis and Catharine, of the Curé d'Ars and of ten thousand others. They knew that they could do little, but they knew that they could catch fire and burn.

However small the light we may be the means of lighting others. Some great palace of darkness with rows of unlighted lamps—one small candle may light them all. One Catholic in a house, &c. It is such material God uses. Every good person in his degree. And in days of special darkness or superficiality God sets some great saint on fire with Himself and through him men return to God, the old thoughts of God revealed in the Incarnation revive.

ST. IGNATIUS

'And Elijah passed by him and cast his mantle upon him. And he left the oxen, and ran after Elijah.'—1 KINGS xix. 19.

THE world is divided into givers and receivers. Everywhere there are those who have and those who need. God has bound the world together by this constant action and interaction of the members of the human race. There are those who have money and those who need it. Those who can work and those who need work to be done.

The sacred writer is describing one of the ways in which the prophetical ministry was propagated in Israel. It was not like the Jewish priesthood, a matter of hereditary descent; the son of a prophet was not necessarily a prophet. Each was the subject of a special vocation, and he was called to his work by some special token or influence. Elisha was ploughing when Elijah passed by. He does not seem to have spoken; he merely cast his mantle upon Elisha and passed on. But the young man's soul is stirred to its depths. We are not told that they had ever met before, but Elisha arose and ran after the prophet.

Is this to be looked at merely as an incident in the life of a prophet, or is it a matter of permanent interest and wide application? I think this call of Elisha has its place not merely in the history of his country, but of mankind.

It is one of those striking instances of personal influence which we come across again and again. The silent prophet passes on his way and drops his mantle, and the soul of another is agitated to its very depths. He yields to an attraction which he does not analyse but obeys, and henceforth the currents of his life are changed—a vocation of which he was apparently hitherto unconscious begins to unfold itself and change the whole tenor of his life. Certainly, brethren, we are all conscious of the action of this strange power that we possess over one another almost unconsciously; many of us can tell the story of how an apparently chance meeting or a friendship has affected our lives for good or evil:—how the first dawn of good or the first shadow of evil was thrown across our path by another.

Such a power, mysterious and awful as it is, is purely human, it is in the mystery of personality, and there is probably no one so low in the human scale who has not got the power of casting the mantle of his influence over another. Personal influence, magnetism, does not lie in strength of will, nor greatness of gifts—it is in itself a gift apart, the channel for carrying other gifts. It has been bestowed upon some men and women who were greatly gifted in other ways and upon some who were not. There it is; anyone who has it can't get rid of it, nor can he tell upon whom it will act, nor is he free to use it or not as he likes—it is often strongest when it is exercised unconsciously. It is by this means causes spread; a man of influence takes up a cause and now God and Satan will endeavour to utilise his influence. But, brethren, such a power existing in man's nature, we can readily understand how quickly it can become a channel for conveying supernatural things to man. The soul stands midway between the seen and the unseen. An unseen world is ever acting upon it, unseen forces are ever dealing with it. If I see how I affect another, I too may be affected by unseen powers. If a man therefore, highly endowed with the power of influencing others, is himself largely under supernatural influences, either good or evil, we can readily see how he can be made the channel for conveying to others these supernatural influences that act upon himself.

Let a man be very near to God, let his love of God be the deepest and strongest thing in his character, let him see life from God's point of view, and let him be such a man as I have spoken of, one who seems to live with open doors through which his personality flows out, and we can readily see what a power for good he can be.

And add to this great personal gifts and a strong and vigorous personality. The effect of such a life upon others will be to bring the supernatural within their reach. The stream of personal influence—one of the mightiest forces on earth—will flow out upon the world instinct with supernatural light and supernatural power; the supernatural will be brought to men through the action of a force that is purely natural. I don't deny that there is such a thing acting in and through men as an influence purely supernatural; no doubt there is, no doubt men of no influence, of no gifts at all can be used by God for great purposes. But God does not hesitate to use the natural gifts He has bestowed upon men.

And this I conceive was one of the sources of the power that acted upon Elisha when Elijah passed by and cast his mantle upon him—wherever he went he moved men.

Brethren, this is but a type of what God does throughout the ages. Elijah appeared in a dark day of Israel's history, when the landmarks of the old faith were giving way under the pressure of new ideas, imported into the land by a strong-minded and bad woman. He stood for the sole strong representative of the old faith.

And at all times in the history of God's people whether of the Old Covenant or the New, when the fire seemed dying out upon the Altar, or in days of intellectual disturbance or moral upheaval, God has never left Himself without witness. He has raised up someone, so that when the enemy came on like a flood he should lift up His standard against him. He has predestined and equipped some man or woman to bring some message to bestir and awaken men's minds and recall them. And humanly speaking the great work that was to be done, the currents that were to spread, depended on these. This is but a type of what God does throughout the ages. Elijah appeared in a dark day of Israel's history, when the landmarks of the old faith seemed to be giving way before the onward sweeping tide of a young and vigorous idolatry. He stood forth the representative and embodiment of the great truths revealed to Israel by God. In times of great trial great causes become identified with individuals. When men looked upon Elijah moving rapidly from one scene of danger to another the whole history of Israel, the whole Mosaic revelation seemed to live and speak in him. Behind his voice and gesture there was felt to be a great cause present, a great truth. His name stood for all that was greatest in the past of Israel. No wonder as he passed and cast his mantle upon Elisha that he arose and followed him. The man with his strongly marked character and whole-souled conviction became the channel for conveying to the younger man stirring impulses from the world beyond.

It has been ever so in the history of the Old Covenant and of the Catholic Church. In an hour of danger, when the fire seemed dying out on the Altar, or in days of intellectual disturbance or of moral upheaval, the warning or the guidance has come through an individual, one man has stood in the breach the embodiment of some special thought inspired by God. Moses—Samuel—David—Daniel. So in the history of the Catholic Church. Every great movement for quickening decaying love or for upholding the truth against the assaults of the enemy has been associated with some person. And humanly speaking, the work that was to be done depended upon whether some man (or some woman) would be true to his vocation and do what God wanted him to do.

We know what a delicate thing vocation is in its beginning, however imperious when it is given its sway. A Voice from the other world breaking in upon all the strong realities of the present, a Voice that might so easily be silenced and that calls we know not whither nor to what. The great awakening that has come through some Saint did not come into his mind as an end to strive after, nor was that primarily his vocation; it all grew out of his love and his union with God.

Thus was it with Saint Ignatius. Anywhere and under any circumstances he would have been a man of influence. His strong personality, his great courage—his unbending will must have made him anywhere a man of influence. How will he use this influence; what will he do with his power and his gifts? He was born in a great religious crisis—the end of one century and the beginning of a new one. The Church was in need of a man. Her forces needed to be rallied, all her earthly resources needed to be taxed. Who living at the time could have foreseen the man who was to take a leading part, to meet the Church's needs in that day and to be a source of power to her for 400 years after?

Already nearly half his life was spent. He had lived in the great world and apparently for it. Who that met him at Court or in the army could have told the power that was in him for good and for helping the world? And then came the supreme moment of his life—you all know the story, how he was wounded at Pampeluna and how when reading the lives of the Saints, he began to ask himself if these men did these things why should not he.

We watch him pass under the shadow of this great struggle. What would be the issue? who could foretell? He was free, absolutely, the choice must be his own. His military career and dreams of love and earthly happiness were on one side and on the other a Voice that called, a hand that beckoned. It was the breaking in upon his life of the supernatural. Could he form an idea of what lay before him if he obeyed? What did he know of the needs of the Church? How could he be sure that he could do anything to stay the influx of the new thought that was sapping the faith of multitudes? And then he gave in; he yielded to that Voice that called, and when he did it he did it with all the generosity and courage of his nature. The chivalry of an age that was dying is in him and comes out again and again.

And thenceforth he sets himself to do two things —unconsciously preparing himself for his work— to break down every barrier between his soul and God, to fight his way to union with Him, and in so doing he was learning lessons to help the world; and the other thing was, to study. We see in these two pursuits the heart and the will that was in him. He will not offer himself an unworthy instrument. He will train and perfect his gifts and powers. From the very first we see that clear judgment that was so marked a feature.

It is not surprising with such work going on behind the scenes, and with such supernatural forces acting upon him and forming him, that wherever he went the spell of his presence fell on others and they began to follow him. And one reason of this power that he had from the very first of drawing others after him, as Elijah drew Elisha, was that wherever he went men felt his extraordinary knowledge of God and the soul, and that will always draw. In the least spiritual age men are moved at the sight of a man who can give up all for the Kingdom of Heaven's sake. But there was in Ignatius yet another reason. It is good, brethren, to see an ideal citizen of the Kingdom of Heaven. It is good amidst the frivolity and superficiality of the world to see a man who lives in constant intercourse with the infinite and the eternal. But there are forms and types of sanctity suited to different times and different people, and there are some forms more attractive than others. Now to what are called men of the world none could appeal so strongly as a man who was essentially a man of the world himself, and who deliberately gave up the world and then came back to help it. The message of Heaven needs not earthly wisdom, nor earthly elegance; yet when it is brought by one who knows all the world has to give and has tasted it all and turned from it, it will have a special power. Some men smile at the halting methods of the priest who preaches God and Heaven to men of the world. What does he know of the great world, of its ideals, of what will move its representatives? And so as Ignatius the Saint, who had all the experience and wisdom of this world and used it in the service of God, as he went in and out amongst men of the world, is it any wonder that many like Elisha felt their hearts stirred as his mantle fell upon them and arose, left all and followed him.

But once more. The times in which Ignatius lived were stirring and full of interest. Two ages met in conflict, the mediaeval and the modern world. The air was astir with thought and changes. He was born at the end of one century and lived half through another—we know something of such a period. Now Ignatius had somewhat of both centuries in him. He had his roots in the Middle Ages, and spread abroad and grew to his strength a man of his own day and generation. The life in such an atmosphere is apt to make

ST. IGNATIUS

a man hard and narrow and a child of the past, or broad and undisciplined, a child of the new age. With Ignatius I think it had a better result; it gave him that great gift in a man of deep convictions—adaptability. He was strong with the strength of the mediaeval ideal : he was enough the child of his age to know its needs and the means whereby it could be influenced and moulded. His ideals were ancient ; his methods largely new. The discipline of authority and tradition controlled and regulated his work from first to last.

ST. THERESA

'And when the man was let down, and touched the bones of Elisha, he revived, and stood up on his feet.'—2 KINGS xiii. 21.

THE historian is describing for us one of those events that at first may look strange and unmeaning, but that on closer examination proves not to be merely an event that causes bewildered surprise. The ministry of Elijah was followed by that of one who was in every way a contrast to him. Elijah was a destroyer, Elisha was a builder-up. Elijah stood alone, the child of the desert wrapped in the solitary grandeur of his own great personality. Elisha dwelt in cities and mingled with the people; his life full of miracles was one of benevolence and kindness. Elijah was wafted into Heaven in a chariot of fire and horses of fire—a fitting end to that extraordinary life; Elisha died in his house full of years and influence. Elijah's life was one long warfare against the weak king and his strong masculine wife, whose influence had ever been in antagonism to the religion of God's people and who spread far and wide throughout the land the idolatrous worship brought from Sidon. Elisha represented the hopes of Israel against the power of Syria. He was the inspirer of the hopes of God's people. He roused the enthusiasm of the army. His last act was placing his hands upon those of the King of Israel to bid him shoot the arrow of his Lord and of deliverance from Syria.

And now he was dead; his sixty long years of prophetic ministry had ended and his voice was no longer heard, and his presence, the source of constant inspiration, was seen no more. And the power of Syria began again to assert itself, and the people were disheartened. It was then that this strange miracle took place and it is easy to see its purpose. The work of great men is soon forgotten, and the power of the living voice is very different from that of the memory of a voice long silent. By a signal and stirring miracle, therefore, wrought at the tomb of the dead prophet—wrought by contact with the bones of the dead—a new interest would be aroused in the memory of Elisha's words and deeds. Once more the enthusiasms that he knew so well how to inspire would be stirred afresh, and the people would go forth to do battle with their enemies with the long forgotten voice of the prophet living and ringing again in their ears. The miracle would assure them that Elisha was still living, and that his prayers had power with God.

But this miracle at the tomb of Elisha is not only an historical incident, it is a type. It is a dramatic representation of the power of the past over the present.

Elisha was dead and buried, and the teaching and inspiration of his life had largely, as is always the case, lost its vividness by which alone it could still act upon the people. The dead lay buried in his tomb. The man who had lived and spoken lay hidden and forgotten, yet no sooner do they bring the dead present in contact with the dead past than it asserts its reviving power and quickens the dead into life again. There is a power in the past to revive the present.

Those dead bones can stir into energy this life that is paralysed or gone. Again and again we find how in the lives of individuals the past, dead and buried, can quicken the present into energy and awaken it from its lethargy.

It is through contact with the great men and deeds of the past that a nation is awakened from its lethargy in the present. It was the memory of God's greatness and love in the past that ever stirred the heart of Israel. It is the memory of the innocence of childhood that has recalled many a man from a life of sin. In the tomb of the past lies the power to rouse the dead to life. And the Catholic Church living in the present, building for the future, strikes her roots deep into the past. She bids us look forward indeed. She bids us work and struggle now, but she ever points us back, uttering in our ears day by day through the passing years the wonders that God has wrought in His saints of old. We hear of the courage, the faith, the sacrifice of those who were men and women of like passions with ourselves, and our hearts burn within us.

Yes, the tombs of the saints have been the scenes of the wakening of many a dead man to life.

And it is so, brethren, in a special degree with the saint of to-day. St. Theresa was born at a moment in the world's history when two ages were wrestling together for the mastery. The Middle Ages were about to pass into the modern world. The whole aspect of life was beginning to undergo a change, and the first stirrings of the activity and energy of the modern world were felt and heard. The noise of religious conflict and the bitter invective of controversy

ST. THERESA

filled the air. The Church began to prepare herself for the new order of things. St. Ignatius was born sixteen years before St. Theresa, and already his drilled and disciplined army was spreading over Europe, rallying round the Holy See, and seizing the arms from the hands of their opponents to fight in the cause of the Church. Soon with the growing needs there spread over Christendom a multitude of devoted men and women who banded themselves together in different orders and congregations to meet every conceivable need, and to all these there has generally been given their due measure of approbation. The world itself, which may reject the claims of the Church, can appreciate its philanthropic work. But this could not be all. It is a glorious thing indeed to minister to the poor and sick, and to educate the ignorant, and to realise the reward 'Inasmuch as ye have done it unto one of the least of these My brethren, ye have done it unto Me.' But there is another side of the life of the Christian Church as there was to the life of its Head. Our Lord's life has in it different types and forms of character from which, as from an inexhaustible fountain, all kinds of people can draw. Out of His thirty-three years on earth there were only three spent, so far as we are told, in the direct ministry for others; though no doubt in another sense every hour of His Incarnate Life was spent for others. But not directly. Thirty out of the thirty-three were hidden at Nazareth, and in His public life we hear of His withdrawing with His disciples to be alone, of nights of solitude and prayer upon the mountain side. If the chief work of man on earth is by the direct ministry to others what was all this for? The hidden life spent itself in such ways. No, we feel as we read the life of Christ that all this is so marked, so strongly in contrast with the rest that it needs an explanation, and it no doubt is that He would in this, as in all else, set us an example. The lesson is that the highest life of man is direct worship of and devotion to God. Out of that inner hidden life came the public life. It was built upon it and rested upon it. For every year in public ten in private. There on the hills of Nazareth that human character grew and formed. The breezes that blew up from the distant sea came laden with the cries of men, burdened with their sorrows and their sins. The sun rose and set over the little village, the child grew to man's estate. He seems to leave the world to itself; but He is living for it, praying for it, offering Himself a sacrifice for it. Those years at Nazareth, those days of labour and nights of prayer have spoken to many as the public life could not; they came back from Heaven in showers of blessing upon a barren and thirsty earth. In all this He would teach us that Christianity is devotion to a Person—not a code of ethics, nor a school of philanthropy—but a personal service, a personal love. He would tell us that more can be done for the world through close and personal union with God than with all the labour of hands and head. That as evil came in through man turning to the Creation from the Creator, evil can be driven out by prayer and love, though men never heard the voice nor saw the face of Him that prayed.

In all the new awakening of the life of active charity in a new world was no place to be found for that other side of Christian life—the life hidden as His was and consecrated and offered with Him in atonement for the world's sin?

If there was not, then we may well ask how could the Church have stood that sudden and extraordinary strain that was put upon her? It wanted a clear vision indeed to see the true need, and a stout will to withstand the rising cry for help in a land over which the blight of schism and rebellion was spreading with such rapidity. It was a woman who stood on the threshold of that new age with its bounding pulses and throbbing temples and eager cries for aid, and said: others can help the world by action, I will help it by love, and by sacrifice and prayer. While men went forth to work she withdrew into a deeper and deeper seclusion that she might find God, and being alone with Him might grow so to know Him, so to live with Him alone, so to yield to the absorbing passion of devotion to Him that she might have such power with Him that her prayers could not be refused—such power against Hell that she might hold it at bay. It makes anyone who has read that history smile when he hears men talk of the cowardice of flying from the world and the selfishness of striving to save one's own soul when there is so much work to be done.

1. Theresa felt that the best way to help the world was to get so close to God that her prayers must have power with Him.

2. The law of vicarious suffering—a fact that makes some angry—she turned her sufferings back upon the world in blessing.

All of us who have ever tried to pray and have taken the first few steps in the path that leads to the temple of prayer know how beset with difficulty it is, how full of discouragement, how uncertain, how after years of effort one finds one has only begun to learn some of its deeper mysteries and its greater difficulties. Obstacles besetting every step forward, within and without.

But she was not content to start upon the road, she would penetrate into the very sanctuary of the Temple itself, where the foot of man had seldom trod, where, if she will enter she must enter without a guide; venturing alone like Peter upon the stormy waters. Ah, brethren, as we think of our early discouragements and our hasty flights, our complaints of coldness and distractions and that God does not hear us, think of her for twenty years in sickness of body and failing health and a soul beset with darkness pressing on. We sometimes think if we were permitted such revelations as she had we too would go on, but we look upon her in the light of her attainments. She had to fight her way step by step in the dark, and when the light came it was so bewildering, so unexpected, so startling, and so strange, that she often knew not whether she was deceived. She was warned back, opposition met her on all sides, but her undaunted courage never failed her. Her characteristics:

1. Courage.
2. Whole-souled surrender.
3. Love.

For her life was not for herself alone—it was for her order. She was opening the way for others to follow. She forced her way up that thorny and intricate path. Her great mental gifts were used to draw for others the chart of those unsounded seas.

ST. THERESA

For what is that hidden life ? It is a life of prayer and sacrifice. It is a life in which the soul sets aside all else that it may draw ever nearer to God and win from Him what it wills for the world.

She knew two things :
1. The power of prayer.
2. The law of vicarious suffering.

Two things will always make her life attractive:
1. It is almost entirely subjective—the history of a soul.
2. She has an extraordinary power of calmly analysing and describing the processes through which she passes.

Men say in the busy world of these later days, with ever increasing population and ever deepening human needs, there is no time for and no place for those who would shut themselves out from lives of active charity. It belonged to a day when the world's pulse beat slower. People have no right to forget others in the selfish efforts to save their own souls. It is true, brethren, there is such a thing as spiritual and religious selfishness, and selfishness never looks so ugly as when it is dressed in the garb of religion. But is it so ? Are these lives selfish ? Not as St. Theresa taught them, not as she lived her life. They are the lives of victims. The love for souls grows deeper. Is it selfish for one to leave home and kindred and to go alone into a far country to make peace between a rebel country and its king ?

One word more. There are the sons and daughters of St. Theresa who wear her habit and follow her footsteps. But these are not her only children.

She has a larger family. There are those all the world over who are as truly though less markedly called to the hidden life. Those whose lives in illness or as invalids are forced back out of the press and competition and are thrown back upon prayer. Or those who, full of enthusiasm, have all their lives been looking forward to work for others and find the time slipping by and their opportunity passing.

1. Her twenty years of mental coldness and physical suffering.

2. Her extraordinary humanness and practical common sense, living as she did in the unseen.

3. Her intellectual power, able to analyse and describe all that passed in her soul. Like one drawing the chart of hitherto unsounded waters.

Nehemiah iv. 16. It came to pass from that time forth that the half of my servants wrought in the work, and the other half of them held both the spears and shields and bows. . . . . .

17 . . . Everyone with one of his hands wrought in the work and with the other held a weapon.

ST. MATTHEW

ONE great advantage of the study of Holy Scripture is that it leads us through all secondary courses directly to God. The tone of thought and study of our day tends to lead the mind to rest with such interest in the workings of the machinery of nature that we need to be brought back again to first principles, and to be reminded that because we have discovered some of the great ways in which nature works out her ends, we are in no sense any nearer to a final explanation. In Holy Scripture we see God.

It is the same in individual life. The Gospel shows us the presence of Christ, and it draws for us the picture of different men and women living more or less careless or sinful lives, and then we see a change; the demoniac becomes clothed and in his right mind, the poor woman that was a sinner becomes the type of modesty and retirement, the persecutor becomes a disciple, the dying thief begins to pray. These are the sort of things we see in life to-day and the Gospel gives us the meaning. It is Christ entering into these lives. The influence of a person acting upon one here, one there. And this is what the Gospel describes as Christianity. This is at once its weakness and its strength. This it is which makes the kind of proofs men ask for impossible, and this it is which makes the proofs which individuals have the strongest in the world. Prove for me the truth of Christianity as you can prove any other scientific fact and I will believe. And to that I answer: thank God I can't, for if I could two things would follow. Every man with a clear head would have no loophole for escape—to be a believer would be a mere matter of cleverness, and besides, it would rob Christianity of its life. You can't scientifically prove the love of a person.

In the Gospels we find ourselves in a world of deeper interest—the moral world of human life, and behind and acting upon it we find a person who claims to be the God of the Old Testament clad in the form of man, and we see lives acted upon and changed by contact with Him. In proportion as He enters into their lives He changes them. He makes the fisherman the great mystic, the fallen woman a model of chastity, &c. This is Christianity, not a mere organisation; the Church is spread throughout the world. There are good and bad Christians; they are good in proportion as Christ enters their life, and as He does men find an objective representation of conscience. I open the Gospel and there I find conscience speaking.

Thus the weakness and strength of the Gospel,— the power of a holy life acting upon men, the most convincing proof to those who know Him. No one can shake your faith in your friend.

So when Christ drew men to Him He didn't merely present them with a creed and say: believe that and you're saved, refuse and you're lost. He drew them to Himself, and as they believed in Him He taught them. They received truth from the lips of one they loved and were led on.

That coming of Christ was different to different people and for different ends.

The great event by the gate of Damascus in the life of Saul of Tarsus was a crash, a lightning flash, a stunning blow, three days of fearful anguish, then a life wholly overturned. Saul professed that he saw Christ on the Throne of God—that was the other side.

We see Saul in his Jewish narrow zeal against Christians, then we see all this changed, the whole character of the man subdued, softened. He is lost sight of for a year or two, when we see him again we scarcely recognise him. What does it mean? He tells us. How could that influence enter and possess such a life? Not by a gradual process of conviction, but like a flash with a crash, a stunning blow.

Different from this was the coming of Christ into the life of St. John the Evangelist. With him there was no such crisis; he passed under an influence that led him on strongly and gently to the highest. He drank from His lips words of power and wisdom that satisfied his soul. How he recalls it all sixty or seventy years after! The day, the very hour.

Then take the change in the life of the Magdalene. She knew not who He was, she only felt that He was the type of what was purest and kindest in man, and as she poured out her soul at His feet peace wrapped her round as the morning light encircles the cold bleak mountain, and she was led on to that of which she never dreamed. In all these cases, so different one from another, there was opened a door to another life.

But amidst all these, none more beautiful and instructive than the saint of your Festival. Who could raise up a sordid money seeker? There are passions that degrade and weaken while they still leave much that is noble ; a drunkard may have a tender heart, or a sensualist has moments of agonising remorse, but the love of money hardens and narrows the whole nature and saps the springs of all natural affection. How can a man who has brought upon himself the scorn of his fellow-countrymen and the contempt of his own people and hired himself into the service of their enemies for the sake of money— how can such a man be touched or reached? Doubtless there were in that life times of longing after better things and bitter revolt against his fate, but habit is strong and under its grasp the will becomes less and less capable of asserting its freedom. How could he be raised? Beneath all the ruins there lay a dormant power of faith, devotion, sacrifice. But who could see, who could tell of its existence?

It was not any conscious influence of religion that raised and rescued him. There was another man in that town who was the very antithesis of himself, One who, instead of using others as a hunting ground for His own greed, was pouring out His very life, taxing nerve and heart beyond the power of human endurance to give. Was there ever greater contrast? And these two met, Jesus of Nazareth and Matthew, and He said to him : get up and leave that sordid life and I will make a man of you. You see the appeal is not to his religious faith—He doesn't touch upon religion, He will not condescend to enter upon the question of His claims or who He was, that would be but waste of time, the appeal is directly to conscience : give up your dishonest money-ruled life and follow Me who am at least unselfish. He threw open the door—nay, He was Himself the door into regions of holiness, &c., but all began here at one great moral act.

It was the same with Pilate. 'Art thou King of the Jews?' 'What is truth?' To all this Christ does not answer. He says to Pilate: You are a Judge, you know what justice is. Be just and if I am innocent don't condemn me. Through that door Christ would lead Pilate on to all the lights and graces of the Christian life.

Brethren, it is so almost always. Behind some strong call to do the right thing or give up something wrong stands Christ, religion, Christian hope, infinite progress. That is the door, pass through and fair visions of green pastures and cool streams open, but you see nothing till you have passed through.

He opens the door to that worldly person amusing herself with questions of controversy and thinking she can take no step till on some subtle question of faith her mind is cleared. He will not clear it; that is not the side upon which He comes to you. He comes to you and says: give up that lazy idle life, step out into a life of active purpose and then I will clear up all these things.

See Matthew; he arises, leaves all. Where is he going? Who has he surrendered to? Here was a man whose work in life was based on selfishness, yet he had talent, the power of an absolute consecration to God and to men. How was he to be drawn upwards, what could break the spell and chain of the present? It was not primarily through religious belief, nor through a gaining of the knowledge of theological truth. No, it was primarily through a moral act, a breaking with what was wrong, a following One who said no word to him about religion but who appealed to him through His own goodness. It seemed to say to him: get up and leave all this sordid money grabbing, break away from that and I will make a man of you. He followed. Brethren, you see a man who led him to do one act, but behind that act lay all possibilities of infinite progress. He followed and he was taught to be a Christian, an Apostle, an Evangelist, but it needed a blind act of surrender. Some scribe or pharisee meets him and says: do you know what you are doing? Do you know who this Jesus is? Do you know that there are various opinions as to His Person and claims? And Matthew answers: no, I only know He has bid me leave what all that's best in me says I ought to leave, I shall follow Him this step and see. And he does and he is led on—more and more of wonder and delight—up into the clear air of the highlands, where all is bracing and pure. He speaks with Him, prays with Him, lives with Him, till he finds at last that this stranger who led him from his money table passes up into the very heavens and sits on the right hand of God and lifts him to sit with Him in heavenly places.

Every age has its difficulties, its tone of thought, its spirit; there have been times of midnight darkness, this is a time of light, so brilliant that it seems as if we need none other. How is the soul to keep hold and to be firm amidst all change? By turning to revelation—there it sees two things: life as it's lived, and behind all God.

EVE

We will consider during Lent some of the women of the Old Testament, and begin to-day with the first—woman in her innocence and purity fresh from the hands of her Maker, ere yet sin had laid its stamp upon her soul and deformed her. As we look back out of the defilement and mistakes and false positions of our present state to that garden of peace and protection, we can see at once what we ought to be and how far we have fallen short of it. We see men and women living motiveless and aimless lives, the great powers that God has given them abused or not used at all, and we may look back to the beginning before the disease had spread and see ourselves as we ought to have been by God's original decree, and how we fell from our high place.

There are now the three great foes: the world, that mass of men who don't look before nor after but live in the present; the flesh, which demands the immediate gratification of the senses; and the great personal deceiver and enemy of our race.

Now in Eden the world did not tempt nor the flesh; there was but one tempter, Satan; there was but one source of temptation, the one forbidden thing, the Tree of Knowledge of Good and Evil. There were but two human beings, Adam and Eve, therefore the sphere of temptation was narrowed, but for that reason only the more intense; to her all temptation had but one source—the forbidden fruit, but one end—her husband.

1. Notice first of all she was created for a special purpose, and she utterly frustrated that purpose through disobedience to the restrictions of the limits within which she was to work. There may be spheres of usefulness that lie open before us which we can't enter because we are forbidden. If I were to do such and such a thing it would largely increase my power of influence with the world; remember, influence flows out spontaneously, it is not premeditated, it is the natural and necessary effect upon others of a life which is fulfilling its own end.

2. Two great instincts in women: (*a*) the power of influencing others; she can't but feel it for it was what she was put on earth to do. (*b*) The readiness to sacrifice herself for those she loves. As Eve stood beneath the Tree of Knowledge to my mind she was enduring a trial not for herself only, but for the one being on earth she loved most. What if she gain and give to him something most worth having in the world; what if she, who was put here to be his helper, could help him in one moment to rise to a height of knowledge only equalled by God. Supposing even she did die, what then; would it not be a great thing to die for her husband's good? Yet as the event showed it was all and only for her husband's harm, yea ruin. How little we know when we pass the line laid down by God for our sphere of action what evil may result from the very best intentions.

3. Then, too, she was in a state of innocence. She

didn't know what evil was—the book of evil was still unopened. Like one going out into the world knowing nothing about it, with a high ideal and a great devotion, and no conception of how one might be deceived by the appearance of things—the one only guide, the guide of God's commands.

The steps by which she fell :
1. Parleying with a distinct command.
2. Doubting.
3. Accusing God of unworthy motives.

Satan exaggerates the prohibition. Can it be that ' the Deity ' hath forbidden you to eat of any tree of the garden ? Has the Deity forbidden all progress ? Does He forbid the enjoyment of the appetites He has created ?

Satan never begins by suggesting some overt act of gross disobedience. He would familiarise the mind with the thought God *could* be hard. Eve says : we may not eat or touch—exaggerates—lest we *die*, not lest we disobey.

Satan seizes the chance : ye shall not surely die.

How long and often we dally with those words : hath God indeed said ?

Then she saw—she took—she ate—she gave to eat.

The most dangerous sins those against the leading purpose of one's life.

Woman made to be man's helpmeet. It's her vocation and her instinct to do this, through this her greatest blessing and her greatest danger and most frequent falls.

As a result of this deep desire in women to sacrifice self for another, she falls or rises. This act of Eve touched her whole position. Her whole life-work.

1. Desire to sacrifice.
2. Desire to keep hold and influence.
3. It was using all her power and place in disobedience.

In more than one parable, and under more than one image, Our Lord warns us of the danger of superficial changes in character. The house built on shifty and unstable soil—the seed on rock—wolf in sheep's clothing—the pressing forward in the spiritual life without beginning at the bottom. There may be many superficial changes while the character remains fundamentally unchanged. This has specially to be borne in mind in a religion like that of Our Lord's, which has to deal with two spheres, the natural and the supernatural. These are not distinct in the sense that we can keep them apart. They are meant for one another as are the seed and the soil. The seed is perfect in itself in a sense, and the soil may be of the best, but the soil can produce no fruit without the seed, and *vice versa*. In the soul these two blend and commingle. The consequence of this is that we cannot neglect nature and develop at the same time grace. Any defect in the soil, anything rocky and hard at once declares itself in the young seed. It is in a sense easier to strive after the supernatural than the natural.

Some devote themselves to the cultivation of all that is natural, others supernatural. But neither can reach their perfection without the other. For the soil of nature was not created sufficient to itself, as an engine is not made to work without steam. We know how easy it is for people to aim at prayer, a lofty purity, a spirit of asceticism, devotion to Our

Lord, the Blessed Virgin, and not to be very particular about truth, justice, temperance, kindness. They divide their souls into water-tight compartments. The waters float but don't soak into the soil of nature; the two must mingle.

A fundamental fault may be left in the foundations of the spiritual life while all the effort is spent in building the superstructure.

1. There are, for instance, faults of temperament, the fault that shows itself first and perhaps last in life. Moses after eighty years—Peter denying our Lord—Philip—Thomas. So a person may find her life spoilt; the supernatural choked by such faults never plucked out.

2. But there are faults deeper, faults against your vocation. Your vocation as truly as St. Peter's to be an apostle, is to the married state—wife, mother. Faults against these are faults against your state. They are like faults against fidelity in a priest, neglect of souls, &c., or against the consecrated life in religion. Your prayers and communions may fail of full fruit because you do not do your best in your home duties.

3. But there are defects that go deeper still. An artist may have the gift of genius and a perfect subject, but a flaw in the material will destroy the most perfect work. The most skilled musician may play the most divine music, but if his instrument is out of tune the music will be far from perfection. So there may be faults in the material. And what is the material? The material out of which a priest is made is his manhood, but out of which a perfect Christian

wife and mother is made is her womanhood. Any
fault in this must mar everything else. The more
perfectly womanly you are, in so far, promises well
for the developments in any of the positions in life to
which God may call you. A fault in the material mars
the best work; and a fault against your position as
a woman is the deepest of all, the poisoning of the
springs, the using the position God has given you in
life for another purpose than that which He intended.
Such a person finds herself with all her powers, &c.,
only she uses them for another end.

Now we know the purpose for which God made
man and woman. He made man in His own image to
develop and perfect the Divine likeness. And He
made woman to help man in this work, to help to raise
man Godward. Therefore woman's position is one
involving fundamentally a relationship to others. She
can't leave this out in the consideration of her life,
for it was for this she was made.

In the opening page of human history we see the
representative woman at once in contact with the
typical temptation of her life. It is in Eden; she and
Adam are alone in the world, as it is in all such temptations. She was alone with the one person whom she
loved. There was no doubt the feeling of a destiny
before them of possibilities and of ambitions, there
opened visions of indefinite growth, and there was the
Forbidden Tree that represented to her and to her husband possibilities closed only by the command of God,
unknown possibilities. We might see how that tree
touched on their whole nature, appealed to every side
of it; but that door was closed by the Divine command. It created then a situation. It *was* a tempta-

tion, the greatest possible. Here then was the testing of Eve. Would she hold up her husband's hands, help to keep him up or to drag him down? It lay in her hands. The tree could move him, but she could move him more. All that power of influence, all her attractions, the attractions of the first-formed woman, unstained by evil,—she might throw it all on God's side, to hold her husband up, and in so doing help him to rise.

We know what she did do (with it came a loss of power, not a gain).

No doubt she saw her husband disturbed and excited, she knew what was in his mind, and she said to herself: he hasn't got the courage to do it himself, I'll do it for him. Women have more moral courage than men. The temptation was to use that power of influence and attraction, the position which God had given her to raise man to his best, to minister on the contrary to what was not best and to strengthen her hold over him and increase his need for her. This is a constant temptation.

1. She used her position just for the one thing which she ought not, to do the one thing she might have helped him not to do. Isn't this the constant temptation of women to use their powers of influence for other than the best?—e.g. in the case of a daughter's marriage or of sons' positions.

Two dangerous times:

(*a*) Marriage.

(*b*) Starting children in life.

2. The desire to sacrifice self to one one loves. By sacrifice we rise or fall. We fall if the sacrifice involves an infringement of what is right.

APPENDIX

FATHER MATURIN'S LAST SERMON

Described by Arthur I. Kegan

A WEEK before Father Maturin sailed on the *Lusitania* he preached his last sermon in St. Patrick's Church, Philadelphia. To those who had often heard him years before in St. Clement's Episcopal Church it was evident his preaching had lost none of that singular charm which in his Anglican days was wont to attract great congregations. Had it been generally known that he was to preach in St. Patrick's that morning many of his Anglican friends and admirers would have been there to hear him. But word had only been passed quietly to a few of his former Episcopalian parishioners who had followed him into the Catholic Church, and these were in attendance.

A score of years had made some changes in him. But they were the changes of growth, not decadence. His step may have been a little slower, his voice not quite so vigorous. His old-time aggressiveness had been softened. There was a look of great sweetness in his face. The old-time flame was still there— less fitful, less passionate, less impatient, if you will, but steadier and steadfast. As one studied the man, no one could doubt he had found the peace and happiness which he had sought so long in vain outside the true Church.

FATHER MATURIN'S LAST SERMON

Father Maturin was always a difficult preacher to report. In the old days his words poured from him in a veritable torrent. But no mere report of his words could have been satisfactory, for at the back of the words was the man, his personality, his mannerisms, the force and fire of his utterance, like a soul on fire. And sometimes, it must be confessed, he was a little difficult to understand—when he spoke in a tone so low that his words did not carry very far from the pulpit. That would be for an instant or two only, but in that instant or two it seemed he was saying the very thing we most wanted to hear.

He had a wonderful voice—clear, musical—and he spoke with the accent of Oxford. There was no attempt at elocution. He was too much in earnest for that. The things he had to say were too vital to be trifled with. And you felt this. He gripped you.

In that last sermon of his in Philadelphia his text was from the Epistle to the Romans (21st verse, 12th chapter), 'Be not overcome of evil, but overcome evil with good.' I can attempt to give only a part of what he said. My notes are incomplete. Such as they are, I give them.

'There is no more common or dangerous error than for people to make generalisations from a little knowledge. Usually such generalisations are full of error. A man has been married, and says marriage is a failure. A man, who has been cheated in business, says the whole world is rotten and dishonest. It is difficult for us to rid ourselves of our own personal experience. The truth generally lies between yea and nay. The middle place between the two will generally be found to be the right one.'

The preacher urged the study of our own nature. No two men are exactly the same, and we can get at the truth regarding human nature by blending the experiences of both. There are people who have the view of human nature that it is all rotten, and, on the other hand, there are men whose view of life is fundamentally opposite. The fact is that in all such considerations there is always our own nature to take into account. Look at a checkerboard; it is black and white. One says it is white with black on it, another that it is black with white on it. There is no saint who has not his defects, no sinner who has not virtues.

' You and I have this combination of good and evil, and our aim should be to overcome the evil with the good. Everything you do is not through one motive. You act, but some of these motives are good and some bad. Wherever a man is there are possibilities of great good and possibilities of great evil. Do not despair, however you may have to fight. How is it that when we would do our best for ourselves we encounter this strange paradox: When I would do good, evil starts out and hampers me ? There are two schools that will meet the young man with their method of combat. One will tell him: destroy the evil. He will say: I'm a mixture of religion and sensuality. Well, says your friend, kill out the evil, conquer your bad temper, destroy your sensuality, and never stop till the evil is crushed beneath your feet. Then you are a man.

' But the man says : I have tried and struggled, yet the beast is only caged. At the end of six months the demon of intemperance arose, and it would have been better if I had never striven. And it is the same with the beast of sensuality. The young man says : God made me with all the evil and good in me. Is the sublime height I am to reach an emasculated personality ? You tell me to annihilate my temper, my affections. I don't want to do it.

' He is quite right. No man can ever do best for himself by simply killing the evil in him. You cannot kill that temper without being weaker : if that is to be a saint, I don't want to be a saint, he says. Is that the best thing—a man without strength ? he asks.

' My ideal of the true Christian man is one who has all in him that God gave him. If you will analyse yourself you will find there is not a thing in you that is evil. In my soul is no evil. What ! says the young man. Good God ! You don't know me !

' *There is not a power in you that is evil. You have misused it !* Take anger. Anger is a sword that God put in our hands to fight the battle of life and to smite evil. When I abuse anger it becomes a vice. People talk as if they had two sets of qualities, one evil, the other good. Nothing of the sort. All is good. *The thief on the Cross stole the kingdom of God and became a saint.*

' A great many people have an idea that sin is some fermentation in their nature. Nothing of the sort. It's the absence of the Holy Ghost. Do as Augustine did when he brought that mighty mind into the service of Almighty God. There is an idea that as soon as a person becomes a Catholic he ceases to be interesting. What makes you admire the bad man. He's so masculine ! But it's an entirely false estimate of masculinity. Tell me if the Magdalen was more interesting before she was converted ? or Augustine ? or Paul ? Those understood that religion is a positive thing, and that no man ever became a servant of Jesus Christ who tried to emasculate himself.

' Some say : I used to go out a great deal among people, but I found I could not without sinning against charity. Good God ! my friends, did God give these hands that you might never use them ? Hands were made to do, eyes to look, lips to speak. If I restrain my lips in silence, it is in order that I may get them under control till I can speak better than ever in the service of God.

' Those colourless people who go about in the world do a great deal of harm to religion, crawling on earth and never lifting their eyes to heaven. Never be content with merely trying not to do wrong. If you have been in the habit of getting angry, I should say : Don't make a resolution not to be angry, but to say something kind. Use those lips in the service of Jesus Christ. A person says : Father, I don't know what to do with my mind ; it's always astir with things I had better leave alone. You can't make your mind a negative thing. My friend, you are trying to drive things out of your mind. Try to bring things into your mind. Convert your mind, fill it with good thoughts. You will find that every person has something great about them if you will only get below the little things.

' Look into yourself, and you will find there is not a faculty you have that is not good. What a splendid faculty is imagination ; yet it has been the curse of many a man's life. And yet there is no more splendid handmaiden to the things of faith. So it is all around.

'Use the lips to overcome evil. Then there is the positive side. So St. Paul makes this splendid analogy. Use all the faculties of your mind and body as the instrument of justice and holiness. Never rest till your hands are stretched out doing good and your lips speaking good. It is easy to discourage, to drive a man almost to despair and the gutter.'

'No man,' continued Fr. Maturin, 'is complete in his recovery from sin till all his faculties are centred in the service of Jesus Christ. That seems to me to be the keynote of the Catholic faith. It takes the beggar off the street. The thing to make a person good is to turn his heart to God. And then to serve Him. To do things for Him. The only way to drive out darkness is to call in light. In many a disease the physician can do nothing but sustain the vitality till it is strong enough to overcome the evil malady.'

A SELECT LIST OF BOOKS.

THE LIFE OF JOHN HENRY CARDINAL NEWMAN. By WILFRID WARD. With 15 Portraits and other Illustrations. 2 vols. 8vo. 36s. net. CHEAP EDITION. With 2 Portraits. 2 vols. 8vo. 12s. 6d. net.

SERMON NOTES. By JOHN HENRY CARDINAL NEWMAN. Crown 8vo. 5s. net.

INDEX TO THE WORKS OF CARDINAL NEWMAN. By JOSEPH RICKABY, S.J., B.Sc. (Oxon.). Crown 8vo. 6s. net.

THE SEQUEL TO CATHOLIC EMANCIPATION : The Story of the English Catholics continued down to the re-establishment of their Hierarchy in 1850. By the Right Rev. MONSIGNOR BERNARD WARD, F.R.Hist.S. With Illustrations. 2 vols. 8vo. 21s. net.

AT HOME WITH GOD : Prie-dieu Papers on Spiritual Subjects. By the Rev. MATTHEW RUSSELL, S.J. 3s. 6d. net.

AMONG THE BLESSED : Loving Thoughts about Favourite Saints. By the Rev. MATTHEW RUSSELL, S.J. With 8 Full-page Illustrations. Crown 8vo. 3s. 6d. net.

SAINT FRANCIS OF ASSISI : a Biography. By JOHANNES JÖRGENSEN. Translated by T. O'CONOR SLOANE, Ph.D. With 5 Illustrations. 8vo. 12s. 6d. net.

LIFE OF ST. FRANCIS OF ASSISI. By FATHER CUTHBERT, O.S.F.C. With 13 Illustrations. 8vo. 6s. 6d. net.

THE ROMANTICISM OF ST. FRANCIS : and other Studies in the Genius of the Franciscans. By FATHER CUTHBERT, O.S.F.C. With Frontispiece. 8vo. 6s. 6d. net.

THE HOUSE AND TABLE OF GOD : a Book for His Children, Young and Old. By the Rev. WILLIAM ROCHE, S.J. With 24 Illustrations from Drawings by T. BAINES, Jun. Crown 8vo. Cloth, 2s. 6d. net. Vegetable Vellum, gilt top, 3s. 6d. net.

A CHILD'S PRAYERS TO JESUS. By the Rev. WILLIAM ROCHE, S.J. With Illustrations by T. BAINES, Jun. Demy 16mo. 1s. net. PRESENTATION EDITION. White cloth, gilt edges, 1s. 6d. net.

⁎ To be had also in two parts, without the Illustrations, price 1d. net each.

MYSTERIES OF THE MASS IN REASONED PRAYERS. By the Rev. WILLIAM ROCHE, S.J. With Frontispiece by T. BAINES, Jun. Crown 8vo. Paper covers, 1s. net ; cloth, 1s. 6d. net.

THE WESTMINSTER LIBRARY.

Edited by the Right Rev. Mgr. WARD and the Rev. H. THURSTON, S.J.

THE PRIEST AND SOCIAL ACTION. By the Rev. CHARLES PLATER, S.J., M.A., Professor of Psychology at St. Mary's Hall, Stonyhurst. With an Introduction by the BISHOP OF NORTHAMPTON. Crown 8vo. 3s. 6d. net.

LONGMANS, GREEN & CO.
LONDON, NEW YORK, BOMBAY, CALCUTTA, AND MADRAS.

A SELECT LIST OF BOOKS.

THE LIFE OF MONSIGNOR ROBERT HUGH BENSON. By the Rev. C. C. MARTINDALE, S.J. With Portraits and other Illustrations. 2 vols. 8vo. 18s. net.

BY THE VERY REV. MGR. ROBERT HUGH BENSON.

SPIRITUAL LETTERS TO ONE OF HIS CONVERTS. With a Preface by A. C. BENSON and a Portrait of Monsignor Benson. Crown 8vo. 2s. 6d. net.

PARADOXES OF CATHOLICISM. Sermons preached in Rome, Easter, 1913. Crown 8vo. 3s. 6d. net.

CONFESSIONS OF A CONVERT. Crown 8vo. 3s. 6d. net.

CHRIST IN THE CHURCH: a Volume of Religious Essays. Crown 8vo. 3s. 6d. net.

THE FRIENDSHIP OF CHRIST. Sermons. Crown 8vo. 3s. 6d. net.

A CHILD'S RULE OF LIFE. Printed in Red and Black, and Illustrated by GABRIEL PIPPET. 4to. Paper covers, 1s. net; cloth, 2s. net.

OLD TESTAMENT RHYMES. Printed in Red and Black, and Illustrated by GABRIEL PIPPET. 4to. Paper covers, 1s. net; cloth, 2s. net.

VEXILLA REGIS: a Book of Devotions and Intercessions on behalf of all our Authorities, our Soldiers and Sailors, our Allies, the Mourners and Destitute, and all affected by the War. Arranged, Translated, and Compiled by the Very Rev. Mgr. BENSON, M.A. With a Prefatory Note by the BISHOP OF SALFORD; and a Frontispiece by T. BAINES, Jun. Fcap. 8vo. 1s. 9d. net.

THE UPPER ROOM: A Drama of Christ's Passion. With an Introduction by His Eminence CARDINAL BOURNE; and 14 Illustrations by GABRIEL PIPPET. Crown 8vo. 3s. net. ACTING EDITION. Paper covers. Without the Illustrations. 7d. net.

THESAURUS FIDELIUM: a Manual for those who desire to lead Prayerful Lives in the World. Compiled by a Carmelite Tertiary (H. M. K.). With a Preface by the Very Rev. MONSIGNOR ROBERT HUGH BENSON. Fcap. 8vo. 3s. net.

THROUGH AN ANGLICAN SISTERHOOD TO ROME. By A. H. BENNETT. With a Preface by Dame SCHOLASTICA M. EWART, O.S.B., Lady Abbess of Bride's Abbey College, Milford Haven. With Illustrations. Crown 8vo. 4s. 6d. net.

THE STRAIGHT PATH. By the Rev. M. J. PHELAN, S.J. Crown 8vo. 2s. 6d. net.

THE CHURCH OF CHRIST, ITS FOUNDATION AND CONSTITUTION. By the Rev. PETER FINLAY, S.J. Crown 8vo. 2s. 6d. net.

FROM FETTERS TO FREEDOM: Trials and Triumphs of Irish Faith. By the Rev. ROBERT KANE, S.J. Crown 8vo. 5s. net.

LONGMANS, GREEN & CO.
LONDON, NEW YORK, BOMBAY, CALCUTTA, AND MADRAS.